Old Testament Yahweh Texts in Paul's Christology

Library of
Early Christology

Larry W. Hurtado
David B. Capes
April D. DeConick
Editors

SERIES INTRODUCTION

Over the past forty years or so, there has been a renewed interest in the origins and early developments of belief in Jesus, many of these studies sometimes referred to as loosely forming a kind of "new religionsgeschichtliche Schule" (new history of religion school). This body of work both resembles and differs from the German scholarship of the original "Schule," particularly in emphasizing more the roots of early Jesus-devotion in the rich and varied Jewish traditions of the Greco-Roman era.

Available from the Library of Early Christology Series

Bousset, Wilhelm. *Kyrios Christos: A History of the Belief in Christ from the Beginnings of Christianity to Irenaeus*

Capes, David B. *Old Testament Yahweh Texts in Paul's Christology*

DeConick, April D. *Seek to See Him: Ascent and Vision Mysticism in the Gospel of Thomas*

Fossum, Jarl E. *The Name of God and the Angel of the Lord: Samaritan and Jewish Concepts of Intermediation and the Origin of Gnosticism*

Gieschen, Charles A.. *Angelomorphic Christology: Antecedents and Early Evidence*

Hengel, Martin. *Between Jesus and Paul: Studies in the Earliest History of Christianity*

Hurtado, Larry W. *Ancient Jewish Monotheism and Early Christian Jesus-Devotion: The Context and Character of Christological Faith*

Juel, Donald H. *Messianic Exegesis: Christological Interpretation of the Old Testament in Early Christianity*

Newman, Carey C. *Paul's Glory-Christology: Tradition and Rhetoric*

Newman, Carey C., James R. Davila, and Gladys S. Lewis, editors. *The Jewish Roots of Christological Monotheism: Papers from the St Andrews Conference on the Historical Origins of the Worship of Jesus*

Segal, Alan F. *The Other Judaisms of Late Antiquity: Second Edition*

Segal, Alan F. *Two Powers in Heaven: Early Rabbinic Reports about Christianity and Gnosticism*

Stuckenbruck, Loren T. *Angel Veneration and Christology: A Study in Early Judaism and in the Christology of the Apocalypse of John*

Old Testament Yahweh Texts in Paul's Christology

David B. Capes

BAYLOR UNIVERSITY PRESS

Published in 1992 by Mohr. Copyright © 1992 J. C. B. Mohr (Paul Siebeck), Tübingen, Germany
Reprinted in 2017 by Baylor University Press, Waco, Texas

All rights reserved. This book may not be reproduced, in whole or in part, in any form (beyond that permitted by copyright law) without the publisher's written permission. This applies particularly to reproductions, translations, microfilms and storage and processing in electronic systems.

Cover design by Savanah N. Landerholm for Baylor University Press

Library of Congress Cataloging-in-Publication Data

Capes, David B.
    Old Testament Yahweh texts in Paul's christology / by David B. Capes.
    vii, 220 p. ; 24 cm.
    Originally published: Tübingen: J. C. B. Mohr, 1992, in series Wissenschaftliche Untersuchungen zum Neuen Testament, 2/47
    ISBN 3-1614-5819-2 (acid-free paper)
    Includes bibliographical references and index.
    1. Jesus Christ—History of doctrines—Early church, ca. 30-600. 2. Bible. New Testament—Relation to the Old Testament. 3. Bible. Epistles of Paul—Criticism, interpretation, etc. 4. God—Name—Biblical teaching. I. Title. II. Series.

BT198 .C279   1992
232'.8'09015

92219486

Baylor University Press ISBN: 978-1-4813-0791-8 (paper)

Printed in the United States of America on acid-free paper.

Preface

I was introduced to the subject matter of this study in a seminar on Pauline Christology at Southwestern Baptist Theological Seminary in Fort Worth, TX. It was led by Professor E. Earle Ellis, who later agreed to serve as my dissertation supervisor. Although I had read through Paul's letters many times, I had never noticed what still strikes me as an astounding fact. Paul, who at one time gloried in his Jewish heritage, applied to his "Lord," Jesus Christ, sacred scripture originally reserved for Yahweh (יהוה), the unspeakable name of God. It is my hope that this investigation will increase our knowledge of Paul's Christology and help to correct mistaken notions regarding how he perceived the relationship between God and Christ.

The present work is a slight revision of my doctoral dissertation entitled "Paul's Use of Old Testament Yahweh Texts and Its Implications for His Christology." Most of the research was carried out from 1986 to 1989. Since then, however, many books and articles have appeared on Paul and early Christology. In some cases I have been able to incorporate these contributions into my own work.

Commonly cited periodicals, series, Jewish Pseudepigrapha, the Dead Sea Scrolls, biblical references, and related ancient writings are abbreviated according to the list provided in "Instructions to Contributors," *Journal of Biblical Literature* 99 (1980): 83-97. Quotations from the Greek New Testament follow *Novum Testamentum Graece*, ed. Eberhard Nestle, Kurt Aland, *et al*, 26th ed. (Stuttgart: Deutsche Bibelgesellschaft, 1979). Translations of scripture belong to the Revised Standard Version (2nd ed., 1971) unless specified otherwise.

I am indebted to John Hansen who provided many hours of technical assistance in completing the manuscript for publication. His enthusiasm for the project nearly rivaled my own. His skill and demeanor have redefined for me the meaning of collegiality. I am also grateful to Randy Hatchett who read the manuscript and offered various suggestions.

In addition to these I wish to thank a number of people who have shaped my thinking regarding Paul and have provided streams of encouragement, wisdom, and criticism over the past several years. These include Robert Sloan, Bruce Corley, Randy Richards, Fred Wood, Marty Reid, Carey Newman, and a host of other colleagues

Preface

and mentors too numerous to mention. Thanks also go to my wife, Cathy, and my three children, Bryan, Daniel, and Jordan. They were always supportive and, nearly always, uncomplaining as I spent many days away and many hours in my study at a time when my boys needed a father and my wife needed a husband. In particular I wish to express my appreciation to my dissertation supervisor, Professor E. Earle Ellis. Over his distinguished career he has provided the world of biblical scholarship with many new insights and a style of reverent scholarship worthy of emulation. I count it a privilege to have served as his graduate assistant and to have worked for a time under his capable hand. In addition, I wish to thank Alan Segal and Carey Newman who encouraged me to pursue the publication of my manuscript.

Finally, I wish to thank Professor Dr. Martin Hengel and Professor Dr. Otfried Hofius for considering this work in Wissenschaftliche Untersuchungen zum Neuen Testament, a series which has done much to further biblical studies. My own work is offered with the sincere but modest hope of fostering discussion upon the person of Christ. Despite centuries of biblical investigation, the nature and work of Christ remains a great mystery.

Houston, Texas   David B. Capes
October 1991

Table of Contents

Preface	iii
Introduction	1
The Significance of the Name "Yahweh"	3
Format of Study	5
The Use of the Pastorals	6
I. ΚΥΡΙΟΣ As a Christological Title in Recent Discussion	9
The Background of Current Research	9
The Theory of an Origin outside Palestine	10
The Thesis of Wilhelm Bousset	10
The Thesis of Ferdinand Hahn	12
The Theory of a Palestinian Origin	14
The Thesis of J. Gresham Machen	14
The Thesis of A. E. J. Rawlinson	16
The Thesis of Oscar Cullmann	18
Summary	20
Conclusion	32
II. ΚΥΡΙΟΣ in the Septuagint and in Paul's Letters	34
The Septuagint's Use of ΚΥΡΙΟΣ	34
ΚΥΡΙΟΣ As a Human Designation	34
ΚΥΡΙΟΣ As a Title for God	37
Paul's Use of ΚΥΡΙΟΣ	43
The Maranatha Invocation	43
ΚΥΡΙΟΣ As a Human Designation	47
ΚΥΡΙΟΣ As a Title for God or Gods	48
ΚΥΡΙΟΣ As a Title for Christ	49
"Jesus Is Lord"	50
Resurrection, Exaltation, and the Lordship of Jesus	53
The Scope of Jesus' Lordship	59
God, the Father, and the Lord, Jesus Christ	62

ΚΥΡΙΟΣ in Ethical Admonitions	69
The Lord's Supper	74
The Earthly Jesus As Lord	78
ΚΥΡΙΟΣ in Paul's Eschatology	82
Summary	88
III. *Yahweh Texts in Paul's Letters*	90
Yahweh Texts with God As Referent	90
The Lord and Righteousness—Rom 4:7-8	90
"The Lord of Hosts"—Rom 9:27-29	93
"The Mind of the Lord"—Rom 11:34	99
"Praise the Lord, Ye Gentiles"—Rom 15:9-11	103
"The Lord Knows the Thoughts of the Wise"—1 Cor 3:20	106
"The Lord Almighty"—2 Cor 6:18	111
Summary	114
Yahweh Texts with Christ As Referent	115
"Calling upon the Name of the Lord"—Rom 10:13	116
"Every Knee Shall Bow"—Rom 14:11	123
"Boast in the Lord"—1 Cor 1:31 and 2 Cor 10:17	130
1 Cor 1:31	130
2 Cor 10:17	135
"The Mind of the Lord"—1 Cor 2:16	136
"The Earth Is the Lord's"—1 Cor 10:26	140
"The Lord Knows Those Who Are His"—2 Tim 2:19	145
Allusions to Yahweh Texts in Paul's Writings	149
Allusions in 1 Corinthians and the Thessalonian Letters	149
Second Corinthians 3:16	155
Philippians 2:10-11	157
Implications for Paul's Christology	160
The Contribution of Lucien Cerfaux	160
Some Modifications to Cerfaux's Conclusions	162
Jesus Is Yahweh	164

Contents

Paul's Christological Use of Yahweh Texts and Monotheism	167
Judaism's Concept of Divine Agency	168
Yahweh As a Corporate Person	173
The Catalysts for Paul's Christological Use of Yahweh Texts	174
Paul's "High" Christology	181
Conclusion	184
Bibliography	187
Index	213

Introduction

In his book, *Christology in Paul and John*, Robin Scroggs analyzed Paul's Christology and concluded that the apostle did not identify Christ with God in any substantive way.[1] Scroggs' work, however, was flawed because (1) he worked with an abbreviated Pauline corpus, (2) he did not deal with the christological designations "wisdom of God" and "image of God,"[2] and (3) he did not pay serious attention to Paul's christological use of the Old Testament. Had he taken these factors into account, he might have concluded otherwise. Although the first two flaws render his conclusion inaccurate, it is the final deficiency which this project addresses.

Scholars generally recognize the importance of the Old Testament for Paul and early Christianity.[3] Furthermore, they acknowledge the debt he owed to the hermeneutical principles laid down by Jewish exegetes.[4] But they also understand that he, along with other Chris-

---

[1] Robin Scroggs, *Christology in Paul and John* (Philadelphia: Fortress Press, 1988), 52.

[2] E. Earle Ellis, review of *Christology in Paul and John*, by Robin Scroggs, in *SWJT* 31 (1989): 55.

[3] Several important contributions to this field of inquiry include: E. Earle Ellis, *Paul's Use of the Old Testament* (Grand Rapids: Baker, 1957); selected essays in idem, *Prophecy and Hermeneutic in Early Christianity: New Testament Essays* (Grand Rapids: Eerdmans, 1978), 147-256; James D. G. Dunn, *Unity and Diversity in the New Testament* (Philadelphia: Westminster, 1977), 80-102; Matthew Black, "The Christological Use of the Old Testament in the New Testament," *NTS* 18 (1971): 1-14; Richard N. Longenecker, *Biblical Exegesis in the Apostolic Period* (Grand Rapids: Eerdmans, 1975); Leonhard Goppelt, *Theology of the New Testament*, vol. 2, *The Variety and Unity of the Apostolic Witness to Christ*, trans. John Alsup (Grand Rapids: Eerdmans, 1982), 51-61; and Richard Hays, *Echoes of Scripture in the Letters of Paul* (New Haven and London: Yale University Press, 1989).

[4] E. Earle Ellis, "Biblical Interpretation in the New Testament," in *Mikra: Text, Translation, Reading and Interpretation of the Hebrew Bible in Ancient Judaism and Early Christianity*, CRINT (Philadelphia: Fortress, 1988), 691-725; and J. Christiaan Beker, *Paul the Apostle: The Triumph of God in Life and Thought* (Philadelphia: Fortress, 1980), 251-52.

tian writers, made Christ's person and work the hermeneutical key to interpreting the Old Testament.[5]

One scholar, L. Joseph Kreitzer, however, recently pointed to a significant weakness in contemporary research when he stated:

> Yet, one specialized feature of the Christian's use of Old Testament texts has not been as thoroughly explored as perhaps it ought to be. This involves the way in which an outright *substitution* of christocentricism for theocentricism occurs with many of the Old Testament quotations and allusions.[6]

While many have taken notice of this "substitution" or shift of referent from God to Christ in Paul's quotations, comprehensive studies into these matters have not been forthcoming. Kreitzer contributed in his own way by analyzing the eschatological perspective of certain Jewish pseudepigraphical writings (1 Enoch, Jubilees, 2 Enoch, 4 Ezra, and 2 Baruch). Accordingly, he offered some suggestions upon how they might have impacted Paul's eschatological teachings, in particular, his view of the messianic kingdom, the parousia, and the final judgment. His investigation into Paul's teachings on "the Day of the Lord" included some important examples of a "referential shift" from God to Christ centered around the κύριος title.[7] He concluded that in Paul's writings a "conceptual ambiguity" existed involving the eschatological roles of God and Christ. This ambiguity reflected "the delicate balance between theocentricity and christocentricity in Paul's thought"[8] and illustrated the close connection between Paul's Christology and eschatology. For Paul, "the Day of the Lord," a doctrine so significant for the Old Testament, had become "the Day of the Lord Jesus Christ."

The present writer hopes that this volume offers a further contribution in this regard as it deals with Paul's christological application of Old Testament texts originally reserved for Yahweh. In addition, it is anticipated that this investigation will correct the claims of scholars, like Scroggs, who believe Paul did not substantially identify Christ with God.

[5.] Longenecker, *Biblical Exegesis*, 207; L. Joseph Kreitzer, *Jesus and God in Paul's Eschatology* (Sheffield, UK: Academic Press, 1987), 18; and Beker, *Paul*, 251-52.

[6.] Kreitzer, *Jesus and God*, 18.

[7.] Ibid., 112-27.

[8.] Ibid., 128-29.

Introduction

The purpose of this project is to analyze Paul's use of Old Testament Yahweh texts and to derive from this analysis some implications for his Christology. In the present study a Yahweh text is a quotation of or an allusion to an Old Testament text which refers directly to the divine name (יהוה) in the HT. However, since Paul's quotations demonstrate affinities with the Septuagint (LXX)[9] and since κύριος replaced the divine name therein, this investigation focuses upon Pauline quotations which contain the κύριος predicate.[10]

The Significance of the Name "Yahweh"

The concept of the divine name in the Old Testament stands in sharp contrast to the same idea in the Hellenistic world. The Greeks had a fascination with the names of their gods and goddesses, treating them at times as magical formulas to conjure up some kind of supernatural aid. They even gave many names to some gods out of the fear that the correct name might be missed, or perhaps to emphasize their greatness and power.[11]

The Old Testament, however, depicts a different concept of the divine name. Rather than being an object of speculation, it presents God as revealing his name to his followers. The *locus classicus* for this is found in Exod 3:13-15:

> Then Moses said to God, "If I come to the people of Israel and say to them, 'The God of your fathers has sent me to you,' and they ask me, 'What is his name?' what shall I say to them?" God said to Moses, "I AM WHO I AM (אהיה אשר אהיה)." And he said, "Say this to the people of Israel, 'I AM (אהיה) has sent me to you.'" God also said to Moses, "Say this to the people of Israel, 'The LORD (יהוה), the God of your fathers, the God of Abraham, the God of Isaac, and the God of Jacob, has sent me to you': this is my name forever, and thus I am to be remembered throughout all generations."

[9.] Ellis, *Paul's Use*, 11-20.

[10.] Not all Pauline quotations which contain the κύριος predicate have the divine name in the HT (e.g., Rom 10:16; 11:3; 12:19; 1 Cor 14:21). These by definition are not dealt with here.

[11.] Hans Bietenhard, "ὄνομα," *TDNT*, 5:243-52.

In this important text God responded to Moses' request by revealing to him the divine name, Yahweh, and identifying himself as the God of his ancestors. In Exod 6:2-3 God clarified that relationship when He said:

> "I am the LORD (יהוה). I appeared to Abraham, to Isaac, and to Jacob, as God Almighty (אל שדי) but by my name the LORD (יהוה) I did not make myself known to them."

These are not, however, the first occurrences of Yahweh (יהוה) in the Old Testament. Genesis 4:26 describes Enosh and his descendants as the first to invoke Yahweh's name, suggesting that the name Yahweh was known in pre-Mosaic times (cf. Gen 9:26). Accordingly, some scholars believe Exodus 3 to be an explanation of a name already known to Moses, a name mediated to him perhaps by his Midianite father-in-law, Jethro.[12] Nevertheless, they are not able to agree on the etymology of Yahweh as the divine name, although the relationship of Yahweh to the verb "to be" (היה) arises from the context of Exod 3:13-15.[13]

Gerhard von Rad warned against reading too much into the name "Yahweh" regarding God's character or nature. He admitted that Old Testament writers customarily considered names to be significant indicators of one's character and person. He suggested, however, that the revelation of the divine name in Moses' time emphasized Yahweh's "being there" for Israel in the midst of their hopeless situation.[14]

Thus, the name "Yahweh" acquired its significance primarily in relation to the Exodus and the establishing of the covenant. This is witnessed by the oft-repeated phrase: "I am the LORD (יהוה) your God, who brought you out of the land of Egypt, out of the house of bondage" (Exod 20:2). Yahweh is God's covenant name revealed to Israel as God's covenant people, thereby assuring them of his pres-

---

[12.] Ludwig Köhler, *Old Testament Theology*, trans. A. S. Todd (Philadelphia: Westminster, 1957), 45-46; and Edmond Jacob, *Theology of the Old Testament*, trans. Arthur W. Heathcote and Philip J. Allcock (London: Hodder & Stoughton, 1955), 48-54.

[13.] A. B. Davidson, *The Theology of the Old Testament* (Edinburgh: T. & T. Clark, 1904), 53-54, suggested that the relation of יהוה to היה may be a play on words and not an indication of etymology. On the possible meanings of the name "Yahweh" see Jacob, *Theology*, 48-54.

[14.] Gerhard von Rad, *Old Testament Theology: The Theology of Israel's Historical Traditions*, trans. D. M. G. Stalker, vol. 1 (New York: Harper & Brothers, 1962), 179-80.

ence as well as reminding them of his demands. It emphasizes God's saving activity on behalf of his people, not only in the past, but also in the future.[15] It does not express his nature; it does express his relation to Israel. It indicates that Yahweh is a national God and that Israel's worship was monolatrous, if not monotheistic, from the beginning.

The covenant people had great reverence for the name "Yahweh" as indicated by the prohibition in Exod 20:7 against using Yahweh's name in vain. They used it in sacrifice, prayer, blessings, curses, and holy war.[16] Although the Old Testament used the name over six thousand times to indicate the God of Israel, according to von Rad the Jews utilized it less and less during the post-exilic period. By the first century the name "Yahweh" was probably not spoken in the synagogues and only seldom, if at all, in certain temple ceremonies.[17]

In light of the reverence attributed to the divine name (יהוה) in the Old Testament and Paul's high regard for scripture,[18] his christological use of Old Testament Yahweh texts offers important insights into his view of Christ.

Format of Study

No investigation into Paul's use of Old Testament Yahweh texts would be complete without first addressing the Greek word used to translate the divine name (יהוה) in the LXX and in the New Testament. Chapter one discusses how scholars understand the origin and content of κύριος as a christological designation. Chapter two carries the investigation further as it focuses upon how Paul's Bible (the LXX) uses κύριος as a designation for men with legitimate claims to

---

[15] Davidson, *Theology*, 55-56, pointed out that the force of the imperfect phrase אהיה אשר אהיה signifies one who comes in full manifestation.

[16] E.g., Gen 12:8; 13:4; 21:33; Num 6:27; Deut 6:13; 10:8; 2 Sam 6:18; 1 Kgs 18:24; Ps 20:8 [7]; 44:6 [5]; 54:1; 118:10.

[17] von Rad, *Theology*, 1:179-87, thought this was suggested by scant usage of the name in later Old Testament literature (e.g., Esther, Ecclesiastes, Song of Solomon, Psalm 42-83). Also compare 1 and 2 Chronicles with the same events told in 1 and 2 Samuel and 1 and 2 Kings.

[18] Paul's view of scripture may be adduced from statements in Rom 1:2, 3:1-2, and particularly 2 Tim 3:16, i.e., that all scripture is "God-breathed" (θεόπνευστος). Moreover, his tendency to quote scripture frequently in defending doctrinal and ethical instruction indicates a high regard for those sacred books.

authority and for יהוה, the divine name for God in the Old Testament. It discusses how Paul employed the title as a designation for men in authority, for God, and in particular for Christ. Finally, it argues that Paul's christological use of κύριος reveals his overall thought structure regarding Jesus' Lordship and informs the investigator as he determines how Paul utilized Yahweh texts. With such conclusions in mind, chapter three engages in an exegetical study of Pauline Yahweh texts to determine whether the apostle applied a particular quotation to God or to Christ. It classifies them as "Yahweh Texts with God As Referent" and "Yahweh Texts with Christ As Referent." In addition it surveys Pauline allusions to Yahweh texts. It concludes with a synthesis of the information and draws from it some implications for Paul's understanding of Christ.

Generally, the present writer follows the lead of H. B. Swete, who offered a definition of a quotation based upon (1) the presence of an introductory formula and (2) verbal affinity with a known translation of the Old Testament.[19] E. E. Ellis improved upon the definition when he listed his own criteria for determining the presence of a quotation: "the presence of an introductory formula or conjunction, the degree of verbal affinity with the OT text, and the intention of the apostle as judged from the context."[20] Allusions, on the other hand, typically lack an introductory formula, have a lesser degree of verbal affinity, and are embedded in the surrounding material so that it is difficult to determine where they begin or end. Nevertheless, the distinction between a quotation and an allusion often cannot be strictly defined.[21] With these criteria in mind, this study will deal with passages commonly recognized as quotations or allusions by Ellis[22] and various biblical commentators.

The Use of the Pastorals

Biblical scholars in the nineteenth century generally assumed that Paul either wrote his letters or dictated them verbatim. Consequently, they held that vocabulary, style, and theological expression

---

[19] H. B. Swete, *An Introduction to the Old Testament in Greek*, 2d ed. (Cambridge: University Press, 1914), 382.

[20] Ellis, *Paul's Use*, 11.

[21] Ibid. Ellis commented: "the gradation from quotation to allusion is so imperceptible that it is almost impossible to draw any certain line."

[22] Ibid., 150-87.

could be used to determine whether or not Paul was the author of a particular letter. Some, having decided that Romans, Galatians, and 1 and 2 Corinthians were Paul's genuine epistles, compared these to the Pastorals and concluded that they could not have been penned by the apostle.[23]

Recent studies, however, have called this assumption into question on two accounts. First, Paul wrote his letters through a secretary who could have exercised considerable influence upon a letter's literary style.[24] Second, in composing the Pastorals, as in other letters, he used pre-formed traditions, hymns, and teaching pieces.[25] Consequently, a letter's vocabulary and style could be due to the use of a secretary or pre-formed materials and not simply to the hand of the stated author.

Since the primary assumption upon which the deutero-Pauline theory was constructed has been dismantled, it is doubtful that the Pastoral's vocabulary, style, and manner of theological expression can be used to exclude them from Pauline authorship. In fact, Pauline authorship of the Pastorals is indicated by (1) the *prima facia* claim to Pauline composition (1 Tim 1:1; 2 Tim 1:1; Tit 1:1), (2) the

---

[23.] Contemporary adherents to this approach include Martin Dibelius and Hans Conzelmann, *The Pastoral Epistles*, Hermeneia, trans. Philip Buttolph and Adela Yarbro (Philadelphia: Fortress, 1972), 1-5; Karl Hermann Schelkle, *Paulus: Leben—Briefe—Theologie*, Erträge der Forschung, vol. 152 (Darmstadt: Wissenschaftliche Buchgesellschaft, 1981), 139-47; Günther Bornkamm, *Paul*, trans. D. M. G. Stalker (New York: Harper & Row, 1969), 242-43; Rudolf Bultmann, *Theology of the New Testament*, 2 vols., trans. Kendrick Grobel (New York: Charles Scribner's Sons, 1951-55), 2:183-86; and Werner Georg Kümmel, *Introduction to the New Testament*, trans. Howard C. Kee (Nashville: Abingdon, 1975), 366-88.

[24.] Otto Roller, *Das Formular der paulinischen Briefe* (Stuttgart: W. Kohlhammer, 1933). That Paul used a secretary is indicated by Rom 16:22 ("Tertius"); 1 Cor 16:21; Gal 6:11; Col 4:18; 2 Thess 3:14; Philem 19. On the possibility and extent of secretarial influence on Paul's letters consult E. R. Richards, "The Role of the Secretary in Greco-Roman Antiquity and Its Implications for the Letters of Paul," (Ph.D. diss., Southwestern Baptist Theological Seminary, Fort Worth, TX, 1988), 326-53. In addition, Paul's co-senders may have had considerable influence upon a letter's literary style (1 Cor 1:1; 2 Cor 1:1; Phil 1:1; Col 1:1; 1 Thess 1:1; 2 Thess 1:1; Philem 1).

[25.] E. Earle Ellis, "Traditions in the Pastoral Epistles," *Early Jewish and Christian Exegesis*, ed. C. A. Evans and William F. Stinespring (Atlanta: Scholars Press, 1987), 239-46. Paul's use of pre-formed material is now accepted in the undisputed letters, e.g., Rom 1:3-4; 1 Cor 8:6; 11:23-26; 15:1-6; Phil 2:6-11; 1 Thess 4:15-17. See E. Earle Ellis, "Traditions in 1 Corinthians," *NTS* 32 (1986): 481-502.

presence of Pauline features in each letter,[26] and (3) the early church's witness to their genuineness.[27] If the Pastorals were not written or dictated verbatim by Paul, they were in all probability written by the careful hand of a trusted secretary to whom the apostle granted considerable latitude in writing.[28] Therefore, they can be classified as from Paul and not relegated to a different time and setting in the early church.[29]

Accordingly, evidence from the Pastorals is used in this project. However, since Yahweh texts are present primarily in the undisputed letters, should evidence from the Pastorals be omitted, it would not substantially alter the thesis or results.

[26.] E. Earle Ellis, *Paul and His Recent Interpreters* (Grand Rapids: Eerdmans, 1961), 49-57. The presence of Pauline materials in the Pastorals caused some to suggest the Pastorals contain genuine Pauline fragments. See P. N. Harrison, *The Problem of the Pastoral Epistles* (London: Oxford, 1921); B. S. Easton, *The Pastoral Epistles* (New York: Charles Scribner's Sons, 1947), 9-15; C. K. Barrett, *The Pastoral Epistles* (Oxford: Clarendon Press, 1963), 4-12; perhaps Bruce Metzger, *The New Testament: Its Background, Growth, and Content*, 2d ed. (Nashville: Abingdon, 1983), 214, 238.

[27.] Irenaeus *Against Heresies* 2.17.7; 3.3.3; Polycarp *Philippians* 4.1; Tertullian *Against Marcion* 2.21; see other sources and canonical lists as cited in J. H. Bernard, *The Pastoral Epistles* (Cambridge: Cambridge University Press, 1899; reprint, Grand Rapids: Baker, 1980), xiii-xxi.

[28.] C. F. D. Moule, "The Problem of the Pastoral Epistles: A Reappraisal," *BJRL* 47 (1964/65): 430-52, suggested the likelihood of Luke as the secretary.

[29.] The following scholars generally agree to Pauline authorship of the Pastorals: Walter Lock, *A Critical and Exegetical Commentary on the Pastoral Epistles*, ICC (Edinburgh: T. & T. Clark, 1924), xxii-xxxi; J. B. Lightfoot, *Biblical Essays* (London: MacMillan & Co., 1904), 397-410; J. N. D. Kelly, *A Commentary on the Pastoral Epistles*, Thornapple Commentaries (New York: Harper & Row, 1963; reprint, Grand Rapids: Baker, 1981), 30-34; Joachim Jeremias, *Die Briefe an Timotheus und Titus* (Göttingen: Vandenhoeck & Ruprecht, 1949), 3-7; and Ellis, *Paul*, 49-57.

I. ΚΥΡΙΟΣ As a Christological Title in Recent Discussion

Paul's use of Old Testament Yahweh texts reflects a larger debate on two ways of approaching New Testament theology. Generally speaking, it is a part of a debate between the History of Religions School, which considers Graeco-Roman influences upon the New Testament to be as important as Jewish factors, and the Salvation History School, which regards Jewish influences as dominant.[1] Although this characterization may be an oversimplification, it nevertheless reflects the tension between the two approaches. The κύριος ("Lord") title as applied to Jesus is part of that argument, for some look for the title's background in Greek, others in Jewish sources.

This chapter presents these two ways of understanding the christological use of κύριος, dealing primarily with the theories of the major proponents on each side. It concludes with a summary and a critique which should demonstrate that the weight of the evidence falls in one direction.

The Background of Current Research

Perhaps the major question confronting biblical interpreters regarding this title involves its setting within the early church. Three options have been suggested.

(1) Some accept the premise that the Aramaic-speaking congregations within Palestine were the first to acclaim Jesus as "Lord" in the divine sense.[2] (2) Others, supposing that such an acclamation among

---

[1] I. H. Marshall, *The Origins of New Testament Christology* (Leicester, UK: Inter-Varsity Press, 1976), 16-18. The History of Religions method searches the environment in which Christianity developed and asserts that most of its teachings are derived from that environment. This is no doubt true. Marshall called this a "reasonable working hypothesis." The real question lies in where one should search for the environment. Since the New Testament quotes extensively from the Old Testament and portrays a Jewish background, is it necessary to look to pagan religions and ideas for their contributions to New Testament theology? This question will be addressed below.

[2] E.g., Vincent Taylor, *The Names of Jesus* (New York: St. Martin's Press, 1953), 38-51.

Jewish monotheists would be impossible, suggest that Greek-speaking churches, outside Palestine, and therefore free from the constraints of biblical monotheism, were the initial catalysts for the acclamation of Jesus as κύριος.[3] (3) Still others attempt to draw upon positive elements of both theories. They assert that Jesus was called "Lord" in the earliest Palestinian churches as demonstrated by the Maranatha invocation of 1 Cor 16:22. However, they claim the term meant something entirely different to those first Jewish believers than it did to later Gentile believers who composed Paul's churches. For Palestinian Jewish Christians, Jesus would be κύριος when he returned. For Diaspora Jewish Christians, Jesus was the exalted κύριος who now reigns at the right hand of God. For Gentile Christians, Jesus was presently κύριος in the fullest sense of divinity. Only for this final group was Jesus considered divine.[4] To discover the origin and content of Paul's use of the title κύριος, each of these theories should be considered in more detail.

The Theory of an Origin outside Palestine

As biblical interpreters seek to discover the origin and content of the christological designation κύριος, some conclude, for a variety of reasons, that Christian churches outside Palestine were the first to apply this title to Jesus. To understand this point of view, it is necessary to examine the contribution of two representative thinkers, Wilhelm Bousset and Ferdinand Hahn.

The Thesis of Wilhelm Bousset

According to Wilhelm Bousset, the title κύριος ("Lord"), as applied to Jesus, originated in the setting of Greek churches outside Palestine. This title displaced the terms "Son of Man" and "Christ," which were human titles prevalent in the Palestinian communities. It became the new title of the Hellenistic churches, which was inherited and used by Paul.[5]

[3.] E.g., Wilhelm Bousset, *Kyrios Christos: A History of the Belief in Christ from the Beginnings of Christianity to Irenaeus*, trans. John E. Steely (Nashville: Abingdon Press, 1970). This book was originally published in German in 1913 and revised posthumously in 1921. Bultmann, *Theology*, 1:51-56, followed Bousset.

[4.] Ferdinand Hahn, *The Titles of Jesus in Christology: Their History in Early Christianity*, trans. Harold Knight and George Ogg (New York: World Publishing Co., 1969), 68-73, 101-13.

[5.] Bousset, *Kyrios*, 121-28. Interestingly, Bousset claimed the seed for the acclamation of Jesus as Lord was found in the Palestinian church in the acts of exorcism in Jesus' name.

Earliest Christianity, with its eschatological "Son of Man" figure, emphasized the future of the Church when the Messiah would return to restore all things (Acts 3:21). As it moved beyond Judea and Samaria to "the uttermost parts of the earth," however, it took on a decidedly Gentile flavor.

Rather than emphasizing the future consummation, Gentile Christianity stressed the present experience of their Lord in the worshiping community. It experienced the presence of the risen Lord in baptism, in celebrations of the Lord's Supper, and in miraculous workings and utterances during worship. Within this context it used the κύριος predicate for Jesus.[6]

Bousset, who approached his task with meticulous care, reasoned that Hellenistic Christianity first grew and developed in Syria where the κύριος title, along with the implications which went with it, was first used in worship. He cautioned, however:

> No one thought this out, and no theologian created it; people did not read it out of the sacred book of the Old Testament. They would hardly have dared without further ado to make such a direct transferral of the holy name of the almighty God—actually almost a deification of Jesus. Such proceedings take place in the unconscious, in the uncontrollable depths of the group psyche of a community; this is self-evident, it lay as it were in the air, that the first Hellenistic Christian communities gave the title κύριος to their cult hero.[7]

Primarily, two reasons stand behind the theory of an origin outside Palestine. First, the monotheistic heritage of the first Palestinian believers would have prevented their assigning to Jesus, a man of recent memory, such a position. Bousset stated:

> Now it becomes clear that it was no accident that we did not encounter the title Kyrios on Palestinian soil in the gospel tradition. Such a development would not have been possible here. This placing of Jesus in the center of the cultus of a believing community, this peculiar doubling of the object of veneration in worship, is conceivable only in an environment in which Old Testament monotheism no longer ruled unconditionally and with absolute security.[8]

[6.] Ibid., 129-33, 151. For a good summary of Bousset's view of the church's worship of κύριος, see pp. 134-38.

[7.] Ibid., 146-47.

Thus, Jesus could have been acclaimed as Lord only outside a Palestinian context.

Second, philological and religious factors within the Greek and Roman culture would have facilitated the ascription of deity to Jesus. Ancient writers used the κύριος predicate widely in reference to the ruler cults common in Roman, Greek, and Egyptian political and religious life. One writer called Augustus "God and Lord Caesar" (θεὸς καὶ κύριος Καῖσαρ Αὐτοκράτωρ).[9] Epictetus referred to Caesar as Lord (κύριος) of all.[10] Other texts also show that, around the first century, rulers were often acclaimed as κύριος.[11]

Not only did worshippers utilize the κύριος predicate in the adoration of their rulers, but they also applied it commonly to the gods of the mystery religions.[12] Supplicants of Isis called her "the Lord God of the earth" (ἡ κύρια τῆς γῆς θεός);[13] and others likewise applied it to Zeus, Poseidon, Helios, Dionysius, Osiris, and other gods.[14]

Therefore, according to Bousset, the κύριος title, as it was used in the emperor cult and in the mystery religions, provided the backdrop for the application of the same title to the cult figure of early Christianity. Thus, it was given to Jesus within, and only within, the environs of the Diaspora churches.

The Thesis of Ferdinand Hahn

Ferdinand Hahn built upon many of the presuppositions and findings of Bousset and the History of Religions School. He was also sensitive, however, to some of the weaknesses of this approach and the need to take more seriously the contribution of the earliest churches to the formation of New Testament Christology. He agreed that the earliest Palestinian communities referred to Jesus as "Lord" but supposed that for them the title had nothing to do with divinity or worship. Noting that the Synoptic Gospels parallel διδάσκαλε and

---

[8.] Ibid., 147.

[9.] BGU, 1197.1.15, cited in Werner Foerster, "κύριος," *TDNT*, 3:1049.

[10.] Epictetus *Dissertationes* 4.1.12.

[11.] Bousset, *Kyrios*, 138-48, gave numerous examples. See also Foerster, *TDNT*, 3:1049.

[12.] Ibid.

[13.] Plutarchus *De Iside et Osiride* 2.367.

[14.] See the texts cited in Foerster, *TDNT*, 3:1047-58.

κύριε, vocative forms for "teacher" and "lord" respectively, he argued that the disciples probably referred to Jesus as their "teacher" (רבי) and their "lord" (מרי). The title κύριος applied to Jesus by the Palestinian disciples was, he concluded, in no way an assertion of deity but was only an assertation that Jesus was their teacher.[15]

Hahn also affirmed with Bousset that κύριος played an essential role in the practices of the mysteries and the emperor cult. He surmised that the title emphasized the unlimited power, authority, and divinity of its bearer. He concluded that this understanding of the title must have had some affect on the gospel's proclamation outside Palestine[16] where Jewish monotheism was not pervasive and where the influx of pagan ideas brought about changes in doctrine, including Christology. Accordingly, he argued that the acclamation "Jesus is Lord" grew out of the Palestinian churches' ideas regarding Jesus' earthly activity and his anticipated return but must be seen as distinct from it. Hahn wrote:

> The kyrios predicate of the Hellenistic church not only had a foreshadowing in the Palestinian sphere, but also took over from thence a concept which in some important respects was already moulded with firm features, and which even later was not given up. This does not preclude the fact that the old Palestinian conception was basically distinct from the Hellenistic one, for elements which came to predominate later are completely absent from it.[17]

By this Hahn meant, above all, that Jesus was worshiped as divine in the Gentile churches. And yet, he claimed, this was not totally new; it was the culmination of a long process of development in which each stage of christological development had its genesis in the preceding stage.[18]

Hahn elaborated on Bousset's theory and introduced another stage between Jesus and Paul. Whereas Bousset believed the Hellenistic Greek Church stood between Paul and the Palestinian

---

[15] Hahn, *Titles*, 73-88. Accordingly, Jesus also did not consider himself the "Lord" in the absolute sense. See John 13:13-14 where the two descriptions are parallel.

[16] Ibid., 68-73. Hahn ignored the possibility that the κύριος title may have exercised some influence on Palestinian thought also.

[17] Ibid., 101.

[18] Ibid., 110. The church assigned to the Exalted One this title as it was "faced with the task of defining the reality of the work and person of Jesus."

Church, Hahn asserted that two communities separated Paul from the earliest Church: (1) the Hellenistic Jewish Church and (2) the Hellenistic Greek Church.[19] In so doing he added further distance between Paul's teachings and the doctrines of the first believers.

Therefore, according to Hahn's theory, the Palestinian churches considered Jesus their rabbi and teacher, while the Gentile churches worshiped him as "Lord." Under this reconstruction Paul's Christology inevitably must be seen as a departure from the Christology of the earliest believers.

The Theory of a Palestinian Origin

Other interpreters, having studied the period and contemporary literature, have concluded that Palestinian churches applied κύριος to Jesus, not merely to express their confidence in him as teacher, but to express their religious devotion to him as well. It is now necessary to consider the contributions of J. Gresham Machen, A. E. J. Rawlinson, and Oscar Cullmann.

The Thesis of J. Gresham Machen

J. Gresham Machen offered one of the most significant rejoinders to Bousset's theory. In his book, *The Origin of Paul's Religion*,[20] he argued against the importance of Graeco-Roman influences on Paul and upheld his Jewish background as the dominant factor in the formation of his religion, particularly his Christology.[21]

Machen challenged Bousset's reconstruction of the christological use of κύριος in several areas. (1) Bousset maintained that "Lord" was not a title of the Palestinian churches due to (a) its infrequent and often unimportant appearances in the Synoptic Gospels and (b) the fact that the Synoptics emerged from the Jerusalem church. Machen countered that κύριος as applied to Jesus in the Gospels often carried great christological import. While admitting the vocative form of the term usually indicated polite address, he nevertheless highlighted several key passages, including Mark 12:35-37, which refer κύριος to Jesus (cf. Matt 7:21 and Luke 6:46). He saw the crux of Mark 12:35-37 in the quotation from Ps 110:1 (LXX, 109:1) which begins, εἶπεν κύριος τῷ κυρίῳ μου ("The Lord said to my Lord"). In

---

[19] Ibid., 68-135.

[20] J. Gresham Machen, *The Origin of Paul's Religion* (New York: MacMillan, 1923).

[21] Ibid., 173-251.

this phrase the first κύριος translates the divine name (יהוה) and the second אדני in the Hebrew text. Machen criticized Bousset for attempting to explain away the christological significance of this verse by appealing to the LXX which does not differentiate between the sacred and secular use of κύριος. He pointed out further that the title "Christ" was not frequent in the Gospels either, yet Bousset believed it to be a designation of the Palestinian church. How then, he asked, can Bousset ascribe "Christ" to the Palestinian church and, at the same time, ascribe κύριος only to churches outside Palestine, given their similar record of infrequent appearances in the Gospels?[22]

(2) Machen disputed Bousset's claim that Paul's christological use of κύριος came, not from Palestine, but from Christian communities in Antioch, Damascus, and/or Tarsus. He appealed to the common sense interpretation of the phrase "brother of the Lord" in Gal 1:19 as evidence that such nomenclature was current in Palestine. He also argued that the Maranatha invocation (1 Cor 16:22) demonstrates that the Aramaic-speaking church in Palestine called Jesus "Lord." Otherwise, he thought, why would it have become what was evidently a sacred word for Paul's Gentile churches? Beyond this, he even raised the possibility that the christological designation κύριος may be traced to Jerusalem due to the influence of the Hellenists (Acts 6).[23]

(3) Machen also challenged Bousset's contention that κύριος became a christological title in churches outside Palestine due to (a) the ecstatic nature of their worship experiences and (b) their consequent belief that their "Lord" was present in these times of worship. He wondered how this could have happened given the apparent intolerance of Christian monotheists like Paul as expressed, for example, in 1 Cor 8:4-6 and 10:14-22. Since these passages reflect admonitions given to Diaspora believers, how did they come to identify Jesus with pagan cult-deities? While Machen granted the syncretistic mood of most pagan groups, he continued to emphasize the evidence that early Christianity was forged in the strong monotheistic heritage of Judaism.[24]

Accordingly, for Machen, the Greek word κύριος, as used in the New Testament, does not indicate dependence upon pagan cults; rather it indicates only dependence upon the Greek language. If the

---

[22.] Machen, *Origin*, 295-98.

[23.] Ibid., 298-302.

[24.] Ibid., 306.

gospel were to make inroads into the Greek milieu, it must do so on the vehicle of Greek language and concepts. Furthermore, since κύριος was used in the LXX for יהוה and since Christianity first grew and developed among readers of the Greek scriptures, the use of κύριος therein sheds more light upon Christian usage than does pagan usage.[25]

Machen believed the origin of Paul's Christology would not be discovered apart from an understanding of his Damascus road experience and the recognition of the truth of his claims about Christ, that is, Jesus was who Paul said, the Savior, the Son of God, the "Lord." Until scholars overcome their anti-supernatural bias, he argued, they would never grasp the background and essentials of Paul's religion.[26]

The Thesis of A. E. J. Rawlinson

A. E. J. Rawlinson presented another major challenge to Bousset's theory.[27] He believed that the key issues could be summarized in terms of the questions: To what extent did Paul the missionary to the Gentiles remain a Jew? To what extent did he succumb to the syncretistic mood of the day?[28]

Bousset held that Paul's faith was ignited not by the historical Jesus nor his Damascus road experience but by "the powerful reality of the Kyrios as Paul experienced it in the first Hellenistic communities."[29] He thus understood Paul's religion as a departure from the faith of the Palestinian Church in which only limited fragments of the apostle's Jewishness remained, namely (1) his tendency to distinguish between God as Father and Jesus as Lord and (2) his view of Christ's return which relied on a Jewish eschatological scheme.[30] All

---

[25] Ibid., 306-8.

[26] Ibid., 309-17.

[27] A. E. J. Rawlinson, *The New Testament Doctrine of the Christ* (New York: Longmans, Green and Co., 1926). The substance of Rawlinson's work was presented at the Bampton Lectures in 1926.

[28] Ibid., 97.

[29] Bousset, *Kyrios*, 116.

[30] Ibid., 205-10. E.g., 1 Cor 8:5-6. For Bousset Jesus was the image of God, not God himself. For this reason one cannot speak of the deity of Christ in Paul. Paul never called him θεός, and he always maintained a clear distinction and subordination (1 Cor 11:3; 3:22-23; 15:25-28). Bousset did concede, however, that despite Paul's desire to maintain this distinction, later believers could not do so since they venerated Jesus as "Lord" in worship. Cf. Rawlinson, *Christ*, 97.

in all, according to Bousset, Paul's basic mindset remained the product of the Hellenistic Church.

Rawlinson countered by saying that Paul would have been astonished by such an idea. Following Schweitzer[31] and arguing upon the basis of Paul's own letters, he concluded that the apostle considered Christianity not a new religion, but "simply Judaism with its centre of gravity shifted in consequence of the new era."[32] For example, Paul spoke of the gospel as "the power of God for salvation to every one who has faith, to the Jew first and also to the Greek" (Rom 1:16). He consistently quoted and argued doctrine from the standpoint of the Old Testament, even though his letters were addressed to primarily Gentile audiences. He often spoke with pride concerning his Jewish background and heritage (e.g., Gal 1:13-14; Phil 3:4-6). He demonstrated little knowledge of Greek literature[33] or philosophy. Moreover, as did other Jews, he considered pagan sacrifices as offerings to demons and not to God (1 Cor 10:20). Given these facts, Rawlinson asked, is it likely that Paul would have borrowed ideas or practices from pagans?[34]

Against Bousset κύριος should not be rigidly distinguished in its secular and sacred usage. Whether applied to gods or to man, it meant that the one called "lord" had a just claim to reverence and honor by his subordinates or worshipers. This is evident in the New Testament's use of Psalm 110. According to Bousset, "lord" (אדני) applied by David to the Messiah could mean "lord" only in the secular sense. But since in Hebrew thought the king was already considered anointed by Yahweh and in some sense divine and since the Messiah was no mere king but Yahweh's special agent of redemption, "lord" in this context cannot have a merely secular connotation.[35]

According to Rawlinson the Maranatha invocation (1 Cor 16:22) is the "Achilles' heel" of Bousset's theory. It gives evidence that the title "Lord" (מרי) was used in the Aramaic-speaking congregations with reference to Jesus. Despite Bousset's contention that this did

---

[31]. Albert Schweitzer, *Paul and His Interpreters: A Critical History*, trans. W. Montgomery (London: Adam and Charles Black, 1912), 227.

[32]. Rawlinson, *Christ*, 98.

[33]. One may note the exceptions in 1 Cor 15:33, which Rawlinson, *Christ*, 99, considered a "schoolboy tag," and Tit 1:12.

[34]. Rawlinson, *Christ*, 99.

[35]. Ibid., 234-35.

not amount to the worship of Christ in the earliest churches,[36] it indicates that inherent within the movement from the beginning was the idea that "Lord" meant Jesus was more than a man.

From this basic way of thinking about Jesus as "Lord," Rawlinson reasoned, the first believers began to worship Christ. Given Bousset's theory, he asked, how did "Lord" come to connote deity for converts if for Palestinian missionaries he was only a man?[37]

In light of this evidence κύριος as a Pauline title for Christ could not have originated in the setting of Greek churches as Bousset contended. Rather it emerged in Palestinian Jewish Christianity.[38]

The Thesis of Oscar Cullmann

Oscar Cullmann in his book, *The Christology of the New Testament*, also challenged the thesis of the History of Religions School. He believed that there was no need to look beyond Palestine for the origin of Jesus' worship as Lord.[39]

Cullmann placed the κύριος title under his discussion of the present work of Christ. Although he recognized the Hellenistic use of the term to be significant in Graeco-Roman religious thought, he stopped short of claiming that this understanding influenced the New Testament writers. He believed Bousset was too quick to propose that the worship of Christ did not occur in Palestine. In fact, he argued that one cannot prove that Hellenistic churches were the first to worship Jesus as divine.[40]

As evidence of this, Cullmann pointed to the Maranatha passage (1 Cor 16:22), the oldest liturgical formula in the New Testament. He considered it to be a prayer ("Our Lord, Come!") that was most likely

---

[36] Bousset, *Kyrios*, 210.

[37] Rawlinson, *Christ*, 234-37.

[38] Ibid., 106. On the broad question at the heart of the debate between the Salvation History School and the History of Religions School, Rawlinson concluded: "any fruitful examination of S. Paul's doctrine of the person of Christ must proceed upon the assumption that its presuppositions are not syncretistic and virtually pagan, but Jewish and Christian, and that the supposed cleavage in respect of Christology and worship between the Christianity of Palestine and that of the Gentile-Christian Church is a chimera."

[39] Oscar Cullmann, *The Christology of the New Testament*, trans. Shirley Guthrie and Charles A. M. Hall (Philadelphia: Westminster, 1959), 203.

[40] Ibid., 206.

used in an eucharistic setting. With Rawlinson, he believed it to be the weak link in Bousset's theory and proof that the original Aramaic-speaking church worshiped Christ. He wrote: "[1 Cor 16:22] shows from the very beginning that it is impossible to explain the Aramaic formula Maranatha successfully except in the way which naturally suggests itself when one approaches it without a preconceived opinion: it is an expression of the cultic veneration of Christ by the original Aramaic-speaking Church."[41]

Moving to the linguistic evidence, Cullmann noted that the Greek word κύριος translated both the Hebrew אדני as well as the Aramaic מרי. Since Jesus' first followers were Palestinian Jews, they no doubt used such terms from the first to describe him. These words could be used either as a designation for deity or as a form of polite address ("Master" or "Sir"). But since in synagogue worship אדני had replaced the sacred name יהוה, Cullmann concluded that אדני was the customary form of address for God in Palestinian Judaism in the first centuries.

Cullmann noticed that in the Septuagint (LXX) κύριος is used to translate אדני and יהוה; it must therefore have also been used to express the divine name in scripture reading in Greek-speaking synagogues. Therefore, he contended that the first believers acknowledged and worshiped Jesus as Lord within Palestine.[42] He reasoned that this practice was carried subsequently to Greek-speaking congregations.

Cullmann understood the problem not in terms of Christ's nature, but in terms of his function. He explained: "When it is asked in the New Testament 'Who is Christ?', the question never means exclusively, or even primarily, 'What is his nature?', but first of all, 'What is his function?'"[43] He went on to state that the various New Testament titles and images ascribed to Christ encompass both his person and his work. Nevertheless, such lofty titles and images raised the question in later years concerning both his relationship to God and his nature. Yet Cullmann considered the "nature" question, as it is often asked, foreign to the New Testament. Accordingly, he concluded that the Hebrew believers who wrote the New Testament were not concerned to speculate concerning his nature; they were engaged

---

[41.] Ibid., 208-214.

[42.] Ibid., 199-203.

[43.] Ibid., 3-4.

rather with the highly difficult task of explaining their experience with Jesus as Savior.[44]

Summary

Bousset's theory of a Hellenistic origin for the christological use of κύριος stands upon three basic presuppositions which deserve examination. (1) A dichotomy between Palestinian Jewish congregations and Hellenistic Greek congregations existed in the early Church. (2) The κύριος title as found in the New Testament is parallel to the title used in Greek paganism. (3) Jewish monotheism precluded a divine ascription being given to Jesus in Palestine. Each of these presuppositions deserves comment and criticism.

First, Bousset assumed that a religious dichotomy existed between Palestinian Jewish churches and Hellenistic Greek churches before Paul's conversion.[45] Each group, he argued, had its own needs, language, and ways of expressing its faith in Christ. Hahn's theory was only an elaboration of Bousset's since it included three communities between Jesus and Paul: (1) the Palestinian Jewish Church, (2) the Hellenistic Jewish Church, and (3) the Hellenistic Greek Church.[46] If this were the structure of the early Church, one may

---

[44.] Since Cullmann, others have sought for the origin of the κύριος predicate within Palestine. E.g., Geza Vermes, *Jesus the Jew: A Historian's Reading of the Gospel* (New York: MacMillan, 1973), 111-21; Joseph A. Fitzmyer, "The Semitic Background of the New Testament *Kyrios*-Title," chap. in *A Wandering Aramean: Collected Aramaic Essays*, Society of Biblical Literature Monograph Series, no. 25 (Missoula, MT: Scholars Press, 1979), 115-42; Richard Longenecker, *The Christology of Early Jewish Christianity* (London: SCM Press, 1970; reprint, Grand Rapids: Baker, 1981), 132, pointed out that κύριος had religious but not cosmological overtones for the Palestinian church. It was only in the encounter between the church and the Greek world that the Lordship of Jesus over the cosmos came into play, although he admitted that Lordship implicitly has cosmological import.

[45.] One criticism which may be leveled against the History of Religions School regards the confusion in terminology between terms like "Hellenistic," "Gentile," "Jewish," and "Diaspora." At times it is difficult to understand what proponents mean by these terms since they do not distinguish between racial, cultural, and geographic categories.

[46.] Hahn, *Titles*, 68-135; Reginald Fuller, *Foundations of New Testament Christology* (New York: Charles Scribner's Sons, 1965), followed Hahn as evidenced by his Table of Contents (pp. 7-10). Hendrikus Boers, "Jesus and the Christian Faith: New Testament Christology since Bousset's *Kyrios Christos*," *JBL* 89 (1970): 455, considered Hahn's work the most significant Christology since Bousset's. He

understand why Bousset, Hahn, and those who follow them have arrived at their conclusions. But was this structure present in the early Church, particularly before Paul's conversion, which could only have been a few years following the crucifixion of Jesus? Beyond this, if this dichotomy were present in the early Church, then it must have been reflected in contemporary Palestinian and Diaspora Judaism also. Was this in fact the case? Did Palestine escape the hellenization begun centuries earlier under the Seleucids and continued under the Romans? Two scholars have addressed these issues extensively: W. D. Davies and Martin Hengel.[47]

W. D. Davies in his book, *Paul and Rabbinic Judaism*, argued that Palestinian Judaism did not differ significantly from Diaspora Judaism. He based his argument upon the fact that (1) Greek was known and taught in Palestine,[48] (2) Greek-speaking synagogues were present in Jerusalem (Acts 6:9), (3) Paul, who had been taught by Gamaliel in Palestine, preferred the Greek Old Testament to the Hebrew,[49] and (4) the rabbis permitted translations of the scripture and religious duties to be carried out in Greek.[50] Davies concluded on the basis of these and other factors that since "there was a considerable reciprocal interchange of thought between the Judaism of Palestine and that of the Diaspora,"[51] no basis exists for viewing Palestinian Judaism as a "watertight compartment" against Graeco-Roman influences. He admitted, however, that his cursory examination of the evidence could not settle the issue. To do so, he insisted, would require "an exhaustive study of Palestinian and Hellenistic

---

criticized Hahn, however, (1) for blurring the distinction between primitive Palestinian Christianity and Hellenistic Christianity and (2) for limiting his investigation to the Synoptics, which in Boer's opinion rendered his reconstruction incomplete. Yet he praised Hahn for smoothing over the caesura between the historical Jesus and the Christ worshiped in the churches.

[47.] More briefly, see Ellis, *Prophecy*, 119-120, 125, 245-46; and I. H. Marshall, "Palestinian and Hellenistic Christianity: Some Critical Comments," *NTS* (1972/73): 271-87.

[48.] Josephus *Antiquities* 20.11. W. D. Davies, *Paul and Rabbinic Judaism: Some Rabbinic Elements in Pauline Theology*, 4th ed (Philadelphia: Fortress, 1980), 5, noted that Greek terms were used to designate Jewish institutions, e.g., the Sanhedrin, and perhaps up to eleven hundred Greek terms are found in the Talmud.

[49.] Davies, *Paul*, 5-6; Ellis, *Paul's Use*, 12.

[50.] See sources cited in Davies, *Paul*, 6.

[51.] Ibid., 8.

Judaism in the first century,"[52] a task which was undertaken by Martin Hengel.

In his book, *Judaism and Hellenism*, Hengel concluded that the hellenization of Palestine, which began in the upper classes of society in the third century B.C., made its way to the general populace in the next two centuries.[53] As evidence he cited: (1) Greek loan words in the Talmud,[54] (2) the use of Greek names in Palestine,[55] (3) the erection of a gymnasium in Jerusalem by the high priest Jason (2 Macc 4:7-17), along with the Greek education attendant with it, (4) the writing of Jewish literature and history in Greek,[56] and (5) tombstone inscriptions written in both Greek and Aramaic.[57] According to Hengel, the usual distinction made in New Testament scholarship between Palestinian and Hellenistic Judaism needed re-examination. Hengel concluded: "From about the middle of the third century B.C. *all Judaism* must be designated '*Hellenistic Judaism*' in the strict sense."[58]

[52.] Ibid., 15.

[53.] Martin Hengel, *Judaism and Hellenism: Studies in Their Encounter in Palestine during the Early Hellenistic Period*, 2 vols., trans. John Bowden (Philadelphia: Fortress, 1974), 1:103-6.

[54.] See sources cited in ibid., 1:61; 2:43-44.

[55.] E.g., two of Jesus' disciples, Andrew and Philip, Mark 3:18; the "Hellenists" in Acts 6; 2 Macc 12:9, "Dositheus"; 2 Macc 14:9, "Theodotus"; 2 Macc 4:11, "Eupolemus"; Jos. *Ant.* 12.189, "Hyrcanus"; CIS 1, 115, 116, 122; and other sources cited in Hengel, *Judaism and Hellenism*, 1:61; 2:44-45.

[56.] E.g., LXX, Additions to Esther, 1 Maccabees, 2 Maccabees; 7Q2 in Qumran, and other sources cited in Hengel, *Judaism and Hellenism*, 1:88-102.

[57.] Ibid., 2:71.

[58.] Hengel, *Judaism and Hellenism*, 1:104; cf. James D. G. Dunn, "Some Clarifications on Issues of Method: A Reply to Holladay and Segal," in *Christology and Exegesis: New Approaches*, ed. Robert Jewett, *Semeia* 30 (Decatur, GA: Society of Biblical Literature, 1985), 99, concluded that most New Testament ideas, words or phrases belong to Hellenistic Judaism. See also J. N. Sevenster, *Do You Know Greek?*, Supplements to Novum Testamentum, vol. 19 (Leiden: E. J. Brill, 1968), 189-91, who collated literary and archeological sources from Palestine and concluded that the Greek language was known and used in Palestine in the first century, perhaps even by Jesus and his disciples in certain areas. Joseph A. Fitzmyer, "The Languages of Palestine in the First Century A.D.," chap. in *A Wandering Aramean: Collected Aramaic Essays*, Society of Biblical Literature Monograph Series, no. 25 (Missoula, MT: Scholars Press, 1979), 29-56.

The evidence cited by Hengel and Davies is sufficient to call into question the presupposition which lay behind Bousset's theory that Palestinian and Diaspora Judaism were basically different entities.[59] It demonstrates that Palestinian Judaism, along with the rest of the world, had gradually succumbed to the invasive power of Hellenism.

Thus, there is no evidence that a dichotomy in the early Church between Palestinian Jewish elements and Diaspora elements ever existed. As Professor Hengel pointed out, prior to the Jerusalem Council (A.D. 48), one may not speak of separate Jewish or Greek churches, but only mixed churches with the Jewish Christians remaining the spiritual leaders and the spokesman of doctrine.[60]

Second, Bousset also presupposed that the κύριος title used in Graeco-Roman pagan religious texts is identical with the κύριος title used for Jesus by Paul and other New Testament writers. As he understood it, pagan influence determined Christian usage. Two factors, however, raise significant doubts regarding his understanding of parallel religious concepts and practices in the Graeco-Roman world: (1) the late date of sources cited and (2) the religious antagonism of Paul to paganism.

(1) Many have been quick to point out parallels between Christianity and other religions present—or assumed to be present—in the New Testament world, more specifically, the christological use of κύριος over against the pagan use of it. The problem of parallels, or alleged parallels, is significant in New Testament studies.[61] In identifying significant parallels, four criteria must be satisfied in order to avoid abuses: (a) the parallels must be real rather than imaginary; (b) they must stem from a relevant, contemporary culture;

---

[59] G. B. Caird, "The Development of the Doctrine of Christ in the New Testament," in *Christ for Us Today*, ed. Norman Pittenger (London: SCM Press, 1968), 68-70, believed it was time to lay aside the misconception that two independent, distinct brands of Judaism and Christianity existed in the first century. Likewise, he considered mistaken the presupposition that Christology moved from a lower to a higher plane when it moved out of Palestine to the Greek world.

[60] Martin Hengel, "Christology and New Testament Chronology," chap. in *Between Jesus and Paul* (Philadelphia: Fortress Press, 1983), 37-47

[61] Larry Hurtado, "New Testament Christology: Retrospect and Prospect," in *Christology and Exegesis: New Approaches*, ed. Robert Jewett, *Semeia* 30 (Decatur, GA: Society of Biblical Literature, 1985), 21, wrote: "We must also recognize the responsibility of all historical work to do justice to the peculiarities of each example of religious phenomena, and we must avoid determining the meaning of a term, concept, belief or practice too heavily on the basis of its occurrence in other sources and groups."

(c) they must be significant rather than coincidental; (d) they must represent a genealogical source and not just an analogous similarity.[62]

When applied to Bousset's hypothesis these criteria call into question his contention that the christological use of κύριος had a true parallel in pagan cult-deities. While it may be argued that his thesis does satisfy certain of these criteria, it does not satisfy all of them.

In constructing his thesis, Bousset was not controlled sufficiently by the data at hand because the sources he used were often too late to have affected nascent Christianity. For example, he consistently held that early Christians were influenced significantly by the practices of the mystery religions despite the fact that (a) the mysteries were not prominent until after the second century A.D., (b) their beliefs and practices were not as widespread as originally thought, and (c) Christian practices and thought stood in sharp contrast to these allegedly common mystery practices.[63] From a methodological standpoint, more significant and closer parallels were available in Paul's Jewish background.[64]

In light of these four criteria above, is it correct to understand the Christian affirmation "Jesus is Lord" in terms of "Caesar is Lord"?[65] Likewise, apart from terminological and some cultic affinities (e.g., a sacred meal), is the Christian message in any significant way related to the mysteries? It seems that the rapid rise of Christianity and its uniqueness rule out anything beyond only incidental, verbal parallels.

[62.] See R. T. France, "The Worship of Jesus: A Neglected Factor in Christological Debate?" in *Christ the Lord: Studies in Christology Presented to Donald Guthrie*, ed. Harold H. Rowdon (Leicester, UK: Inter-Varsity Press, 1982), 20-21; Grant Osborne, "Christology and New Testament Hermeneutics: A Survey of the Discussion," in *Christology and Exegesis: New Approaches*, ed. Robert Jewett, *Semeia* 30 (Decatur, GA: Society of Biblical Literature, 1985), 53, followed France.

[63.] Martin Hengel, *The Son of God: The Origin of Christology and the History of Jewish Hellenistic Religion*, trans. John Bowden (Philadelphia: Fortress, 1976), 25-30. See also the work of the following scholars: Machen, *Origin*, 293-317; Hurtado, "Christology," 19-20; and A. D. Nock, *Early Gentile Christianity and Its Hellenistic Background* (New York: Harper & Row, 1964), xi-xvii.

[64.] Fitzmyer, "*Kyrios*-Title," 115-27; see the discussion of Machen, Rawlinson, and Cullmann above, pp. 14-19.

[65.] Hengel, *Son*, 30, considered the ruler cult's terminology to have been "at best a negative stimulus, not a model" for early Christians.

(2) Paul and his co-workers were responsible for translating the Christian message for their Gentile audiences,[66] a message which centered around the person and work of Jesus. They would not have passively permitted the alteration of their gospel under pagan influence as Bousset imagined, particularly in light of the tenor of Galatians.

This is all the more evident when one considers how Paul felt about pagan practices. In 1 Cor 10:20 he indicated that pagan sacrifices to idols were offerings to demons; therefore, believers were not to participate in them. For Paul to have allowed his belief in "Jesus as Lord" to be distorted through the influx of such pagan ideas seems unlikely. Although he desired to win the Gentiles with his message, he would not have run the risk of losing the essentials of that message by adopting pagan concepts.

Admittedly, the Gentile believers, influenced by their own background, determined to some extent what they heard and how they interpreted the gospel. When Paul and his entourage moved on to plant other churches, they were left to work out for themselves the gospel's implications. Yet they received letters from their apostle which continued to affirm the same Jesus whom he had preached when they first met (Gal 1:6-9).

Therefore, Bousset's assumption that the christological use of κύριος arose from Graeco-Roman influence upon the rapidly expanding young churches may also be called into question. It ignores the possibility, even the probability, that Christian beliefs arose primarily in connection with Palestinian Judaism.[67]

Third, Bousset argued that Jewish monotheism would have prevented the acclamation, "Jesus is Lord," and accordingly the christological use of κύριος must have arisen outside Palestine. This argument faces three weighty objections: (1) the attitude of Paul himself, (2) the possible views of Paul's opponents, and (3) the nature of pre-Christian Jewish monotheism.

(1) The apostle Paul claimed to have been "circumcised the eighth day, of the people of Israel, of the tribe of Benjamin, a Hebrew born of Hebrews (Ἑβραῖος ἐξ Ἑβραίων); as to the law a Pharisee, as to zeal a persecutor of the church, as to righteousness under the law blameless" (Phil 3:5-6). With these phrases he underscored that he

---

[66.] Fuller, *Foundations*, 203.

[67.] Hurtado, "Christology," 20, remarked that it would be unwise to assume that influence ran in only one direction. Christianity no doubt affected its culture.

was born into the heart of Judaism and was not merely a loose practioner of his faith. As a Pharisee he would have carefully observed the Mosaic law which included the belief that God is One, as demonstrated in the *Shema* (Deut 6:4-6).[68] In addition, he persecuted the Church at first due to his zeal for the traditions of his fathers and his desire to excel in the practice of Judaism (Gal 1:13-14).

As a Jew Paul was a monotheist. Frequently he spoke of God as being one (e.g., 1 Cor 8:4; Rom 3:29-30; Gal 3:20; Eph 4:6; 1 Tim 2:5). Despite this, however, he was not offended by the declaration "Jesus is Lord" and often proclaimed it to be the heart of his gospel (Rom 10:9; 1 Cor 12:3; Phil 2:9-11).

Therefore, if this profession were possible upon the lips of Paul, the zealous Jew, it was hardly less so within the first Palestinian churches. Against this Bousset could only argue that the Christian Paul represented Diaspora Judaism and not Palestinian Judaism. However, this line of reasoning falls if, as has been argued above, the alleged dichotomy between Diaspora Judaism and Palestinian Judaism did not exist.

(2) Not only did the claim "Jesus is Lord" not violate Paul's Jewish sensibilities but according to his letters, it apparently did not cause his opponents offense either. While the identity of these opponents is a difficult and unsettled question,[69] and even less is known about their doctrinal beliefs,[70] nevertheless, a few aspects of their teachings may be noticed.

Although Paul's opponents appear in a different light in Galatians, Philippians, and other letters, they probably belonged to the same general group.[71] They came from outside the church (2 Cor 11:4)[72] and probably had a Jewish background as implied by 2 Cor 11:22:

---

[68]. Joachim Jeremias, *Jerusalem in the Time of Jesus* (Philadelphia: Fortress Press, 1969), 246-67.

[69]. For a survey of recent trends in this research, see E. Earle Ellis, "Paul and His Opponents," chap. in *Prophecy and Hermeneutic in Early Christianity* (Grand Rapids: Eerdmans, 1978), 80-115.

[70]. Victor Paul Furnish, *II Corinthians*, The Anchor Bible (Garden City, NY: Doubleday, 1984), 53.

[71]. Ellis, "Opponents," 112.

[72]. This seems to be the force behind the participle, ὁ ἐρχόμενος.

Are they Hebrews ('Εβραῖοι)? So am I. Are they Israelites? So am I. Are they descendants of Abraham? So am I.[73]

Taken together, these passages seem to indicate that Paul's opponents arose from the primitive Palestinian churches. These rivals antagonized Paul by disparaging his apostolic ministry (2 Cor 10:2-12) and by boasting of their own spiritual status as well as their charismatic endowments.[74] They were preaching "another gospel" (εἰς ἕτερον εὐαγγέλιον), although it was in fact no gospel at all (ὃ οὐκ ἔστιν ἄλλο, Gal 1:6), for they required their converts to be circumcised and to follow the law of Moses (Gal 5:2, 12; 6:12f.).

Is there any evidence that his opponents had a different Christology? Some scholars, appealing to 2 Cor 11:4, have thought so, although they have offered differing opinions on who these opponents might be. In 2 Cor 11:4 Paul said: "For if some one comes (ὁ ἐρχόμενος) and preaches another Jesus (ἄλλον Ἰησοῦν) than the one we preached, or if you receive a different spirit (πνεῦμα ἕτερον) from the one you received, or if you accept a different gospel (εὐαγγέλιον ἕτερον) from the one you accepted, you submit to it readily enough." Evidently, the apostle spoke of a real, not a hypothetical situation in the church.[75] He understood that a group had arrived to undermine his work.[76]

Noting the key phrase, "another Jesus" (ἄλλον Ἰησοῦν),[77] some scholars think that Christology formed a major difference between

---

[73]. Furthermore, they claimed to be "apostles of Christ" (2 Cor 11:13). While Paul used the term "apostle" to refer to those sent out by the churches (2 Cor 8:23), this phrase, "apostle of Christ," may be used in a technical sense to refer to those directly commissioned by the risen Jesus (1 Cor 9:1; 1 Cor 15:8f.). Ellis, "Opponents," 105-6, stated: "In all likelihood the term is so applied to the opponents and thereby presupposes their personal acquaintance with Jesus."

[74]. Ibid., 104-5.

[75]. Εἰ with the present indicative κηρύσσει indicates this and 2 Cor 11:1-3, 19-20 confirms it. See Furnish, *II Corinthians*, 488.

[76]. At first glance ὁ ἐρχόμενος seems to suggest an individual antagonist. This position is adopted by Barrett, *2 Corinthians*, 275. However, it is more likely that Paul had a group of troublers in mind. Dieter Georgi, *The Opponents of Paul in Second Corinthians* (Philadelphia: Fortress Press, 1986), 307, n. 256; Ellis, "Opponents," 102-8.

[77]. There appears to be no significance in the change from ἄλλον referring to Jesus and ἕτερον referring to gospel and spirit. See BAGD, "ἕτερον," 315. Furnish, *II Corinthians*, 488. *Contra* Walter Schmithals, *Gnosticism in Corinth*, trans. John

Paul and his opponents.[78] Walter Schmithals, for example, arguing that Paul used the proper name Ἰησοῦς to speak of the earthly Jesus or Χριστὸς κατὰ σάρκα, contended that the opponents were gnostics who viewed the incarnate Christ as "the execrable dwelling of the heavenly spiritual being."[79] Against this, however, is the opponent's self-designation as Hebrews, Israelites, and descendants of Abraham (2 Cor 11:22).[80] Furthermore, any gnostic problem in Corinth—if it existed at all—would have been indigenous to the area, while it is clear Paul's adversaries were outsiders.[81]

Dieter Georgi, agreeing that Paul employed Ἰησοῦς to refer to Jesus' earthly life and ministry, considered the phrase, "another Jesus," in 2 Cor 11:4 to represent a substantial christological difference between Paul and his opponents, not just a mere contrast of opinion.[82] He suggested that Paul's opponents saw Jesus as a charismatic "divine man" (θεῖος ἀνήρ).[83] His suggestion, however, fails at one essential point. There is no evidence that "divine man" speculation was current in the Hellenistic Judaism at that time.[84]

In the end, the phrase "another Jesus" reveals little, if anything, regarding the identity or beliefs of Paul's opponents. Since it parallels "another spirit" and "another gospel," it cannot be used as proof that Christology formed the main point of contention between the apostle and his adversaries. As Furnish said: "It is therefore quite possible that here, along with references to *another Spirit* and *another gospel*, this characterization of his rivals as preaching *some other Jesus* is intended only as a general condemnation of their teaching—and, if so, it would not be any more precise than the criticism Paul directs against his opponents in Galatia, Gal 1:6-9."[85]

E. Steely (Nashville: Abingdon Press, 1971), 132-33.

[78] Gerd Theissen, *The Social Setting of Pauline Christianity: Essays on Corinth*, trans. John H. Schütz (Philadelphia: Fortress Press, 1982), 40-54, suggested that both social and theological problems separated Paul from his opponents.

[79] Schmithals, *Gnosticism*, 134.

[80] Georgi, *Opponents*, 273.

[81] Furnish, *II Corinthians*, 501; Ellis, "Opponents," 105-6.

[82] Georgi, *Opponents*, 273.

[83] Ibid., 274

[84] Carl Holladay, *Theios Aner in Hellenistic Judaism: A Critique of the Use of This Category in New Testament Christology* (Missoula, MT: Scholars Press, 1977), 233-42.

Although Paul defended his apostleship and his doctrine of salvation by grace through faith, he was never driven to defend his doctrine of Christ. The most likely reason for this is that his opponents, who probably came from the Palestinian church, had no doctrinal reason to oppose his Christology. Had Paul's doctrine of Jesus' Lordship essentially altered the earliest Church's Christology, would it not have occasioned attacks from his opponents? These Jewish monotheists did not discredit his Christology because they probably agreed with it.[86] Although this may be an argument from silence, it is consistent with what is known of Paul's Christology and explains the absence of christological polemics in his letters.

(3) The nature of pre-Christian Jewish monotheism presents another problem for Bousset's reconstruction. It most likely was not the unitarian monotheism of the later rabbis,[87] but it appears to have understood God's unity within a multiplicity.

As scholars have long recognized, the Old Testament views man as extending beyond the individual to encompass a corporate reality.[88] Likewise, it portrays God in corporate categories which are

---

[85.] Furnish, *II Corinthians*, 501; cf. Ellis, "Opponents," 107, who noted that Paul did not criticize their background, their pneumatic powers or their theology; rather he found fault with their huckstering God's Word (2:17; 4:2), their opposition to his apostleship, and their libertine practices. Also Johannes Munck, *Paul and the Salvation of Mankind* (Atlanta: John Knox Press, 1959), 175, perceived no definite doctrine in 2 Corinthians to reveal what Paul's opponents believed.

[86.] Larry Hurtado, *One God, One Lord: Early Christian Devotion and Ancient Jewish Monotheism* (Philadelphia: Fortress, 1988), 4, noted that "although Paul had clashes with people who troubled his churches and whose view of Christian faith he found seriously defective, and although he had differences with the Jerusalem church over matters connected with the mission to the Gentiles, nothing in Paul's letters indicates any awareness that his fundamental view of Christ was unique or that he had made any serious innovation in the way Christians before him had regarded the exalted Jesus, however much he may have had his own emphases in the articulation of his message."

[87.] The later rabbinical view is demonstrated in the "two powers" controversy outlined by Alan Segal, *Two Powers in Heaven: Early Rabbinic Reports about Christianity and Gnosticism*, Studies in Judaism in Late Antiquity, vol. 25 (Leiden: E. J. Brill, 1977), 33-155.

[88.] See A. R. Johnson, *The One and the Many in the Israelite Conception of God* (Cardiff: University of Wales Press, 1961), 1-13; idem, *Sacral Kingship in Ancient Israel*, 2d ed. (Cardiff: University of Wales Press, 1967); H. Wheeler Robinson, *Corporate Personality in Ancient Israel*, rev. ed. (Philadelphia: Fortress Press, 1980), 25-60; R. P. Shedd, *Man in Community: A Study of St. Paul's Application of Old Testament and Early Jewish Conceptions of Human Solidarity* (London:

adopted and expanded in the intertestamental period so that he appears in many manifestations including "the angel of the Lord,"[89] the divine "Word" (e.g., Isa 9:8; 55:10-11), and "Wisdom."[90]

The concept of corporate personality comes over into the New Testament regarding man[91] as well as God. Given this background and the expectation that Yahweh would come to deliver Israel,[92] Ellis concluded that "the followers of Jesus would have been prepared, wholly within a Jewish monotheistic and 'salvation history' perspective, to see in the Messiah a manifestation of God."[93] All they needed was the catalyst to identify Jesus as this divine manifestation; that was provided by the resurrection and subsequent appearances of the Risen Lord.

Thus, pre-Christian Jewish monotheism should be seen as a different entity from later rabbinic monotheism due to the Hebrew concept of corporate personality. It was not unitary but could include divine manifestations as identical, yet distinct from God. It does not follow then that Jewish monotheism would have precluded the identification of Jesus with God.

Epworth Press, 1958), 29-41; and Ellis, "Biblical Interpretation," 716-20.

[89]. The "angel of the Lord" tradition was based apparently upon Exod 23:20-21, which describes the angel in whom the name of God dwells. See also Gen 16:7-14; 22:11-18; Exod 14:19-20; perhaps Dan 10:2-9; 11QMelchizedek, "Melchizedek." It comes to expression in *Apoc. Abr.* 10:3-4 where God sends his angel Yahoel (apparently Yahweh + El) to strengthen Abraham. Yahoel comes in the likeness of man (10:4) and is distinct from God (10:3) but also worshiped as God (17:13). Cf., also *Sanh.* 38b, "Metatron." See Jarl E. Fossum, *The Name of God and the Angel of the Lord: Samaritan and Jewish Concepts of Intermediation and the Origin of Gnosticism*, WUNT 36 (Tübingen: J. C. B. Mohr, 1985).

[90]. E.g., Prov 8:22-31; Wis 7:21-27. Hurtado, *One God*, 17-92, offered a description of Jewish divine agency in three categories: (1) divine attributes as divine agents, e.g., Wisdom and Logos, (2) exalted patriarchs, and (3) principal angels. He argued (pp. 93-128) that the binitarian devotion to God and Jesus represented a mutation of Jewish monotheism based upon the Jewish concept of divine agency.

[91]. E.g., "the two shall be one flesh" (Eph 5:31; Matt 19:5); baptism "into Moses" (1 Cor 10:2); mankind as "in Adam" (1 Cor 15:22; Rom 5:12-19); believers as "in Christ" (1 Cor 15:22) or members of "the body of Christ" (1 Cor 10:16-17; 12:12-13); see Moule, *Origin*, 47-96; also E. Earle Ellis, *Pauline Theology: Ministry and Society* (Grand Rapids: Eerdmans, 1989), 55-57.

[92]. Isa 40:3-5, 10-11; Mal 3:1; *Pss. Sol.* 17:36; *T. Sim.* 6:5; *T. Levi* 5:2; *T. Jud.* 22:2; *T. Naph.* 8:3; *T. Asher* 7:3; and other sources cited in G. R. Beasley-Murray, *Jesus and the Kingdom of God* (Grand Rapids: Eerdmans, 1986), 3-68.

[93]. Ellis, "Biblical Interpretation," 719.

Therefore, in light of Paul's use of κύριος and of corporate conceptions of God in ancient Jewish monotheism, the claim by Bousset and others that Jewish monotheism would have precluded the use of the title with reference to Jesus hardly seems plausible.

No compelling reasons, therefore, can be found to adopt Bousset's presuppositions. His assertion that a dichotomy existed in the early Church between a Palestinian Jewish branch and a Gentile branch, his philological arguments which claim influence by pagan sources on New Testament Christology, and his contention that Jewish monotheism precluded any claim to Jesus' Lordship in Palestine fail to meet the facts inside Paul's letters as well as in extra-biblical sources.

Accordingly, Bousset's thesis did not adequately account for Paul's use of κύριος.[94] Although he demonstrated dramatically that the Greek and Roman world knew and used the κύριος concept in connection with their mystery religions and ruler worship,[95] he went too far in assuming the absence of such a concept in the Aramaic-speaking church. Further, Paul's Maranatha invocation (1 Cor 16:22) may ultimately be the "Achilles' heel" of his theory.[96] Bousset's suggestion that this "old cultic formula" emerged not from Palestine, but from the multi-lingual churches in Antioch, Damascus, and Syria hardly seems credible. Palestine is the most likely provenance of such a formula.[97]

In *Kyrios Christos*, Bousset proved that κύριος was a term used widely in the veneration of political leaders and in the cultic practices associated with the mystery religions. If so, κύριος is just the term one would expect to be applied to Jesus as King and as the object of worship in the Christian churches. He did not demonstrate that the acclamation of Jesus as "Lord" was exclusive to the Gentile churches or that the Christology of Gentile believers was a radical departure from the faith of the early Palestinian churches.[98]

---

[94] Note the arguments of Machen, Rawlinson, and Cullmann above, pp. 14-19.

[95] Hengel, *Son*, 77-79, n. 135 and 136, called it a "senseless undertaking" to try to derive from the mysteries the terminology and concepts of Lordship which the New Testament applied to Jesus. Κύριος, in fact, was generally not used in the mysteries. More important is the fact that "we have no evidence for mysteries in Syria in the first century BC."

[96] This phrase will be discussed below, pp. 43-47.

[97] Hahn, *Titles*, 102-3.

[98] The same difficulties which plague Bousset's theory also render Hahn's seeming

Conclusion

The theory of a Palestinian origin for the christological use of κύριος, as presented by Machen, Rawlinson, Cullmann, and others, appears to be in harmony with the data at hand in Paul's letters and the New Testament.

Despite the syncretistic mood of his day, Paul remained a Jew and continued to pay homage to his own religious heritage which determined his mindset as well as his general approach to the person and work of Christ. Yet he lived at a time when Judaism, even within Palestine, was colored by Hellenistic ideas.[99]

This does not mean that Hellenism dominated Judaism nor that pagan religions radically changed the essential doctrines of the Jewish faith. Hellenism affected Palestine primarily in the arena of language.[100] Specifically, it brought the κύριος title, a title which could refer to anyone who exercised authority. During the first century, when the Christian faith addressed Greek-speaking congregations, the term κύριος was available to be applied to Christ.

Paul's frequent quotations[101] of and allusions[102] to the Old Testament, even in letters addressed primarily to Gentile congregations, indicate that his mind was steeped in the concepts and language of his Bible. Given the fact that he preferred the LXX,[103] in which κύριος represented the divine name, his application of this title to Jesus must have meant that he considered Jesus to be more than a man.

---

compromise approach less useful. Though it has some interesting features, it, nevertheless, builds upon many of Bousset's presuppositions and consequently is unacceptable.

[99.] Hengel, *Judaism and Hellenism*, 1:104.

[100.] Davies, *Paul*, 1; Hengel, *Judaism and Hellenism*, 1:103-6. See idem, *Son*, 2, where Hengel discussed the 'apotheosis of the crucified Jesus' which he considered to have taken place by the forties (A.D.). He stated (p. 2): "Indeed, one might even ask whether the formation of doctrine in the early church was essentially more than a consistent development and completion of what had already been unfolded in the primal event of the first two decades, but in the language and thought-forms of Greek, which was its necessary setting."

[101.] Ellis, *Paul's Use*, 11, indicated Paul quoted the Old Testament ninety-three times. For a list of these see pp. 150-52 and pp. 156-87.

[102.] Ibid., 153-54. Ellis listed 107 allusions by Paul to the Old Testament.

[103.] Ibid., 12.

The Maranatha invocation (1 Cor 16:22) provides further evidence. This prayer, directed to the Lord Jesus for his return, indicates that Paul and the early Church considered Jesus more than a rabbi. All in all, the theory of a Palestinian origin for the christological use of κύριος seems to fit the evidence more precisely than Bousset's thesis.

One final question needs to be addressed: if a concept may be explained by the immediate background of a writer, is it necessary to look beyond that background to understand it? The answer should, in most cases, be answered negatively. However, this is precisely what Bousset did. He looked beyond the Palestinian church for the origin of the christological use of κύριος when, as the evidence shows, it was possible to explain it entirely within a Palestinian setting.

Therefore, one may conclude that the κύριος title stands within the religious milieu of first century Jewish practice. There is no need to look beyond Palestinian Christian experience for the background of the claim that "Jesus is Lord." Neither is there any reason to deny that veneration, worship, and prayers directed to Christ took place first within the earliest churches.

II. ΚΥΡΙΟΣ in the Septuagint and in Paul's Letters

Having completed an analysis of κύριος in scholarly debate, it is now fitting to investigate briefly how this term was used in the Septuagint and in Paul's letters. With these areas in mind, it will then be possible to see how the apostle used Old Testament Yahweh texts.

The Septuagint's Use of ΚΥΡΙΟΣ

ΚΥΡΙΟΣ As a Human Designation

Although the Septuagint used κύριος primarily as a title for God, on many occasions it employed the term as a way to delineate those who possess authority over other people or other things. In Gen 27:29, for example, when Jacob stole Esau's blessing, Isaac uttered:

> Let peoples serve you,
>   and nations bow down to you.
> Be lord (γίνου κύριος) over your brothers,
>   and may your mother's sons bow down to you.

In this text κύριος translates the Hebrew word גביר which carries the idea of "ruler." Later, when the deed became manifest, Esau pled with his ailing father for his blessing. Isaac lamented (Gen 27:37):

> Behold, I have made him your lord (εἰ κύριον αὐτὸν ἐποίησά σου), and all his brothers I have given to him for servants, and with grain and wine I have sustained him. What then can I do for you, my son?

Significantly, κύριος occurred earlier in the blessing in v. 27 referring to God and translating the tetragram, יהוה. In the second occurrence it referred to Jacob's position as head or "ruler" of the family and implied that the promise which came to Abraham would be passed through his descendants.

In Exodus chapter twenty-one, after giving the Ten Commandments, God commanded Moses to set before the Israelites other ordinances. The first of these were instructions on the treatment of slaves. Hebrew slaves were to be freed in the seventh year by their owners according to the Law. If one entered the master/slave relationship single, he was to be freed single; if one entered the relationship married, he was to be freed along with his spouse. Another condition prevailed, however, when the master provided the slave with a wife: "If his master (ὁ κύριος) gives him a wife and she bears him sons or daughters, the wife and her children shall be her master's (τῷ κυρίῳ αὐτοῦ) and he shall go out alone" (Exod 21:4). In this passage κύριος translates the Hebrew אדון[1] and refers properly to one who owned and exercised authority over his servants (e.g., Exod 21:5, 6, 8).

Later, in the same chapter, the Law addressed another incident, this time involving livestock: "When an ox gores a man or a woman to death, the ox shall be stoned, and its flesh shall not be eaten; but the owner of the ox (ὁ κύριος τοῦ ταύρου) shall be clear" (Exod 21:28). In the HT בעל[2] designated the owner of the ox. In other passages where κύριος is found in the LXX, it was used to refer to the owner of a house (Exod 22:8 [HT, 22:7]) and the owner of a donkey (Isa 1:3). The Hebrew word בעל thus emphasized one who possessed something or someone.

בעל could also refer to the god worshipped by the Canaanite people. However, κύριος translated בעל only when it was used in the secular sense. When referring to the Canaanite god Baal, the LXX has Βάαλ,[3] αἰσχύνη,[4] or εἴδωλον.[5]

Κύριος also appears within the same passage as both a title for God and a designation for a man in authority. In 1 Sam 1:15 Hannah replied to Eli: "No, my lord (κύριε), I am a woman sorely troubled; I have drunk neither wine nor strong drink, but I have been pouring out my soul before the Lord (ἐνώπιον κυρίου)." The first κύριος

---

[1] Κύριος translates אדון in all its pointings nearly two hundred times in the LXX. See Edwin Hatch and Henry A. Redpath, *A Concordance to the Septuagint and the Other Greek Versions of the Old Testament (Including the Apocryphal Books)*, 2 vols. (Graz, AUS: Akademische Druck-U. Verlagsanstalt, 1954), 2:800-838. Cf., Gottfried Quell, "κύριος," *TDNT*, 3:1058-59.

[2] Κύριος renders בעל fifteen times in the LXX referring to human authority figures. Eleven times it is used in Exodus 21-22. It is also found in Gen 49:23; Judg 19:22-23; Isa 1:3; and Job 31:39.

[3] E.g., 1 Kgs 18:18, 21, 22; Judg 8:33; Judg 9:4, Βααλβερίθ; Num 25:3, 5 and Deut 4:3, Βεελφεγώρ.

[4] 1 Kgs 18:19, 25.

[5] 2 Chron 17:3; 2 Chron 28:3; Jer 9:14. Cf., Hahn, *Titles*, 71-72.

translates אדני and refers to Eli as the husband or "lord" of his wife; the second translates יהוה and refers to the Lord God of Israel.

Elsewhere Hannah said (1 Sam 1:26-28):

> Oh, my lord (κύριε)! As you live, my lord, I am the woman who was standing here in your presence, praying to the Lord (πρὸς κύριον). For this child I prayed; and the Lord (κύριος) has granted me my petition which I made to him. Therefore I have lent him to the Lord (τῷ κυρίῳ); as long as he lives, he is lent to the Lord (τῷ κυρίῳ).

The text quite naturally swings from the use of κύριος referring to Eli (אדני) to the use of κύριος referring to God (יהוה). This appears to have created no difficulties for those translating the sacred text.

The same practice may be noted in what many consider a messianic context. Psalm 110 (LXX, Psalm 109) demonstrates this dramatically. It begins with the following phrase:

[ET] The Lord says to my lord

[LXX] εἶπεν ὁ κύριος τῷ κυρίῳ μου

[HT] נאם יהוה לאדני

In the verses which follow, the "lord" (Messiah ?) sits at the right hand of the "Lord" God, while God establishes his rule over all, including his enemies. In this text the first κύριος translates the divine name; the second translates אדני and refers properly to the Messiah-king. Since this word translates both in such close proximity, one may conclude that the κύριος title enjoyed much latitude in its application to men in authority and to God.

In summary, the LXX utilizes κύριος frequently as a designation for men who possessed some type of authority, including heads of families, husbands of wives, owners of livestock, owners of slaves, and ultimately the Messiah. In these instances it uses κύριος for various Hebrew terms among which are גביר, אדון, and בעל.

The use of κύριος to translate the tetragrammaton in certain passages where it also translates גביר, אדון, and בעל demonstrates the versatility of this word as a designation for human authority figures. Even in Ps 110:1 [LXX, Ps 109:1], where κύριος occurs referring both to God and the king (Messiah ?) respectively, no indication exists that confusion between them could have been possible. This fact suggests that the translators did not delineate rigidly between a sacred and secular use of κύριος. As Rawlinson concluded, the designation κύριος for human authorities meant primarily that these men had a just claim to reverence and honor.[6]

ΚΥΡΙΟΣ As a Title for God

In the LXX κύριος translates the divine name יהוה over six thousand times in all its pointings and the combination, יהוה צבאות ("Lord of hosts").[7] Particularly in the Psalms, it renders the abbreviated form יה approximately twenty times.[8] The term is also used to translate אלהים ("God") nearly one hundred and ninety times.[9] It also translates the shortened form אל sixty times,[10] although manuscript evidence is not uniform in this matter[11] and the Greek word θεός is found in some manuscripts. Twenty-one times κύριος renders אלוה;[12] it may also stand for the combination, אלהי צבאות ("God of hosts").[13] In addition it translates the most common Old Testament term for "Lord," אדון, in the absolute[14] as well as in construct.[15] Κύριος is also used in interpretive renderings as in Isa 17:10 where it translates צור ("rock").[16] Although this term may translate several Hebrew words for God,[17] it is overwhelmingly the word of choice for the divine name by the translators of the Greek Old Testament.[18]

[6.] Rawlinson, *Christ*, 234-35.

[7.] Hatch and Redpath, *Concordance*, 2:800-838; cf. Quell, *TDNT*, 3:1059.

[8.] Ps 68:4 [LXX, 67:4; HT, 68:5]; Ps 77:11 [LXX, 76:11]; Ps 115:17, 18 [LXX, 113:25, 26]; Ps 118:17, 18, 19 [LXX, 117:17, 18, 19]; Ps 122:4 [LXX, 121:4]; Ps 130:3 [LXX, 129:3]; Ps 135:3, 4 [LXX, 134:3, 4].

[9.] E.g., Gen 19:29; 21:2, 6; Exod 3:4; 13:19; 18:1; 20:1; Lev 2:13; Judg 6:20; 7:14; 9:57; Ps 77:1 [LXX, 76:1]; Prov 3:4; Isa 61:10; 62:5; Dan 1:2, 9, 17; 9:18. See Hatch and Redpath, *Concordance*, 2:800-838; also Quell, *TDNT*, 3:1059-60.

[10.] E.g., Josh 3:10; Ps 15:1; Ps 85:8 [LXX, 84:8]; Isa 40:18. Hatch and Redpath, *Concordance*, 2:800-838; cf., Quell, *TDNT*, 3:1059.

[11.] Generally, Alexandrinus has κύριος, while Vaticanus has θεός.

[12.] Job 3:4, 23; 4:9, 17; 5:17; 6:8, 9; 10:2; 11:5, 6, 7; 15:8; 16:21, 22; 19:6, 21; 21:19; 27:8; 29:4; 31:6: 33:26.

[13.] In HT Jer 35:17; 38:17; 44:7; see Quell, *TDNT*, 3:1059-60.

[14.] E.g., Gen 18:2; 23:5, 6, 11, 15; Josh 3:11; Mic 4:13; Zech 1:9; 4:4, 5, 13, 14; Mal 3:1; Isa 36:8, 12; Dan 1:10.

[15.] E.g., Gen 18:27, 30, 31, 32; 19:18; 20:14; 24:9, 10; Exod 4:13; 21:4; Ps 2:4; 22:30 [LXX, 21:30]; 37:13 [LXX, 36:13]; 79:12 [LXX, 78:12]; Hos 12:15 [LXX, 12:14]; Amos 3:7-8; Obad 1:1; Isa 29:13; 30:16, 20; Dan 1:2.

[16.] Isa 17:10 reads: "For you have forgotten the God of your salvation, and have not remembered the Rock of your refuge." The LXX has: Διότι κατέλιπες τὸν θεὸν τὸν σωτῆρά σου, καὶ κυρίου τοῦ βοηθοῦ σου οὐκ ἐμνήσθης.

Another term, δεσπότης, translates יהוה in Jer 15:11.[19] Occasionally, δέσποτα κύριε renders אדני יהוה,[20] however, usually this phrase is translated κύριε κύριε.[21] Particularly in Ezekiel, the Hebrew phrase אדני יהוה is translated by the single κύριος, even though some manuscripts add Ἀδωναΐ.[22] Thus, κύριος appears to have been the best alternative for translating the divine name.

Κύριος is also used in combination with other titles and phrases to render the divine name. In some instances, יהוה is translated κύριος θεός.[23] In other instances, interpretive translations are given, such as in Isa 12:5 where the tetragrammaton is rendered τὸ ὄνομα κυρίου ("the name of the Lord"). Thus, rather than singing praises "to the Lord" as the HT declares, the LXX exhorts to "Sing the name of the Lord (ὑμνήσατε τὸ ὄνομα κυρίου), for he has done glorious things, announce these in all the earth." Likewise, τὸ στόμα κυρίου ("the mouth of the Lord") translates יהוה in Isa 24:3 (cf. Isa 25:8):

> The earth shall be utterly laid waste and utterly despoiled; for the Lord has spoken this word.

The HT carries the final phrase: כי יהוה דבר את־הדבר הזה. The LXX translates it: τὸ γὰρ στόμα κυρίου ἐλάλησε ταῦτα. Rather than rendering the Hebrew literally, the translator chose to embellish the text with a more anthropomorphic expression. The Lord certainly speaks, but his mouth, as it were, forms the words. In each of these cases, the variation is slight; nevertheless, liberty is taken with the text for either theological or poetic reasons.

The combination of Greek titles used to translate יהוה and the interpretive renderings point to one undeniable fact: the translators

---

[17.] Added to the evidence above is its use to translate אלה (Dan 2:18, 19, 20, 23, 37; 3:28), מרא (Dan 2:47), and שליט (Dan 4:14).

[18.] Quell, *TDNT*, 3:1058-60.

[19.] Foerster, *TDNT*, 3:1081-82, considered δεσπότης a more natural translation of Yahweh in light of current usage.

[20.] E.g., Gen 15:2, 8; Jer 1:6; 4:10.

[21.] Deut 3:24; 9:26; Josh 7:7; Judg 6:22; 16:28; 2 Sam 7:18, 19, 20, 28, 29; cf., Quell, *TDNT*, 3:1059-60.

[22.] E.g., Ezek 5:5, 7, 8; 6:3, 11; 7:2, 5; 9:8; 11:7, 8, 13, 16, 17; 12:19, 23, 25, 28; 13:3, 9; 17:3, 9, 16, 19, 22; 30:2, 6.

[23.] Isa 26:12; 38:22; 41:17, 21; 42:6, 8, 13, 21; 43:1, 10, 12, 14, 15; 44:2; 45:1, 3, 5, 6, 7, 8; Jer 5:18; 23:30, 37.

of the sacred text considered Yahweh to be a high and holy name, and they were careful not to detract from its grandeur. At times they felt the need to embellish their rendering to convey somehow the authority contained therein.[24] The liberty they took should not be construed as lack of respect; on the contrary, it should be understood as representing deep awe and reverence.

When, therefore, substitute words were offered during synagogue readings to avoid using the divine name, they were chosen with the upmost care to convey, as much as possible, the content of the holy name. אדון became the replacement name for יהוה among Aramaic synagogues, while κύριος was used in the Diaspora. This shows, among other things, that the development arose from a Jewish, not a Greek, source.[25] It also shows that the κύριος predicate was adequate, not merely as a title for God, but ultimately as a name for God also. Foerster wrote: "The consistent use of κύριος in the absolute suggests God's legitimate, unrestricted and invisible power of disposal over all things, His ἐξουσία."[26]

It is important to note, however, that κύριος cannot be an exact synonym for the sacred tetragram, יהוה. In the words of one scholar, it is "an expository equivalent" for the divine name.[27] This is because κύριος, like אדני and מרי, can be used of human authorities as well as God, while יהוה can refer only to God. Nevertheless, for Greek-speaking Jews κύριος stands in the place of יהוה.[28]

Recent discoveries, however, have challenged the connection between κύριος and the divine name in the LXX. Greek texts of the Old Testament have been found which predate our earliest texts of the Septuagint. Although they are not particularly numerous, they disclose one important fact: they leave the divine name יהוה untrans-

---

[24] Jacob Neusner, *What Is Midrash?* (Philadelphia: Fortress, 1987), 23-30.

[25] Hahn, *Titles*, 71-72.

[26] Foerster, *TDNT*, 3:1081.

[27] Quell, *TDNT*, 3:1058.

[28] Ibid., 3:1058. The name of God, i.e., Yahweh, implies man's experience of him, not as an abstract principle or as absent potentate, but as divine encounter. The revelation of God is within history, not above history or beyond history. Foerster, *TDNT*, 3:1062, wrote: "The term 'Lord' is thus a summation of the beliefs of the OT. It is the wholly successful attempt to state what God is, what the Holy One means in practice for man, namely, the intervention of a personal will, with approximately the pregnancy and binding force which constitute the distinctive mark of the name Yahweh."

lated,[29] transcribed by ΙΑΩ[30] or written with the Greek letters ΠΙΠΙ.[31] The last was used, presumably, because of its similar appearance to the Hebrew word.[32]

In light of these texts, the argument is made that, before and during the first century, Greek versions of the Old Testament generally left the divine name untranslated. Thus, during that time, κύριος did not replace the divine tetragram יהוה. The popular occurrence of κύριος in the LXX, the texts of which come many years after the first century, must be due to the practices of early Christian scribes. One writer has even speculated that Paul and other New Testament writers originally placed the tetragrammaton in their quotations of and allusions to the Old Testament. As the letters or gospels were copied, he argued, the abbreviation (*nomina sacra*) of κύριος replaced יהוה. This ultimately led to confusion between the "Lord God" and the "Lord Jesus" in the mind of the readers.[33]

This theory faces several serious objections. First, it is based on evidence which is sparse and not uniform. One fragmentary Greek text of Kings discovered in the Geniza at Cairo uses the tetragrammaton, but in one case (2 Kings 23:34) it has the Greek abbreviation for κύριος.[34] Since the text is fragmentary, it may well have contained the Greek abbreviation or the word itself in other places.[35] After all, one would expect to find the divine name untranslated in

---

[29] E.g., *P.Fouad* 266; also Aquila fragments of Ps 22:20, 24 from Geniza in Cairo. See C. Taylor, *Hebrew-Greek Cairo Genizah Palimpsests from the Taylor Schechter Collection Including a Fragment of the Twenty-Second Psalm according to Origen's Hexapla* (Cambridge: University Press, 1900).

[30] See sources cited in Hans Conzelmann, *An Outline of the Theology of the New Testament* (New York: Harper & Row, 1969), 83-84.

[31] See Hatch and Redpath, "ΠΙΠΙ," *Concordance*, 2:1135; see also Henry A. Redpath, *Concordance to the Septuagint and Other Greek Versions of the Old Testament: Supplement* (Oxford: Clarendon Press, 1906), 126.

[32] See particularly, W. G. Waddell, "The Tetragrammaton in the LXX," *JTS* 45 (1944): 158-61; also Philipp Vielhauer, "Ein Weg zur neutestamentlichen Christologie?" in *Aufsätze zum Neuen Testament* (Münich: Chr. Kaiser Verlag, 1965), 147-50; Conzelmann, *Outline*, 82-84; and Fitzmyer, "*Kyrios*-title," 117-27.

[33] George Howard, "The Tetragram and the New Testament," *JBL* 96 (1977): 63, 77-79.

[34] F. C. Burkitt, *Fragments of the Books of Kings according to the Translation of Aquila from a Manuscript Formerly in the Geniza at Cairo* (Cambridge: University Press, 1897), 16.

[35] Fitzmyer, "*Kyrios*-title," 122.

at least some Greek versions, especially in the bilinguial areas around Palestine and Syria.

Second, this theory does not adequately address the practices of Greek synagogues when reading the Old Testament. If one assumes that the tetragrammaton remained in the Greek texts, what happened when these texts were read aloud in worship? Was the divine name pronounced? Was nothing said? Did another word replace the tetragrammaton? The most reasonable assumption is that the divine name was not spoken but was replaced by a Greek word which would be readily understood as a divine acclamation. Bousset has already demonstrated that such a word was available in the κύριος predicate. It seems likely then in the context of Diaspora synagogue meetings that κύριος was the common replacement for the divine name in worship and in the Greek version of the Old Testament.

Third, this theory fails to account for the consistency with which New Testament writers quoted the Old Testament. Even the casual observer of the New Testament Greek texts notices that κύριος replaces יהוה. If the tetragrammaton were present in the Greek texts quoted by all the New Testament writers, is it reasonable to assume that they, independent of one another, would choose the same Greek word to replace the divine name? A more reasonable hypothesis is that a Greek text—or group of texts—already existed by the first century in which κύριος translated יהוה and that the New Testament writers wrote with these texts in mind.

In light of the arguments above, the theory that the presence of κύριος for the divine name in later LXX texts was due solely to the influence of Christian scribes does not take into account all the evidence.[36] Evidently devout Jews in the Diaspora also cherished the κύριος predicate as a replacement for יהוה. Regarding the tetragrammaton in the Greek Old Testament, one scholar wrote:

> Rather, we should probably think of a fluid tradition from the outset, perhaps originally the Hebrew or Aramaic script, but with a great deal of variety including Greek transliteration and also Greek translation. And this last would be exclusively *kyrios*.[37]

[36.] See other arguments against this theory in Fitzmyer, "*Kyrios*-title," 118-23.

[37.] D. R. de Lacey, "'One Lord' in Pauline Christology," in *Christ the Lord: Studies in Christology Presented to Donald Guthrie*, ed. Harold H. Rowdon (Leicester, UK: InterVarsity Press, 1982), 194.

Other contemporary Jewish writers offer a similar, yet at times different, use for κύριος.[38] Josephus, for example, normally used another Greek word, δεσπότης, as an equivalent for Yahweh.[39] He used κύριος only once to translate יהוה in a citation of Isa 19:19 where he represented τῷ κυρίῳ in the LXX by κυρίῳ τῷ θεῷ (*Ant* 13.68).[40]

Josephus' use of δεσπότης for יהוה indicates either his lack of awareness of the κύριος predicate's role in religious circles or his reluctance to utilize it so because of its identification with the divine name. It may be due partly to his relationship with high-ranking Roman officials including Vespasian and Titus. Since the emperor cult acclaimed "Caesar is ΚΥΡΙΟΣ," for practical reasons he may have wanted to avoid attributing the same title to Yahweh.

It is significant, however, that Christian scribes, who were primarily responsible for the preservation of Josephus' works, did not "christianize" his text by replacing δεσπότης with κύριος. Would they, then, have made such changes in the Septuagint?

Turning now to other contemporary evidence, κύριος is frequently used for God in the Apocrypha. It occurs over one hundred and sixty times as a divine term in Sirach.[41] Although δεσπότης does sometimes refer to God,[42] it is all but eclipsed by the term κύριος.[43] Outside the Apocrphya, in Psalms of Solomon, which often imitates the style of scripture, it is retained as a name for God.[44]

[38.] Since much of Philo's works has to do with interpreting scripture, κύριος is found commonly therein. E.g., Philo *Mut Nom* 19; 15; 24; *Leg All* 1.95-96; *Plant* 86-89; and *Som* 1.163.

[39.] Jos. *Ant* 1.20; 1.72; 2.270; 4.40; 5.41; 5.93; 11.64-65; and 8.111.

[40.] Although Josephus claimed to have translated (μεθηρμηνευμένην) from the Hebrew scriptures (*Ant* 1.5), a careful analysis reveals that he in fact utilized both a Semitic and a Greek text. H. St. John Thackeray, *Josephus: The Man and the Historian* (New York: Jewish Institute of Religion Press, 1929), 81, concluded: "Throughout the Pentateuch his main authority is a Semitic text, and the use made of the so-called 'Septuagint' is slight; here he is presumably justified in claiming that the translation is his own. From Samuel onwards to the end of the historical books the position is reversed; the basis of his text is a Greek Bible, and the Semitic text is only a subsidiary source." Cf., also the prayer of a Gentile proselyte (δεσπότα κύριε, *Ant* 20.90).

[41.] E.g., Sir 1:1, 8, 11, 12, 13, 14, 18, 20; 2, 1, 7, 8, 10; 5: 3, 4; 10:4, 13; 17:29.

[42.] E.g., 1 Esdr 4:60; Jdt 7:11; Wis 6:7; 11:26; Sus 1:5; Ep Jer 1:6; 3 Macc 6:10.

[43.] E.g., 1 Esdr 1:1; 5:60; 6:2; Tob 2:2; 3:11; Bar 1:5; 2:1; Sus 1:23, 35; Bel 1:25; Wis 1:1, 7; 3:8; 1 Macc 4:10, 24; 7:37, 41; 2 Macc 1:8; 2:10; 10:38; 3 Macc 2:2; 5:7.

One may conclude that the κύριος title is a common appellative for God in the LXX and other Jewish writings. When referring to God, it is used most frequently to translate the divine name, Yahweh, and therefore has a firm place within first century Jewish worship and religious practices.[45]

Paul's Use of ΚΥΡΙΟΣ

The apostle Paul employed κύριος as a designation for men in authority, the God of Israel, pagan gods, and, primarily, Jesus Christ. Before engaging in a survey of his use of the title, it is necessary to turn briefly to what is perhaps the earliest connection between Jesus and the term "Lord" in Paul's letters.

The Maranatha Invocation

First Corinthians 16:22 may very well contain the earliest christological confession. While writing the farewell in his own hand (16:21), Paul included this Greek transcription of the old Aramaic formula (μαράναθά). The same form is found in the Didache (10:6). It is also found in Rev 22:20, only here it has been translated into Greek (ἔρχου κύριε Ἰησοῦ). Thus, the formula was not exclusive to Paul and seems rather well-fixed in early Christian usage.

Most scholars agree that this phrase arose early in the Aramaic-speaking churches of Palestine.[46] Cullmann noted: "The early date of this formula is proved by the fact that the Apostle preserves its original Aramaic form in a letter written in Greek to a Greek-speaking church."[47]

[44.] de Lacey, "'One Lord'," 194-95.

[45.] de Lacey, "'One Lord'," 194, noted that the anartharous form (κύριος) occurs more frequently than ὁ κύριος; this suggests that Jewish writers during this period understood it more as a name for God than a title. He concluded: "If *kyrios* did not stand originally for YHWH in the LXX, then it is fortuitous that it remains primarily the name of God, and of no other deity, in the Old Testament."

[46.] Werner R. Kramer, *Christ, Lord, Son of God*, trans. Brian Hardy (Naperville, IL: A. R. Allenson, 1966), 99-107; Fuller, *Foundations*, 156-58; and France, "The Uniqueness of Christ," 209, concluded: "For a formula of the Aramaic-speaking church to be so widely known that it could be used without explanation in a letter to Corinth, it must have been already a venerable tradition; so that prayer to Jesus was clearly an accepted pattern long before Paul wrote, and the christological implications of this are obvious."

[47.] Cullmann, *Christology*, 208-210; also Siegfried Schulz, "Maranatha und Kyrios

Unfortunately, the Aramaic phrase's meaning is not entirely clear. There are basically two possibilities: (1) it may be understood to mean "Our Lord, Come!" [μαράνα θά = מרנא תא], that is, as a prayer for the Lord's return or (2) it may be taken as the confession, "Our Lord has come!" [μαράν αθά = מרן אתה].[48] Although the phrase may be taken either way grammatically, in light of its use in Rev 22:20, it is best understood as a plea for the Lord's return.[49]

In the context of the passage, Paul clearly referred to Jesus as the *maran*, for the next verse states: "The grace of the Lord Jesus be with you." But did the phrase always refer to him? Professor Bultmann denied it strongly. In the earliest Aramaic-speaking churches, he argued, the plea was meant for God. The phrase was transferred to Jesus only later, when missionaries preached the gospel among Greeks and Romans.[50] But a relevant question emerges which must be answered: Did the early church ever envision the coming of God? Other than this *maranatha*, which is unclear, no references in the New Testament speak of the Father's coming, only the Son's. It may be granted that Jewish eschatological hopes in general looked for God's personal intervention,[51] yet evidently the first believers' experience of Christ restructured these aspirations so that they were translated to their Risen Lord. Thus early Christians anticipated Jesus' coming. Likewise, in regard to this *maranatha*, the most natural conclusion is that petitioners directed this prayer to the coming Lord Jesus.[52]

A further question remains: How does one understand here the *maran*? Is he divine or human? It has been long known that מרה

Jesus," *ZNW* 53 (1962): 125, said: "The formulaic character of 'Maranatha' is presented clearly from the fact that in Greek-written texts to Greek-speaking communities it has remained untranslated."

[48] Longenecker, *Christology*, 121-24; Cullmann, *Christology*, 208-10; also K. G. Kuhn, "μαράναθά," *TDNT*, 4:466-72. Kramer, *Christ, Lord, Son*, 99-107, understood there to be three possibilities: (1) the prayer, "Our Lord, Come!" as a plea for the parousia, (2) the confession of the past saving events "Our Lord has come!" or (3) the declaration of the presence of the Lord within the context of the Lord's Supper, "Our Lord is here!"

[49] Hahn, *Titles*, 93-101; Longenecker, *Christology*, 121-24; and Marshall, *Origin*, 101-102.

[50] Bultmann, *Theology*, 1:51-53.

[51] Beasley-Murray, *Jesus and the Kingdom*, 3-62.

[52] Hahn, *Titles*, 93-101.

could refer either to a human authority figure—such as a teacher, a husband, or a slave owner—or to God himself.[53]

Perhaps the greatest breakthrough in this question has come from the caves at Qumran. In 1966 Professor Joseph A. Fitzmyer published a fragmentary scroll from cave one which has become known as the Genesis Apocryphon (1QapGn).[54] In 1QapGn the Aramaic noun מרה is used to refer to human authority[55] as well as to God.[56] In other texts found outside Qumran the same Aramaic root refers to God.[57]

The most significant occurrences of מר, however, are when this form is found in the *status absolutus*.[58] Until the discovery in the Judean desert, this particular Aramaic word was found only in construct with other nouns in phrases like "Lord of heaven and earth." Again, the Genesis Apocryphon appears to fill the gap. In 1QapGn 20.12-13 מרה is used in the absolute:

Blessed be you, almighty God, my Lord, for all eternity!
For you are the Lord [מרה] and the Ruler over all.

Later, in the same context, the word occurs in the confession: "You are the Lord [מרה] to all the kings of the earth."[59] In another manuscript at Qumran (11QtgJob), the Aramaic מרא occurs in the

---

[53.] Fuller, *Foundations*, 156-58; Longenecker, *Christology*, 122-24; and Marshall, *Origins*, 99.

[54.] Joseph A. Fitzmyer, *The Genesis Apocryphon of Qumran Cave 1: A Commentary* (Rome: Pontifical Biblical Institute, 1966).

[55.] 1QapGn 2.9; 2.13; 2.24; 20.25; 22.18.

[56.] 1QapGn 2.4 "by the great Lord" [במרה רבות]; 7.7 "Lord of the heavens" [מרה שמיא]; 12.7; 20.12, 13, 14, 15; 21.2; 22.16; 22.21 "Lord of heavens and earth"; 22.32 [אלהא מרי]. See also 1Q20 2.5 "eternal Lord" [מרה עלמה].

[57.] See A. E. Cowley, *Aramaic Papyri of the Fifth Century B. C.* (Oxford: Clarendon Press, 1923), *AP* 30:15 in which God is called "the Lord of the heavens" [מרא שמיא]. This gives evidence that for several hundred years before Christ the Aramaic root מר was used in relation to God. The same phrase occurs in Dan 5:23. See also 1 Enoch 106:11.

[58.] Fitzmyer, "*Kyrios*-title," 116-17. According to Fitzmyer, one may claim a connection between מרה and κύριος only if the following criteria are met: (1) the Aramaic word cannot contain a suffix or belong to a chain of construct forms, (2) the Aramaic word must stand either in the absolute state or the emphatic state, and (3) the Aramaic word must not be attributive.

[59.] 1QapGn 20.15. Although this מרה is in the *status absolutus*, the prepositional phrase following it acts like a genitive; for that reason it is less clear.

absolute as a title for God and parallel to the customary word for God אלהא.⁶⁰

This brief survey of the philological evidence seems to suggest that the Aramaic word מרה occupied an important place in the religious language of first century Jews.⁶¹ It was therefore available to be used in reference to the center of Christian worship, the Lord Jesus.⁶²

The Maranatha invocation of 1 Cor 16:22, therefore, represents an old Palestinian formula of prayer, directed to the Lord Jesus. It is a plea for him to come in power and glory. Had these first believers only considered Jesus *maran* as their rabbi, prayer would not have been directed to him. Rather, it demonstrates decisively that the early Aramaic believers considered Jesus more than a man, and in fact, placed this Coming One at the center of their worship and adoration. Paul adopted this Aramaic phrase and used it, without explanation, to include in his closing remarks to the Corinthian church.

Although this phrase may at first seem far removed from an investigation of Paul's use of κύριος, it in fact informs in at least two points. First, it demonstrates that early Aramaic believers called Jesus "Lord" (מרן) in their language, thus Greek churches were not the originators of this christological category with their κύριος title. Second, since מר was a term currently used for God in Jewish literature and since Paul's μαράναθά represents a prayer to Jesus for

---

⁶⁰· 11QtgJob 24.6-7. Fitzmyer, "*Kyrios*-title," 124-25; Black, "Christological Use," 10-11, suggested that Enoch 1:9 is "a credible source" for the Maranatha invocation. Enoch 1:9 indicates *mara* does refer to deity. Black also cited evidence from the Targums, Daniel, and Elephantine papyri and concluded (p. 11): "*Maranatha*, applied to Jesus and derived by way of a Christian interpretation of Enoch 1:9, does seem to establish the Aramaic provenance of a *maran* or a *maranatha* christology which, if it did not precede it as its source, must have arisen at least concurrently with the *Kyrios* christology of the Greek-speaking churches."

⁶¹· The conclusion of Vermes, *Jesus*, 121, seems valid here: "Thus in Jewish Aramaic the designation, '(the) lord', is appropriate in connection with God, or a secular dignitary, or an authoritative teacher, or a person renowned for his spiritual or supernatural force. The field in fact—and contrary to the opinion generally held by NT experts—is entirely open."

⁶²· Schelkle, *Paulus*, 183, wrote: "Darnach hat die palastinenische Gemeinde Christus als Herrn geglaubt und verehrt." Otherwise see Schulz, "Maranatha," 133-38, who argued that the Maranatha invocation refers to Jesus in his coming judgment as the eschatological Son of Man. It is not a designation of deity in the sense of the hellenistic κύριος. Such an understanding, according to Schulz, does not compromise the spirit of Judaism at the time, which he called a mixed-bag of religious ideas.

his return, there is no basis for denying that Jesus was the object of veneration and worship in these churches, and not just their absent rabbi. For them, as for their Greek-speaking brethren, Jesus was more than a man. Therefore, the confession κύριος Ἰησοῦς, as well as Paul's κύριος Christology, does not represent a significant departure from the faith of the first Aramaic believers.

ΚΥΡΙΟΣ As a Human Designation

As in other parts of the New Testament,[63] Paul used "lord" (κύριος) in a secular sense as a designation for men who hold some kind of the authority over others. In this regard, for example, the household codes in Colossians refer to the master/slave relationship. In Col 3:22 Paul exhorted the slaves to "obey in everything those who are your earthly masters (τοῖς κατὰ σάρκα κυρίοις)." He based the slaves' obedience to their masters "according to the flesh" not on the fear of men, but on the fear of the "Lord." He went on to say (Col 3:23-24): "Whatever your task, work heartily, as serving the Lord (τῷ κυρίῳ) and not men, knowing that from the Lord (ἀπὸ κυρίου) you will receive the inheritance as your reward; you are serving the Lord Christ (τῷ κυρίῳ Χριστῷ)." Thus, Paul based the slaves' obedience to their masters upon the notion that they were actually serving the Lord Jesus.

Paul, however, reserved the "last word" for the slave-owners themselves (Col 4:1): "Masters (οἱ κύριοι), treat your slaves justly and fairly, knowing that you also have a Master in heaven (κύριον ἐν οὐρανῷ)." The play on words here is obvious. According to Paul, both Christ and the Christian slave-owners are κύριοι; yet the authority of the latter is in no way comparable to that of the former. Their slaves may answer to them, but they will ultimately answer to one who is Lord of all. He believed that the "Lord" of every man, whether slave or free, is the Lord Jesus Christ. As these slave-owners submit to his rule in their lives, the result will be fair treatment for those under their care (cf. Eph 6:5-9).

[63.] See, for example, Mark 12:9, "lord" of the vineyard; Luke 16:3, "master" of the servant. In 1 Pet 3:6 Sarah calls Abraham "lord." In Acts 25:26 Festus refers to Nero as "lord." In Matt 27:63 the chief priests and the Pharisees address Pilate as "lord." One might also include in this category references to Jesus prior to the resurrection by his disciples and others. When they address Jesus as "lord" (κύριε), it is for them only a polite form of address, as any student would address his teacher. Yet, at the same time, the Gospel writers seem to be saying more about Jesus than this (cf. Matt 7:21; Mark 12:35-37). Perhaps the title is present in anticipation of his crucifixion and resurrection, an event which the authors understood to be the goal of their message.

Unrelated to the master/slave relationship is the use of κύριος in Gal 4:1. In this section Paul compared life under the law with life under faith. Taking his cue from 3:29 where he calls believers "heirs," he employed a figure of speech to explain further how the law functioned before faith came.[64] Evidently, in this analogy, the image is of a son whose father died while he was still quite young. Prior to the heir's coming of age, he is no better off than a slave (δούλου). He is under the care of others who watch out for his interests. All this is true, Paul affirmed, even though the heir is "owner of all the estate (κύριος πάντων ὤν)."[65] He proceeded to explain the former bondage of believers to the elemental spirits and God's act of sending forth his Son to make possible their redemption and adoption as sons. Although these represent important passages in their own right, the interest here is limited to the simple fact that Paul, as did other New Testament writers, utilized κύριος to refer to those who legally possess power and authority over other people. This practice is completely in line with the common convention of the day. It is plain, however, that, particularly in the household codes, Paul contrasted the slave-owners' authority, signified by the term "lord," and Christ's authority as "Lord." He believed Christ's dominion encompassed any claim to human power.

ΚΥΡΙΟΣ As a Title for God or Gods

There are a few places in Paul's letters where it appears κύριος refers to God. This is mainly the case in Old Testament quotations which refer to Yahweh.[66] Since this forms one of the main areas of discussion in this project, it will be best to discuss these at a later time. For now, suffice it to say that Paul does quote Old Testament κύριος texts with God in mind. Chapter three will be dedicated to an analysis of these passages.

Related to this is the use of κύριος to refer to pagan gods and deities. Paul's discussion concerning food offered to idols in 1 Corinthians offers a case in point. Having stated that an idol has no real

---

[64] Herman N. Ridderbos, *The Epistle of Paul to the Churches of Galatia*, NICNT (Grand Rapids: Eerdmans, 1953), 151-52.

[65] Foerster, *TDNT*, 3:1086, saw κύριος functioning more adjectivally here "with a suggestion of lawful, not actual, ownership."

[66] Ibid., 3:1086-87. Foerster cited these as cases in point: Rom 4:8; 9:28, 29; 11:3; 11:34; 15:11; 1 Cor 1:31; 3:20; 10:22, 26; 2 Cor 3:16; 8:21; 10:17; 2 Thess 1:9; and 2 Tim 2:19. The same is true for the λέγει κύριος texts, e.g., Rom 12:19; 2 Cor 6:17.

existence and having affirmed that there is only one God (8:4), he wrote (8:5-6):

> For although there may be so-called gods (λεγόμενοι θεοί) in heaven or on earth—as indeed there are many 'gods' (θεοί πολλοί) and many 'lords' (κύριοι πολλοί)—yet for us there is one God (εἷς θεός), the Father, from whom are all things and for whom we exist, and one Lord (εἷς κύριος), Jesus Christ, through whom are all things and through whom we exist.

This passage is difficult to interpret; yet it is clear that he intended to contrast the many gods and the many lords of the pagan world with the one true God and the one true Lord, Jesus Christ. The difficulty lies, however, in his ambivalence to the whole question of these other gods' existence. While many contemporaries viewed their ancient world as filled with divine beings going to and fro upon the earth, in this verse Paul neither denied nor affirmed their real existence. Perhaps Barrett is correct when he suggested that Paul voiced his opinion on the matter in 1 Cor 10:20, when he reasoned that whatever pagans sacrifice to an idol is actually offered to demons. Thus, the gods and lords mentioned in 8:5 would refer to evil spirits which were worshiped by pagan Gentiles.[67] While these were no doubt real beings in Paul's understanding, and while they were hailed as "lords" by their supplicants, they nevertheless were not competing with God the Father and the Lord Jesus for divine status. According to Paul, there is one true God and one true Lord; all the rest are simply lesser, evil spirits. Nevertheless, Paul did utilize the κύριος title when referring to these so-called "lords."

ΚΥΡΙΟΣ As a Title for Christ

In a few instances Paul utilized κύριος for human authority figures, pagan gods, or the one God of the Old Testament. Yet, in the vast majority of cases, he employed κύριος with Jesus in mind.[68]

Other than Christ (Χριστός), the most frequently used christological title in Paul's letters is "Lord" (κύριος). Κύριος occurs 275 times in a variety of contexts.[69] He used it alone[70] and in combination with other ascriptions to refer to his Lord, Jesus Christ.[71]

[67.] C. K. Barrett, *The First Epistle to the Corinthians*, HNTC (New York: Harper & Row, 1968), 192, 236-37.

[68.] Goppelt, *Theology*, 2:79, stated that it is "almost exclusively a designation for Christ."

[69.] E.g., Rom 1:4; 1 Cor 6:11; 2 Cor 12:8-9; Gal 1:3; Eph 5:20; Phil 3:8; Col 2:6; 1

"Jesus Is Lord"

Paul was not the first to acclaim Jesus as κύριος. He inherited this designation from the earliest churches as his use of the Maranatha invocation attests (1 Cor 16:22). Likewise, in several places, he referred to what seems to have been a christological confession, κύριος Ἰησοῦς (Rom 10:9; 1 Cor 12:3; Phil 2:11). He used it without any explanation. This suggests that the churches were familiar with it already.

Perhaps this essential Christian teaching explains, to some extent, why Paul persecuted the Church.[72] Prior to his conversion, he considered Jesus, not Lord, but a sinful man who by virtue of his crucifixion suffered under the curse of God (Deut 21:23; Gal 3:13). Thus, as a persecutor of "the Way," he regarded the confession "Jesus is Lord" tantamount to blasphemy against Yahweh. But, on the Damascus road, his experience with the risen Christ convinced him that Jesus was not dead but alive, not cursed but vindicated by God; therefore, he now believed the Christian confession to be true.[73] Subsequently, he adopted this christological title to speak of his own experience of Jesus.[74] This experience was not limited simply to

---

Thess 2:15; 2 Thess 1:2; Philem 5; 1 Tim 1:12; and 2 Tim 4:8. The title is lacking only in the letter to Titus.

[70.] Rom 10:13; 14:9; 1 Cor 2:8; 4:5; 1 Cor 6:13, 17; 9:5; 11:26; 14:37; 2 Cor 3:16, 17; 5:5; Gal 1:19; 5:10; Phil 1:14; Col 1:7; 3:13; Philem 16; Eph 2:21; 4:4-6; 1 Thess 1:6; 4:15, 16; 2 Thess 1:9; 3:1; 1 Tim 1:14; 2 Tim 1:8, 16; 2:22; 4:8, 22.

[71.] The combinations are (1) "Lord Jesus," Rom 14:14; 1 Cor 5:4, 5; 11:23; 2 Cor 1:14; 8:9; Philem 5; Phil 2:19; Col 3:17; Eph 1:15; 1 Thess 2:15, 19; 3:11, 13; 4:1, 2; 2 Thess 1:7, 8; (2) "Jesus Christ our Lord," Rom 1:4; 5:21; 7:25; 1 Cor 1:9; (3) "Lord Jesus Christ," Rom 1:7; 5:1; 13:14; 1 Cor 1:2, 3; 6:11; 15:57; 2 Cor 1:2, 3; 11:31; 13:14; Gal 1:3; 6:14, 18; Phil 1:2; 3:20; 4:23; Col 1:3; Philem 3, 25; Eph 1:2, 3; 5:20; 1 Thess 1:1, 2; 5:9, 12; 2 Thess 1:1, 2; 2:2; 3:12; 1 Tim 6:3, 14; (4) "Christ Jesus our Lord," Rom 6:23; 8:39; 1 Cor 15:31; Col 2:6; (5) "Christ Jesus the Lord," Eph 3:11; 1 Tim 1:2, 12; 2 Tim 1:2; and (6) "Jesus our Lord," Rom 4:24.

[72.] Willi Marxsen, "Christology in the NT," *IDBS*, 149, speculated that although the apostle never explained why he persecuted the Church, two possibilities emerge: (1) its teaching against the law and the sacred things of Judaism and (2) its claim that Christ is Lord.

[73.] Seyoon Kim, *The Origin of Paul's Gospel* (Grand Rapids: Eerdmans, 1981), 104-5; Marxsen, *IDBS*, 149, agreed: "Paul's Christology is actually nothing other than the unfolding of his Damascus experience against the background of his activity as persecutor."

[74.] Kim, *Origin*, 104-5; see the following κύριος passages which may allude to Paul's Damascus Christophany: 1 Cor 9:1; 2 Cor 3:16-18; 4:5; 10:8; 13:10; and Phil 3:8.

cultic activities; for the apostle, Jesus' Lordship was intensely personal. Seyoon Kim noted: "Paul's experience of the risen and exalted Jesus as the Lord had a unique personal dimension beyond the dimension of the cultic acclamation in worship and of the confessional formula."[75]

In the confession κύριος Ἰησοῦς, "Jesus" functions as the subject and "Lord" as the predicate.[76] Paul's use of it suggests the Church already had a clear idea what κύριος meant. According to Lucien Cerfaux κύριος represented "a basic intuition in Christianity, and one of its most essential doctrines."[77] As it was spoken by the new convert or by the church at large, it was a recognition of Jesus' status, power, and authority. It was a surrender to his rule in their lives. Temporally, it emphasized the present as the risen Christ reigns over his Church. This fact becomes apparent, particularly when Paul used κύριος in ethical admonitions.

Some scholars differentiate between the shorter confession, "Jesus is Lord" (κύριος Ἰησοῦς), and the fuller, "Jesus Christ is Lord" (κύριος Ἰησοῦς Χριστός). Werner Kramer, for example, claimed that in the Greek-speaking Gentile churches "Christ" became attached to the name Jesus as a sort of double name.[78] Thus, whenever the fuller confession appears, he argued that this indicates a Hellenistic origin and/or connection. This, however, is probably not the case.

Christ, of course, is a title which refers to Jesus' messianic office. Its use within Jewish-Christian circles would obviously carry the most importance. Many scholars believe that the title lost its messianic significance in the Greek churches which Paul addressed. Consequently, Richard Longenecker thought the confession "Jesus is Christ" predominated in the earliest Jewish churches, whereas Paul's Gentile churches confessed "Jesus is Lord."[79] Kramer considered this the case even when "Christ" has the definite article and when it serves as the subject of the sentence.[80] Yet, interestingly enough, Kramer

---

[75] Ibid., 108.

[76] Kramer, *Christ, Lord, Son*, 65-66.

[77] Lucien Cerfaux, *Christ in the Theology of Paul*, trans. Geoffrey Webb and Adrian Walker (New York: Herder and Herder, 1959), 464.

[78] Kramer, *Christ, Lord, Son*, 67

[79] Longenecker, *Christology*, 133.

[80] Kramer, *Christ, Lord, Son*, 213-15.

seemed to refute his own argument when he also noted that the two terms "Lord" and "Christ" never appear side-by-side.[81] It is never "Lord Christ Jesus," but always "Lord Jesus Christ" (e.g., Rom 5:1, 11; 16:20; 1 Cor 1:2, 10; 5:4; 6:11; 2 Cor 8:9; Gal 1:3; 6:18; Eph 5:20; 1 Thess 5:28; 2 Thess 3:6; and Philem 3). He proceeded to argue that this separation indicates that "Christ," which was originally a title in Jewish-Christian churches but which had lost its messianic significance in Paul's Greek churches, retained some of its original import. He stated:

> It remained customary to keep them apart, so much so that the custom was still followed, even when all awareness of the original significance of *Christ* as a title had disappeared. So the custom survives as a witness to something forgotten.[82]

But was it indeed "something forgotten"? Were there any Pauline churches without at least some Jewish members? The letters suggest not. Paul's churches, in general, must have had at least a minor Jewish constituency. Is it therefore conceivable that such Jewish members would have allowed the title "Christ" to become a meaningless addition to the name "Jesus"? Such a possibility would be hard to imagine. Likewise, would Paul, "the Hebrew of the Hebrews" (Phil 3:5), the persecutor of the Church, and the one who burned with zeal for the traditions of his fathers (Gal 1:13-14), have allowed the blessed messianic hope to be submerged completely in hellenistic categories during his missionary endeavors. Again, such a possibility would be hard to imagine.

It seems best therefore to understand the fuller confession "Jesus Christ is Lord" and the expressions derived from it as formal, more stylized ways of expressing this essential Christian doctrine than the shorter "Jesus is Lord."[83]

More will be said regarding this confession in the discussions which follow on Rom 10:9-13 and Phil 2:6-11. For now, suffice it to say that Paul knew and used the confession "Jesus is Lord" (κύριος Ἰησοῦς); and he probably found it in use already in the churches prior to his conversion.

---

[81] Note the exception to this in Col 3:24.

[82] Kramer, *Christ, Lord, Son*, 213.

[83] See below, pp. 63-69.

Resurrection, Exaltation, and the Lordship of Jesus

For Paul and the early church, the resurrection established the Lordship of Christ.[84] There were other reasons for ascribing to Jesus this exalted title, not the least of which may have been Jesus' own self-understanding, reflected especially in his use of Ps 110:1 (Mark 12:36 and par.). Nevertheless, the resurrection stands as the climactic event which inaugurated Jesus' sovereign reign as the κύριος. This is seen particularly in Acts 2:32-36:

> This Jesus God raised up (ἀνέστησεν), and of that we all are witnesses. Being therefore exalted (ὑψωθείς) at the right hand of God, and having received from the Father the promise of the Holy Spirit, he has poured out this which you see and hear. For David did not ascend into the heavens; but he himself says, 'The Lord said to my Lord, Sit at my right hand, till I make thy enemies a stool for thy feet.' Let all the house of Israel therefore know assuredly that God has made him both Lord (κύριον) and Christ, this Jesus whom you crucified.

Peter's Pentecost sermon climaxed with this magnificent statement of God's vindication of his servant from the tragedy of death by crucifixion. These verses connect two key ideas with regard to Christ's Lordship: (1) resurrection and (2) exaltation to the right hand of God (based upon Psalm 110). This passage also portrayed the close tie the title "Christ" shared with κύριος, for God made him both Lord and Christ (καὶ κύριον αὐτὸν καὶ χριστὸν ἐποίησεν ὁ θεός).

Paul revealed his familiarity with the connection between Jesus' resurrection and his role as Lord primarily in Romans. In Rom 14:8-9 he stated:

> If we live, we live to the Lord, and if we die, we die to the Lord: so then, whether we live or whether we die, we are the Lord's. For to this end Christ died and lived again, that he might be Lord both of the dead and of the living.

The noun κύριος occurs three times in various cases in these two verses, and the verb form κυριεύσῃ occurs once. The "Lord Jesus" is without question the "Lord" who is meant, for the title "Christ" also appears along with the fact of his death and resurrection. Although the verb ἔζησεν means "to live," the idea means clearly "to live again," that is, as a result of resurrection. The phrase "for to this

---

[84.] Longenecker, *Christology*, 128-40; Cerfaux, *Christ*, 464; Foerster, *TDNT*, 3:1088; and Kramer, *Christ, Lord, Son*, 67.

end" (εἰς τοῦτο γάρ), above all, expresses purpose. Thus, in God's plan Christ died and rose to establish his Lordship over the living and the dead. In Rom 14:8-9 Paul makes an unmistakable connection between the resurrection and the κύριος predicate.

Likewise at the beginning of the letter, resurrection and lordship are related. In Rom 1:3-4 Paul wrote: "the gospel concerning his Son, who was descended from David according to the flesh and designated Son of God in power according to the Spirit of holiness by his resurrection from the dead, Jesus Christ our Lord." Many scholars believe that a traditional christological confession stands behind this passage.[85] They cite several criteria for determining this.[86] Paul probably quoted this pre-formed tradition to bridge the gap between himself and the Roman church, a church he did not establish.

If a pre-formed tradition is at the center of these verses, it must have emerged in the twenty years following the resurrection. Moreover, since it refers to the Davidic descent of Jesus, it must be rooted in the earliest Palestinian communities. Therefore, Rom 1:3-4 may be one of the earliest pieces of christological tradition in Paul's letters.

Generally scholars think Paul altered the original creed in one way or another to reinforce his own theological position.[87] Proposed

---

[85] Robert Jewett, "The Redaction and Use of an Early Christian Confession in Romans 1:3-4," in *The Living Text*, ed. D. E. Groh (Lanham, MD: University Press of America, 1985), 99-100; and C. H. Dodd, *The Epistle of Paul to the Romans*, MNTC (New York: Harper & Bros. Publishers, 1932), 4-5. Dissenting opinions are indeed few. See J. C. O'Neill, *Paul's Letter to the Romans* (Baltimore: Penguin Books, 1975), 26-27, who argued that vv. 3-4 were added later by a zealous scribe wanting to expand upon the content of the gospel. His position lacks credibility, however, for several reasons, not the least of which is the total absence of textual evidence. The only manuscript which omits these verses is G, a ninth century uncial manuscript; and this omission is itself suspect. All the earlier, better witnesses provide clear support that these verses were original.

[86] Jewett, "Romans 1:3-4," 100-102; Ernst Käsemann, *Commentary on Romans*, trans. Geoffrey W. Bromiley (Grand Rapids: Eerdmans, 1980), 10. Some of the criteria are (1) the antithetical parallelism, e.g., κατὰ σάρκα/κατὰ πνεῦμα, (2) the use of participles, (3) the use of typically un-Pauline words, phrases, and theological ideas, e.g., the Son of David Christology.

[87] Bultmann, *Theology*, 1:49, suggested the original formula began with a reference to Sonship and omitted the phrases "according to the flesh" and "according to the spirit of holiness." Eduard Schweizer, "Römer 1,3f. und der Gegensatz von Fleisch und Geist vor und bei Paulus," *EvT* 15 (1955), 563-65, advocated that only the phrase "in power" was a Pauline addition. C. K. Barrett, *A Commentary on the Epistle to the Romans*, HNTC (New York: Harper & Row, 1957), 18-20, carried Schweizer further and added that the phrase "by the resurrection from the dead" was also a Pauline interpolation. Oscar Cullmann, *The Earliest Christian*

schemes are often built upon the presuppositions of the History of Religions school which postulates a wide variance in the early Church between the Jewish Christian Church, the Hellenistic-Jewish Church, and the Gentile Christian Church. This notion should be abandoned for the evidence portrays the earliest churches as melting pots of Greek and Jewish thought which should not be defined too narrowly.[88] Nevertheless, reconstruction of the original tradition is difficult, and certainty will never be guaranteed.

The center of this passage is the Sonship of Jesus as demonstrated by the prescript given the creed, "concerning his Son" (περὶ τοῦ υἱοῦ αὐτοῦ), as well as the two stages of Sonship presented. In the first stage, Jesus is the Son of David "according to the flesh." This refers to Jesus' role as Messiah. The messianic hope was attached to David and his family above all by 2 Sam 7:12-16. Mainline and sectarian Judaism utilized this promise throughout the Old Testament and intertestamental periods to express their hope of deliverance.[89] After the resurrection, the early church recognized Jesus as the promised "seed of David" and expressed this sentiment in their creeds and confessions.

The interest here, however, is primarily in the second half of this pre-formed tradition. Whereas the first part describes "his Son" as the messianic descendant of David, the second part describes his appointment as "Son of God in power" by the resurrection.[90] To this Paul added the postscript "Jesus Christ our Lord," which stands in apposition to the entire creed. While his Lordship is more apparent after the resurrection, it must not be relegated only to that stage.

Confessions, trans. J. K. S. Reid (London: Lutterworth, 1949), 55-56, believed Paul used the creed unchanged. Käsemann, *Romans*, 13, echoed a similar sentiment saying Paul added nothing to the body of the creed, but he did give it a prescript ("concerning his son") and a postscript ("Jesus Christ our Lord"). Jewett, "Romans 1:3-4," 113, advocated a three-stage development in which Paul inherited a previously redacted Jewish-Christian confession to which he added "in power" and the genitive ἁγιωσύνης.

[88.] Hengel, *Between Jesus and Paul*, 30-47, suggested that most christological development occurred in the Greek-speaking Jewish Christian churches of Jerusalem, Caesarea, Antioch, and Damascus. But this church was not far removed, as some have suggested, from the *Urgemeinde*, which from the beginning was a *Mischgemeinde* of Greek- and Jewish-speaking believers.

[89.] See 1 Chron 17:11-13; Ps 2:7; 89:26; 110:3; 2 Esdras 7:28-30; 1 Enoch 105:1-2; and 4QFlor 1:10-13.

[90.] Hengel, *Son*, 59-60; and Cullmann, *Christology*, 292.

Part two begins with ὁρισθέντος, a typical divine passive participle with the meaning "to appoint."[91] Its use in the genitive links it with "his Son" (1:3) and with the first part of the confession. The appointment is to the status of Sonship, used here in its full form, "Son of God" (υἱοῦ θεοῦ). This appointment, however, stands above his status of messianic Sonship and expresses Sonship on a higher plane. This becomes apparent when one realizes that the prepositional phrase ἐν δυνάμει modifies, not the participle, but the noun phrase υἱοῦ θεοῦ.[92] The meaning immediately becomes clear. God has appointed Jesus to be the "Son of God in power."

Paul introduced the role of the Spirit into this christological equation with the phrase κατὰ πνεῦμα ἁγιωσύνης.[93] It stands in contrast to the phrase "according to the flesh" in the first half of the confession. It lies immediately after the phrase "in power" and underscores the role "power" and "Spirit" play in Paul's christological scheme.[94]

The supreme show of power and Spirit was the resurrection. The final phrase in the tradition, ἐξ ἀναστάσεως νεκρῶν, emphasizes that this unique event established the second stage of Jesus' saving work. It is both a temporal and a causal modifier of the participle ὁρισθέντος, for Jesus entered the new phase only *after* the resurrection. Moreover, *because* of the resurrection, he is declared "Lord."[95]

[91.] K. L. Schmidt, "ὁρίζω," *TDNT*, 5:452-53.

[92.] C. E. B. Cranfield, *A Critical and Exegetical Commentary on the Epistle to the Romans*, ICC, 2 vols. (Edinburgh: T. & T. Clark, 1975), 1:62; Käsemann, *Romans*, 12. Marie Joseph Lagrange, *Saint Paul: Epitre aux Romains* (Paris: J. Gabalda, 1922), 7, stated: "il sera constitué Fils de Dieu puissant, c'est-à-dire exerçant sa puissance, par opposition à son état d'humiliation dans la chair.... Ce sense nous parait donc plus sur que de joindre ἐν δυνάμει à ὁρισθέντος.

[93.] Such a reference to the Spirit occurs nowhere else in Paul and is best understood as evidence of the confession's Semitic background. The Hebrew רוח הקדש literally means "spirit of holiness."

[94.] On the relationship between δύναμις and πνεῦμα, see E. Earle Ellis, "Christ and Spirit in 1 Corinthians," in *Prophecy and Hermeneutic in Early Christianity* (Grand Rapids: Eerdmans, 1978), 63-71. "Spirit" and "power" are closely connected in the following texts: Rom 15:18-19; 1 Cor 2:4-5; 5:3-4; 15:43-45; 2 Cor 6:6-7; Gal 3:5; Eph 3:16; and 2 Tim 1:7.

[95.] Heinrich Schlier, "Zu Rom 1,3f," in *Neues Testament und Geschichte: Historisches Geschehen und Deutung im Neuen Testament. Oscar Cullmann zum 70. Geburtstag*, ed. Heinrich Baltensweiler and Bo Reicke (Zürich: TheologischeVerlag, 1972), 214; Barrett, *Romans*, 19-20, thought this phrase was a Pauline interpolation; Käsemann, *Romans*, 12, however, disagreed. If it were,

The verse ends with the words, "Jesus Christ our Lord." This no doubt is a Pauline postscript, added by the apostle to emphasize the present ruling station of the Son. It is the exalted "Son of God in power" who rules over the Church and is identical with the κύριος. This postscript ties together two key christological titles, "Son of God" and "Lord," in such a way that it is difficult to distinguish between them (see also 1 Cor 1:9). All in all, however, Paul's use of this pre-formed confession demonstrates the connection between resurrection and the κύριος predicate as it referred to Jesus.

Related to the concept of resurrection are the passages which speak of Christ's exaltation. One may note here in passing Phil 2:6-11, which will be discussed more fully later. The second half of this hymn declares that God highly exalted him (ὁ θεὸς αὐτὸν ὑπερύψωσεν) and graciously bestowed on him the name "Lord." While the resurrection is not mentioned specifically, it certainly may have stood in the mind of Paul as he transmitted this pre-formed hymn to the Philippian congregation. The idea of exaltation recalls both the resurrection and the ascension of Jesus to "the right hand of God," a tradition based upon Psalm 110.

The apostle Paul was familiar with the scriptural tradition which associated Psalm 110 with the risen Lord Jesus (e.g., Rom 8:34; 1 Cor 15:25; Eph 1:20; and Col 3:1). This particular passage was well-fixed in early Christian usage as other New Testament passages suggest (Acts 2:34; Heb 1:3, 13; 8:1; 10:12; Mark 12:36; 14:62; Matt 22:44; 26:64; Luke 20:42; and 22:69). It may very well be the most important Old Testament text to impact christological development with regard to the κύριος title.[96] Whether or not Paul understood Jesus to be the author of this scriptural connection is impossible to know;[97] he certainly never attributed it to Jesus. Nevertheless, no doubt exists that Paul utilized the concepts present in this Old Testament passage and referred them to his Lord, Jesus Christ.

More than any other phrase from Ps 110:1, Paul emphasized that the risen Lord was "at the right hand of God."[98] In Rom 8:34, he

---

he thought that the original would lack "both precision and also the concluding emphasis, which is by no means accidental."

[96.] Hengel, *Son*, 78-80.

[97.] The Synoptic Gospels suggest that Jesus made the connection (Matt 22:44; 26:64; Mark 12:36; 14:62; Luke 20:42; 22:69). The frequency of this *testimonia* in various New Testament writers demonstrates that this appeal is quite early, arising from the earliest levels.

described Christ as "the one who died (ὁ ἀποθανών)," "the one who was raised (ἐγερθείς)," and one who is also seated "at the right hand of God (καί ἐστιν ἐν δεξιᾷ τοῦ θεοῦ)." In Eph 1:20 he addressed the great work to effect man's salvation and portrayed God as the agent and Christ as the sphere of redemption (ἐν τῷ Χριστῷ). He believed this plan was accomplished "in Christ when he raised him from the dead (ἐγείρας αὐτὸν ἐκ νεκρῶν) and made him sit at his right hand in the heavenly places (καθίσας ἐν δεξιᾷ αὐτοῦ ἐν τοῖς ἐπουρανίοις)." Likewise, at the beginning of Paul's exhortation to believers in Colossians 3, the apostle appealed to their relationship with Christ as the basis for their new life. He wrote: "If then you have been raised with Christ (Εἰ οὖν συνηγέρθητε τῷ Χριστῷ), seek the things that are above, where Christ is, seated at the right hand of God (ἐν δεξιᾷ τοῦ θεοῦ καθήμενος)." In each of these passages, Paul associated resurrection and exaltation to the right hand of God.

The "right hand of God" had a rich history in Old Testament literature, particularly the Psalms.[99] It stood as a symbol of divine power which accomplished creation,[100] effected redemption,[101] and stood as a present help in dire circumstances.[102] The phrase was also a rich symbol outside Old Testament literature being found in magical spells, non-sectarian writings, and the rabbis.[103] According to Matthew, Jesus referred to it in the context of the great judgment which is to take place at the end (Matt 25:31-46). When the Son of Man comes in glory, he will sit upon the throne and gather the nations around him. He will separate the sheep from the goats and place the

---

[98.] F. F. Bruce, *Paul: Apostle of the Heart Set Free* (Grand Rapids: Eerdmans, 1971), 115, noted that Paul seldom referred to Christ at the right hand of God. Nevertheless, it denoted supreme authority in Jewish terminology. Bruce suggested Paul may have used it sparingly so that his Gentile converts would not be bound to such a spatial way of thinking about the exalted Christ.

[99.] Ps 16:7; 20:8; 43:3; 47:10; 59:5; 62:8; 118:15. In these texts ἡ δεξιά translates ימין.

[100.] Isa 48:13: "My hand laid the foundation of the earth, and my right hand (HT, וימיני; LXX, ἡ δεξιά μου) spread out the heavens; when I call to them they stand forth together."

[101.] Exod 15:6, 12; Ps. 17:7 [LXX, 16:7]: "Wondrously show thy steadfast love, O savior of those who seek refuge from their adversaries at thy right hand (HT, בימינך; LXX, τῇ δεξιᾷ σου)."

[102.] Ps 60:5 [LXX, 59:7]: "That thy beloved may be delivered, give victory by thy right hand (σῶσον τῇ δεξιᾷ σου) and answer us!"

[103.] Walter Grundmann, "δεξιός," *TDNT*, 2:37-38.

sheep upon his right hand (ἐκ δεξιῶν αὐτοῦ), the goats on his left. This eschatological scene follows the ancient idea that "the right hand is the favourable one, the side of bliss and salvation."[104]

Paul, and the other New Testament writers, inherited this rich tradition, and, from the beginning, associated it with the risen Jesus via Psalm 110. Thus, he viewed Jesus alongside God exalted to the right hand, the place of honor and power, as both Christ and Lord of the world. This fulfills and transcends the messianic promises of the Old Testament and links Jesus unquestionably with the rule, power, and deity of God.[105]

The Scope of Jesus' Lordship

According to Rom 14:8-9, Jesus' death and subsequent resurrection resulted in his Lordship over both the realm of the living and the dead. The aorist form of the verb κυριεύσῃ in verse nine should be understood as ingressive and renders the phrase: "so that he might be established as Lord (κυριεύσῃ) over the living and the dead." By this, Paul meant that the same Jesus who was crucified and resurrected continues to live and to exercise his dominion over those who had already died as well as those who live. Inherent within this idea is the fact that the risen Christ is Lord over all creation. Regarding this verse Moule stated: "This, to be sure, is a *kuriotes* over human persons only; but to be Lord of the domain of dead and living is, nevertheless, a 'cosmic' position."[106]

1 Cor 8:6 contains a pre-formed christological tradition[107] which makes the scope of Jesus' Lordship more explicit: "Yet for us there is one God, the Father, from whom are all things and for whom we exist, and one Lord (εἷς κύριος), Jesus Christ, through whom are all things and through whom we exist." It describes the Lord as the one through whom (δι' οὗ) all things (τὰ πάντα) have been created[108] and through him (δι' αὐτοῦ) redemption is assured.[109] It parallels the one God and the one Lord and portrays the Lord Jesus Christ as mediator of

---

[104] Grundmann, *TDNT*, 2:38.

[105] Ibid., 2:39-40.

[106] Moule, *Origin*, 44.

[107] Kramer, *Christ, Lord, Son*, 95; Ellis, "Traditions in 1 Corinthians," 494f.; cf. Fee, *First Corinthians*, 373-74.

[108] Creation certainly seems to be what the tradition implies in this first clause; see Barrett, *First Corinthians*, 192.

[109] Ἡμεῖς refers to believers who have been redeemed through faith in Christ.

creation and salvation.[110] By using "all things" (τὰ πάντα), it includes the living and the dead as well as other aspects of creation.

Other Pauline passages spell this out further. Colossians 1:15-20 declares:

> He is the image of the invisible God,
> The first-born of all creation;
> For in him all things were created,
> In heaven and on earth,
> Visible and invisible,
> Whether thrones or dominions
> Or principalities or authorities—
> All things were created through him and for him.
> He is before all things,
> And in him all things hold together.
> He is the head of the body, the church;
> He is the beginning,
> The first-born from the dead,
> That in everything he might be pre-eminent.
> For in him all the fulness of God was pleased to dwell,
> And through him to reconcile to himself all things,
> Whether on earth or in heaven,
> Making peace by the blood of his cross.

Although this passage does not contain the title "Lord," it affirms ideas which are consistent with Paul's κύριος Christology, which may be presupposed by the author. The cosmic scope of Christ's Lordship with regard to creation and salvation is undeniably the primary thrust of this piece.[111]

[110.] Kramer, *Christ, Lord, Son*, 95. Εἷς θεός was typical of the language used in the Gentile mission. Cf. Gal 3:20; Jam 2:19; 4:12; 1 Thess 1:9; Heb 6:1. It is reminiscent of Deut 6:4. In the face of the pagan polytheistic practices encountered in the Gentile mission, its use was most likely polemical. The first part of the confession was typically Jewish. The addition of "and one Lord, Jesus Christ" makes the piece distinctively Christian. Other passages in Paul which speak of the Lord's mediation in creation and redemption are Rom 5:1, 11, 21; 7:25; 1 Cor 15:57; Col 1:15-20; and 1 Thess 5:9. The key phrase is "through our Lord Jesus Christ." As a divine agent in creation one may recall the role of Wisdom in Jewish writings, e.g., Prov 8:27-31 and Wisd 7:21.

[111.] Paul Beasley-Murray, "Colossians 1:15-20: An Early Christian Hymn Celebrating the Lordship of Christ," in *Pauline Studies: Essays Presented to Professor F. F. Bruce on His 70th Birthday*, ed. Donald A. Hagner and Murray J. Harris (Grand Rapids: Eerdmans, 1980), 179, wrote: "Jesus Christ is Lord—Lord over all. This is the theme of the Colossian hymn."

At the beginning of verse sixteen the confession states "all things" (τὰ πάντα) were created "in him" (ἐν αὐτῷ). Included within "all things" are heavenly and earthly things (τὰ πάντα ἐν τοῖς οὐρανοῖς καὶ ἐπὶ τῆς γῆς), visible and invisible things (τὰ ὁρατὰ καὶ τὰ ἀόρατα), and the powers which rule over man and creation (εἴτε θρόνοι εἴτε κυριότητες εἴτε ἀρχαὶ εἴτε ἐξουσίαι). At the end of the same verse it affirms again that "all things were created through him and for him" (τὰ πάντα δι' αὐτοῦ καὶ εἰς αὐτὸν ἔκτισται). The Lord is "before all things" (πρὸ πάντων), and in him "all things" (τὰ πάντα) hold together. The scope of Jesus' reign, therefore, begins with the creation of the universe and continues with his sustaining of the same.

In 1:18 the emphasis shifts from his Lordship over creation to his Lordship over the new creation. As Lord he is head of the Church (ἡ κεφαλὴ τοῦ σώματος τῆς ἐκκλησίας), the Beginning (ὅς ἐστιν ἀρχή), the First-born from the dead (πρωτότοκος ἐκ τῶν νεκρῶν), so that he might be first in all things (ἵνα γένηται ἐν πᾶσιν αὐτὸς πρωτεύων). In 1:20 it states "all things" (τὰ πάντα) are reconciled "through him" (δι' αὐτοῦ) "to himself" (εἰς αὐτόν), things on earth as well as things in heaven (εἴτε τὰ ἐπὶ τῆς γῆς εἴτε τὰ ἐν τοῖς οὐρανοῖς).

The key word in both sections of the hymn about Christ in regard to the scope of his Lordship is πᾶς. There can be little doubt that this word has cosmic and universal import in the New Testament and especially here in Paul.[112] The apostle believed that Jesus' Lordship, which was established at the resurrection, extended over all creation.

The Philippian hymn reinforces this idea (Phil 2:10-11): "At the name of Jesus every knee should bow, in heaven and on earth and under the earth, and every tongue confess that Jesus Christ is Lord, to the glory of God the Father." By including "every knee" (πᾶν γόνυ) and "every tongue" (πᾶσα γλῶσσα) in this context, it extends Jesus' Lordship beyond the Church to all creation. It also includes three categories which correspond to all aspects of the created universe (ἐπουρανίων καὶ ἐπιγείων καὶ καταχθονίων). Though it uses different terms than the Colossian hymn, the basic teaching is the same: Jesus is Lord over all the cosmos.

As Lord over the cosmos, however, Jesus does not supplant God's position.[113] The confession in 1 Cor 8:6 includes the creative and

---

[112] Bo Reicke, "πᾶς," *TDNT*, 5:893-96

[113] Kramer, *Christ, Lord, Son*, 83, stated: "It is true that in a certain sense the

redemptive function of God the Father as well. Likewise, in Phil 2:11 every tongue will declare Jesus κύριος "to the glory of God the Father." Thus, Jesus' Lordship over the cosmos neither threatens the position of God the Father nor violates the spirit of biblical monotheism.

The apostle to the Gentiles was not interested in speculation concerning the nature or substance of this Jesus whom he preached. He was concerned primarily with declaring the Lordship of the One who apprehended him in such a way that no doubt remained in Paul's mind that he rules over the realm of the living and the dead.[114]

Κύριος, therefore, "signifies the status of honor and majesty which Jesus has *vis à vis* the Church and the world—a status which is final and of eschatological import."[115] When the Church acclaimed "Jesus is Lord," it placed itself voluntarily and, before God, forensically under his rule; and the ramifications of this extended to every area of their corporate and individual lives.

God, the Father, and the Lord, Jesus Christ

Paul's letters generally followed the literary patterns of that day. Hellenistic letters began with an indication of the sender and the recipients along with a greeting (prescript) and ended with further greetings in some kind of closing formula.[116] Recent discoveries of ancient papyri have expanded our knowledge of early Greco-Roman letter writing patterns and have revealed both the similarities and differences between Paul's letters and other letters written in that day.

Lord thus takes to himself the absolute status of God, in that he is 'God in relation to the world' or to the Church. But God is neither displaced nor absorbed by the *Lord*." He went on to insist that the title "Lord" emphasized the present ruling of Jesus over the Church.

[114]. According to Longenecker, *Christology*, 135-38, the confession "Jesus is Lord" regarded history and religion. Moule, *Origin*, 43-44, allowed that the passages which refer to the cosmic Lordship of Christ may have developed out of the Jewish Wisdom tradition; however, he argued that it may have simply arisen out of the experience of Jesus' "aliveness beyond death." His Lordship over the living and the dead would lead logically to his Lordship over creation. While not denying that development may have occurred here, Moule insisted that the key elements for this idea were there from the beginning.

[115]. Kramer, *Christ, Lord, Son*, 75.

[116]. Kümmel, *Introduction*, 248.

Two types of letter patterns may be recognized: (1) formal letters which amount to great works of literature and (2) less-stylized, occasional letters which deal with more mundane situations.[117] Attempts to force Paul's letters into either category have failed and some, like Amos Wilder, prefer to understand New Testament epistolary style as distinct and probably affected little by Greco-Roman patterns.[118] His letters were both occasional and literary works. They were directed to specific needs at specific churches; yet they transcended the moment to become magnificent expressions of Christian faith and theology.[119] One need look no further than to the Roman letter to come face to face with perhaps the greatest treatise on Christian theology ever written.

Paul followed contemporary epistolary practice by including certain stereotyped forms in his introductory formulae, thanksgivings, and farewells. In these sections he often utilized the formula, "God the Father of our Lord Jesus Christ," or a variation of it.

Paul's salutations amounted to a hybrid of the Hellenistic greeting, χαίρειν,[120] altered to χάρις ("grace"), along with the common Jewish greeting shalom, "Peace."[121] Thus, his typical salutation read:

[117.] Adolf Deissmann, *Light from the Ancient East*, trans. Lionel R. M. Strachen (London: Hodder & Stroughton, 1910), 147, 290-301, argued Paul's letters were not the formal *Episteln* but were the occasional *Briefe*. Beda Rigaux, *The Letters of St. Paul: Modern Studies*, trans. S. Yonick (Chicago: Franciscan Herald Press, 1968), 118, agreed. He continued saying this "does not mean that the Pauline letters should be regarded as ephemeral compositions intended to be read once to the community and subsequently forgotten. Such letters are also apostolic acts, and like preaching, are truly the words of God." Paul himself instructed that the letters be read to the entire congregation (1 Thess 5:27; Col 4:16). D. J. Selby, *Toward an Understanding of St. Paul* (Englewood Cliffs, NJ: Prentice-Hall, 1962), 239, argued that the letters directed to individuals were intended also for the local assembly based upon the use of second person plural pronouns (e.g., Tit 3:15; Philem 25).

[118.] Amos Wilder, *Early Christian Rhetoric: The Language of the Gospel*, 2d ed. (Cambridge: Harvard University Press, 1971), 44.

[119.] William G. Doty, *Letters in Primitive Christianity*, in the Guides to Biblical Scholarship Series (Philadelphia: Fortress Press, 1973), 26.

[120.] This is an infinitive of the word meaning "to rejoice." It is used here, however, with the simple idea "Greetings!" or in English, "Hello!"

[121.] Kümmel, *Introduction*, 248, believed Paul's prescript followed more closely the Oriental-Jewish pattern. See Bezadel Porten, "The Address Formulae in Aramaic Letters: A New Collation of Cowley 17," *RB* 90 (1980): 396-415.

> Grace to you and peace from God our Father and the Lord Jesus Christ
>
> χάρις ὑμῖν καὶ εἰρήνη ἀπὸ θεοῦ πατρὸς ἡμῶν καὶ κυρίου Ἰησοῦ Χριστοῦ

Paul designated both God the Father and the Lord Jesus as dispensers of grace and peace to the Church. He summed up the entire gospel under these great concepts; so it serves as a fitting introduction to all of Paul's correspondence. For Paul the gospel was a gospel of grace and peace.

God the Father *and* the Lord Jesus Christ bring these blessings into men's lives by faith. They are unified in function.[122] Such a connection is possible only if God and the Lord reside at the same level in Paul's thought.[123] To suggest that God the Father is the source and Jesus the Lord mediates grace and peace to believers is to be guilty of reading into the salutation what is not there. Paul made no such distinction of function in the salutations.

Paul customarily followed the salutation of his letters with a thanksgiving.[124] These were typically less stereotyped than his salutations. Second Corinthians 1:3 represents a good example of the Pauline thanksgiving which includes the phrase being discussed:

> Blessed be the God and Father of our Lord Jesus Christ
>
> Εὐλογητὸς ὁ θεὸς καὶ πατὴρ τοῦ κυρίου ἡμῶν Ἰησοῦ Χριστοῦ

The exact wording is found in Eph 1:3, while the sister letter to it, Colossians (1:3), has a less formal version:

> We always thank God, the Father of our Lord Jesus Christ, when we pray for you
>
> Εὐχαριστοῦμεν τῷ θεῷ πατρὶ τοῦ κυρίου ἡμῶν Ἰησοῦ Χριστοῦ πάντοτε περὶ ὑμῶν προσευχόμενοι

Likewise, 1 Thess 1:2-3 contains a reference to God the Father and the Lord Jesus Christ with an even less formal style:

> We give thanks to God always for you all, constantly mentioning you in our prayers, remembering before our God and Father your work of faith and labor of love and steadfastness of hope in our Lord Jesus Christ.[125]

[122.] Kramer, *Christ, Lord, Son*, 154.

[123.] Cerfaux, *Christ*, 473-74.

[124.] Galatians is the only exception.

Following the introductory remarks, Paul thanked God for the blessings which he, his co-workers, and all believers receive in Christ (e.g., Eph 1:3-14). In so doing, he followed the common convention of his day, for thanksgivings, blessings, and doxologies to God were typical in Judaism.[126] Despite this, some scholars claim that Paul adopted it from the Hellenistic churches.[127] The presence of such thanksgivings in Judaism and the reference to God as "Father," which was a term close to the Aramaic church, militate against understanding these Pauline passages as arising out of Hellenistic Christianity. There is in fact no reason to take them as pre-Pauline. Paul probably brought together the formula, "God the Father of our Lord Jesus Christ," with the thanksgiving material in creating a unique Christian blessing for God's goodness.[128]

Paul also used this formula in the body of several letters in what appear to be benedictions and doxologies of praise. While such benedictions and doxologies appear to mark the end of the letter, they often simply serve as a transition into the apostle's closing comments.[129] One may note, for example, 1 Thess 3:11-13:

> Now may our God and Father himself, and our Lord Jesus (αὐτὸς δὲ ὁ θεὸς καὶ πατὴρ ἡμῶν καὶ ὁ κύριος ἡμῶν Ἰησοῦς), direct our way to you; and may the Lord (ὁ κύριος) make you increase and abound in love to one another and to all men, as we do to you, so that he may establish your hearts unblamable in holiness before our God and Father, at the coming of our Lord Jesus with all his saints (ἔμπροσθεν τοῦ θεοῦ καὶ πατρὸς ἡμῶν ἐν τῇ παρουσίᾳ τοῦ κυρίου ἡμῶν Ἰησοῦ μετὰ πάντων τῶν ἁγίων αὐτοῦ).

In another context, when Paul called upon God to bear witness to his truthfulness, he used the same formula (2 Cor 11:30-31):

> If I must boast, I will boast of the things that show my weakness. The God and Father of the Lord Jesus (ὁ

---

[125] The RSV separates the references to God the Father and the Lord Jesus Christ. The Greek text, however, has them together: μνημονεύοντες ὑμῶν τοῦ ἔργου τῆς πίστεως καὶ τοῦ κόπου τῆς ἀγάπης καὶ τῆς ὑπομονῆς τῆς ἐλπίδος τοῦ κυρίου ἡμῶν Ἰησοῦ Χριστοῦ ἔμπροσθεν τοῦ θεοῦ καὶ πατρὸς ἡμῶν.

[126] Hermann W. Beyer, "εὐλογέω," *TDNT*, 2:755-61.

[127] Kramer, *Christ, Lord, Son*, 93.

[128] Gottlob Schrenk, "πατήρ," *TDNT*, 5:1007; *contra* Kramer, *Christ, Lord, Son*, 93.

[129] 1 Thess 3:11-3; 2 Thess 2:16; and Rom 15:6.

θεὸς καὶ πατὴρ τοῦ κυρίου Ἰησοῦ), he who is blessed forever, knows that I do not lie.

Thus, Paul exercised great latitude in using this expression and did not limit it to his formal salutations and thanksgivings.

Given Paul's use of this formula in salutations, thanksgivings, and in the body of his letters in a rather stereotypical style, one might well expect to find it used also in his farewells. This, however, is not the case.

Paul referred to God only twice in his farewells: (1) in the (trinitarian ?) closing to 2 Corinthians[130] and (2) in his farewell to the brothers in the Ephesian letter.[131] Only in the Ephesian farewell did he use the formula "God the Father and the Lord Jesus Christ." In 2 Corinthians he mentioned only God without πατήρ.

In most of the farewells, Paul referred only to the Lord Jesus Christ. First Corinthians 16:23 serves as an example:

The grace of the Lord Jesus be with you.

ἡ χάρις τοῦ κυρίου Ἰησοῦ μεθ' ὑμῶν.

In other letters Paul added or subtracted certain phrases or qualifiers. For example, he qualified the Lord Jesus with the personal pronoun, ἡμῶν ("our"), in several letters, indicating the close relationship between the risen Lord and the community to which he wrote.[132] In Philippians, Galatians, and Philemon, he altered the final prepositional phrase, "with you," to read "with your spirit."[133] In 2 Timothy (4:22) he stated the farewell differently:

[130.] 2 Cor 13:14: ἡ χάρις τοῦ κυρίου Ἰησοῦ Χριστοῦ καὶ ἡ ἀγάπη τοῦ θεοῦ καὶ ἡ κοινωνία τοῦ ἁγίου πνεύματος μετὰ πάντων ὑμῶν = "The grace of the Lord Jesus Christ and the love of God and the fellowship of the Holy Spirit be with you all."

[131.] Eph 6:23-24: εἰρήνη τοῖς ἀδελφοῖς καὶ ἀγάπη μετὰ πίστεως ἀπὸ θεοῦ πατρὸς καὶ κυρίου Ἰησοῦ Χριστοῦ. ἡ χάρις μετὰ πάντων τῶν ἀγαπώντων τὸν κύριον ἡμῶν Ἰησοῦν Χριστὸν ἐν ἀφθαρσίᾳ = "Peace be to the brethren, and love with faith, from God the Father and the Lord Jesus Christ. Grace be with all who love our Lord Jesus Christ with love undying."

[132.] Rom 16:20: ἡ χάρις τοῦ κυρίου ἡμῶν Ἰησοῦ μεθ' ὑμῶν = "the grace of our Lord Jesus be with you". 1 Thess 5:28: ἡ χάρις τοῦ κυρίου ἡμῶν Ἰησοῦ Χριστοῦ μεθ' ὑμῶν = "the grace of our Lord Jesus Christ be with you." 2 Thess 3:18: ἡ χάρις τοῦ κυρίου ἡμῶν Ἰησοῦ Χριστοῦ μετὰ πάντων ὑμῶν = "the grace of our Lord Jesus Christ be with you all."

[133.] Gal 6:18: ἡ χάρις τοῦ κυρίου ἡμῶν Ἰησοῦ Χριστοῦ μετὰ τοῦ πνεύματος ὑμῶν, ἀδελφοί = "the grace of our Lord Jesus Christ be with your spirit, brethren." Phil 4:23: ἡ χάρις τοῦ κυρίου Ἰησοῦ Χριστοῦ μετὰ τοῦ πνεύματος ὑμῶν = "the grace of the Lord Jesus Christ be with your spirit." Cf. Philm 25.

The Lord be with your spirit. Grace be with you.
ὁ κύριος μετὰ τοῦ πνεύματός σου. ἡ χάρις μεθ' ὑμῶν.
In Colossians and the other Pastoral Epistles, he eliminated the reference to the "Lord" altogether. So the farewell to the Colossian church reads simply: "Grace be with you" (ἡ χάρις μεθ' ὑμῶν).[134]

From this brief survey of Pauline farwells, one may conclude that Paul made use of a stereotyped farewell formula in the majority of his letters. While the precise wording was not fixed, it included a reference to "grace" and "the Lord Jesus." With only two exceptions, no mention is made of God in these passages. The subjective genitive κυρίου demonstrates that the Lord Jesus is the source of grace, the one who dispenses salvation in this age, as well as the age to come.[135] Since no verb is present in these farewells, it may be taken either as indicative ("grace is yours")[136] or optative ("grace be to you").[137] The translations above assume the latter and consider these as Paul's benedictory wishes for his congregations.[138]

To summarize, Paul utilized stereotyped formulae in his salutations, thanksgivings, and farewells. In general his salutations and farewells appear more fixed than his thanksgivings. In these he frequently used the phrase "God our Father and the Lord Jesus Christ." While some contend that this phrase originated in the Hellenistic churches, this is not necessarily the case;[139] rather it seems to be a unique Pauline creation.[140] It demonstrates that Paul

---

[134.] Col 4:18. 1 Tim 6:21 is verbatim with the Colossian farewell. In Titus (3:15), however, Paul added πάντων: ἡ χάρις μετὰ πάντων ὑμῶν = "grace be with you all."

[135.] Kramer, *Christ, Lord, Son*, 90.

[136.] Gerhard Delling, *Worship in the New Testament*, trans. Percy Scott (Philadelphia: Westminster Press, 1962), 75.

[137.] Harry Gamble, *The Textual History of the Letter to the Romans: A Study in Textual and Literary Criticism*, Studies and Documents Series, no. 42 (Grand Rapids: Eerdmans, 1977), 65-67.

[138.] Ibid. Gamble pointed out that the customary closing in Greek letters was ἔρρωσο (= "Be strong"). This farewell, having a wish-like character, may indicate Paul's intent.

[139.] Greetings were typical of contemporary letter writing. *Contra* Kramer, *Christ, Lord, Son*, 151, who held that formula "Lord Jesus Christ" must have developed in the Hellenistic churches. See above, pp. 51-53.

[140.] Gordon D. Fee, *The First Epistle to the Corinthians*, NICNT (Grand Rapids: Eerdmans, 1987), 839. Since Paul's letters begin and end with "grace," Fee saw a continuity here which calls into question any theory of origination before Paul. He perceived Christianity as related to and consistent with Judaism,[141] and it carries Jesus' favorite designation for God, i.e., "Father."

This phrase also underscores the relationship between God the Father and the κύριος. In these texts, in fact, κύριος comes close to the title υἱός.[142] It is interesting to note that Paul more often linked "Father" with "Lord" than he did "Father" with "Son."[143] In light of the obvious verbal association and its use in the Gospels, this seems rather odd. The solution for this lay in the fact that the confession, "Jesus is Lord," characterized the churches, while Jesus' Sonship presented his unique relation to the Father.[144] Paul, when writing to his churches, felt the need to establish common ground in their common confession. Jesus stands as "Lord" in relation to the Church, whereas in relation to the Father he stands as Son. Moreover, Paul understood God to be the Father of all Christians, not only the Father of Jesus. For this reason, πατήρ is added to θεός to present in these formal passages God's Fatherhood in relation to the churches.

One final factor needs to be mentioned. The phrase "God the Father and the Lord Jesus Christ," present in Paul's salutations, thanksgivings, and other doxological passages, indicates a functional identity between the Father and the Lord. They are jointly the source of grace and peace. Praise, thanksgiving, and blessing belong to them. There remains, however, no confusion for Paul in respect to their ultimate position. The placing of "God the Father" before "the Lord Jesus Christ" indicates Jesus' subordination to God as other Pauline passages, such as 1 Cor 15:24-27, attest:

> Then comes the end, when he [Christ] delivers the kingdom to God the Father after destroying every rule and every authority and power. For he must reign until he has put all his enemies under his feet. The last enemy to be destroyed is death. "For God has put all things in subjection under his feet." But when it says, "All things are put in subjection under him," it is plain

---

wrote: "This phenomenon tends to make the question of its prior origin in the liturgy of the church especially tenuous, all the more so since all the other evidence is later than Paul." See also Beker, *Paul*, 265.

[141.] Cerfaux, *Christ*, 473-74.

[142.] Note Rom 1:3-4 where κύριος stands in apposition to the phrase "Son of God in power."

[143.] Schrenk, *TDNT*, 5:1009.

[144.] Ibid.

that he [God] is excepted who put all things under him [Christ]. When all things are subjected to him [Christ], then the Son himself will also be subjected to him [God] who put all things under him [Christ], that God may be everything to every one.

This somewhat confusing passage, taken with the evidence given above, teaches the ultimate subordination of the Son to the Father. Nevertheless, Jesus remains in unique relation with God as the κύριος of the Church.

ΚΥΡΙΟΣ in Ethical Admonitions

While κύριος serves as a christological title in nearly every part of Paul's letters, it occurs most frequently in the hortatory sections. When the apostle dealt with practical matters relating to conduct and practices within the churches, he generally made reference to Jesus as κύριος. Although these sections may not comprise the bulk of his writings, they, nevertheless, represent the great passion he had for applying the gospel to daily life.

For Paul, the gospel contained both an indicative and an imperative. He characterized the indicative of the gospel with the phrase ἐν Χριστῷ and associated it generally with the title "Christ"; on the other hand, he characterized the imperative with the phrase ἐν κυρίῳ and associated it generally with the title "Lord."[145] This section will examine these observations and offer some analysis.

The phrase, "in Christ" (ἐν Χριστῷ), due to its frequent appearances in Paul's letters, has received a great deal of attention by scholars.[146] It is best understood in light of his eschatology and his understanding of Christ as the Second Adam: "For as in Adam (ἐν τῷ 'Αδάμ) all die, so also in Christ (ἐν τῷ Χριστῷ) shall all be made alive" (1 Cor 15:22).[147] It signifies that all who belong to Christ have been transferred into the new age inaugurated by his death and resurrec-

---

[145.] Beker, *Paul*, 273-74.

[146.] For a survey of how recent scholars have dealt with this phrase see Richard Longenecker, *Paul: Apostle of Liberty* (New York: Harper & Row, 1964; reprint, Grand Rapids: Baker, 1976), 160-70.

[147.] *Contra* Albert Schweitzer, *The Mysticism of Paul the Apostle*, trans. William Montgomery (London: A. & C. Black, 1931), 122ff., who held to a mystical understanding. On the First Adam/Second Adam teaching of Paul see Davies, *Paul*, 36-58. Albrecht Oepke, "ἐν," *TDNT*, 2:542, saw the phrase as having local *and* instrumental meaning; see also Beker, *Paul*, 272.

tion. Understood in this way, the phrase arose out of Paul's background in rabbinic Judaism as W. D. Davies argued:

> Paul accepted the traditional Rabbinic doctrine of the unity of mankind in Adam. That doctrine implied that the very constitution of the physical body of Adam and the method of its formation was symbolic of the real oneness of mankind. In that one body of Adam east and west, north and south were brought together, male and female, as we have seen. The 'body' of Adam included all mankind. Was it not natural, then, that Paul when he thought of the new humanity being incorporated 'in Christ' should have conceived of it as the 'body' of the Second Adam, where there was neither Jew nor Greek, male nor female, bond nor free.[148]

If this interpretation truly reflects Paul's "in Christ" concept, it should follow then that other phrases used with the title "Christ" would also be related to incorporation language. This is in fact the case. For example, Paul wrote: "But you were washed, you were sanctified, you were justified in the name of the Lord Jesus Christ (ἐν τῷ ὀνόματι τοῦ κυρίου Ἰησοῦ Χριστοῦ) and in the Spirit of our God" (1 Cor 6:11). Perhaps he could have utilized the short-hand "in Christ" here to substitute for the longer, and more formal, "in the name of the Lord Jesus Christ." Furthermore, he spoke of being baptized into Christ (εἰς Χριστόν; Gal 3:27; Rom 6:3) and putting on Christ (Χριστὸν ἐνεδύσασθε; Gal 3:27). Likewise, he claimed believers were crucified with Christ (Χριστῷ συνεσταύρωμαι; Gal 2:20), buried with him (συνετάφημεν . . . αὐτῷ; Rom 6:4), resurrected with him (συνήγειρεν; Eph 2:6), seated in the heavenlies with him (συνεκάθισεν ἐν τοῖς ἐπουρανίοις ἐν Χριστῷ Ἰησοῦ; Eph 2:6), and will one day live with him (συζήσομεν αὐτῷ; Rom 6:8). To these examples one may also add phrases in which "Christ" is used as a genitive of possession, signifying the believer's belongingness to Christ.[149] In each of these cases, Paul had in mind the incorporation of the believer into the person of Christ as it related to his eschatological scheme.

Beker noted that the phrase ἐν Χριστῷ occurs primarily in three contexts: "(1) in relation to concepts of salvation; (2) in relation to the

---

[148] Davies, *Paul*, 57.

[149] Victor Furnish, *Theology and Ethics in Paul* (Nashville: Abingdon, 1968), 179. Κλητοί Ἰησοῦ Χριστοῦ (Rom 1:6); οἱ τοῦ Χριστοῦ (1 Cor 15:23; Gal 5:24); ὑμεῖς Χριστοῦ (1 Cor 3:23; Gal 3:29); and Χριστοῦ εἶναι (2 Cor 10:7).

communal structure of the church; (3) in relation to the apostolate and other apostolic persons."¹⁵⁰ Thus, one may say ἐν Χριστῷ represents the indicative of the gospel, understood as Christ's coming, death, resurrection, and the inauguration of the new age with all of its attendant features as they impact the Church (*Gabe*). Ἐν κυρίῳ, on the other hand, signifies the imperative of the gospel, understood as the demand made upon believers in light of God's saving activity in Christ (*Aufgabe*).¹⁵¹

For Paul, ἐν Χριστῷ became ἐν κυρίῳ when he discussed the Lordship of Christ and the believer's expected response of obedience to him. He gave his ethical instructions within the context of a Christian's incorporation into and belonging to Christ. Evidently, he believed that since Jesus reigned as Lord of the cosmos, and since believers belong to him, that his authority ought to extend to the day-to-day details of their lives.¹⁵²

Therefore, Paul employed ἐν κυρίῳ frequently in his letters, primarily in hortatory sections. He exhorted believers to "stand firm in the Lord" (Phil 4:1) and to "rejoice in the Lord" (Phil 3:1; 4:4). He instructed Christian children to obey their parents "in the Lord" (Eph 6:1). He delivered exhortation "in the Lord" (1 Thess 4:1; 5:27). He sent greetings "in the Lord" (1 Cor 16:19; Romans 16 *passim*). Finally, he encouraged the Corinthian brethren with these words: "Therefore, my beloved brethren, be steadfast, immovable, always abounding in the work of the Lord, knowing that in the Lord (ἐν κυρίῳ) your labor is not in vain" (1 Cor 15:58).

[150.] Beker, *Paul*, 273, followed Fritz Neugebauer, "Das paulinische 'in Christo,'" *NTS* 4 (1958): 124-38. On (1) see Rom 3:24; 6:11, 23; 8:2, 39; 2 Cor 5:19, 21; Gal 2:17; 3:14, 26; 1 Thess 5:18. On (2) see Rom 6:11; 8:1; 12:5; 2 Cor 5:17; Gal 1:22; 2:4, 17; 3:28; 1 Thess 2:14. On (3) see Rom 9:1; 15:17; 16:3, 7, 9, 10; 1 Cor 4:15, 17; 15:31; 16:24; 2 Cor 2:14, 17; 12:2, 19; 13:4.

[151.] On the indicative/imperative structure in Paul see Rudolf Bultmann, "Das Problem der Ethik bei Paulus," *ZNW* 23 (1924): 123-40. Note also Beker, *Paul*, 272-78, who understood this in terms of its apocalyptic fulfilment. For him the point is not individual and Christocentric, but cosmic and theocentric. He wrote (p. 277): "The scheme of the indicative and imperative must be lifted out of its Christocentric and anthropocentric moorings and placed in the theocentric-cosmic perspective of Paul's Christology."

[152.] Kramer, *Christ, Lord, Son*, 169, thought Paul utilized "Lord" primarily when concrete issues were at stake. The title "Lord" attached to ethical injunctions gave them a sense of urgency. If the church confessed "Jesus is Lord!" they ought to be willing to live under his Lordship.

Paul was not limited to the ἐν κυρίῳ formula in using κύριος in ethical admonitions.[153] He employed it throughout his instructions to the churches. Three examples should offer sufficient warrant.

First, in 1 Cor 5:1-5 Paul offered his advice on the problem of the incestuous man. Having stated the nature of the transgression (5:1), he advised that this character be removed from the church (5:2). He continued:

> When you are assembled *in the name of our Lord Jesus* (ἐν τῷ ὀνόματι τοῦ κυρίου ἡμῶν Ἰησοῦ) with my spirit, *with the power of our Lord Jesus* (σὺν τῇ δυνάμει τοῦ κυρίου ἡμῶν Ἰησοῦ), you are to deliver over such a man to Satan for the destruction of the flesh, so that his spirit may be saved *in the day of the Lord* (ἐν τῇ ἡμέρᾳ τοῦ κυρίου).[154]

In these verses, Paul referred to the "Lord" three times in his appeal to the Corinthians to move quickly to expel this overt sinner from their midst.

Second, in Romans 14 Paul encouraged the Roman Christians to refrain from passing judgment on each other with regard to certain dietary customs. He wrote (Rom 14:5-9; italics added):

> One man esteems one day as better than another, while another man esteems all days alike. Let every one be fully convinced in his own mind. He who observes the day, observes it *in honor of the Lord* (ὁ φρονῶν τὴν ἡμέραν κυρίῳ φρονεῖ). He also who eats, eats *in honor of the Lord* (καὶ ὁ ἐσθίων κυρίῳ ἐσθίει), since he gives thanks to God; while he who abstains, abstains *in honor of the Lord* (καὶ ὁ μὴ ἐσθίων κυρίῳ οὐ ἐσθίει) and gives thanks to God. None of us lives to himself, and none of us dies to himself. If we live, we live *to the Lord* (τῷ κυρίῳ), and if we die, we die *to the Lord* (τῷ κυρίῳ); so then, whether we live or whether we die, we are *the Lord's* (τοῦ κυρίου ἐσμέν). For to this end Christ died and lived again, that *he might be Lord* (κυριεύσῃ) both of the dead and of the living.

---

[153]. Rom 12:11 may be included here: "serve the Lord" (τῷ κυρίῳ δουλεύοντες). Also Col 3:17 says: "And whatever you do, in word or deed, do everything in the name of the Lord Jesus (πάντα ἐν ὀνόματι κυρίου Ἰησοῦ), giving thanks to God the Father through him."

[154]. 1 Cor 5:4-5, author's translation, italics added.

In this passage, κύριος occurs several times in regard to the problem at hand. Later Paul added: "I know and am persuaded *in the Lord Jesus* (ἐν κυρίῳ Ἰησοῦ) that nothing is unclean in itself; but it is unclean for any one who thinks it unclean" (Rom 14:14, italics added). The title Χριστός does appear in this text, yet, as stated above, it recalls primarily the indicative of the gospel, in this case the death and resurrection of Jesus. The imperative of the gospel is left to the title κύριος. Christians live to the Lord. They die to the Lord. They belong to the Lord. Therefore, Paul could ask (14:10): "Why do you pass judgment on your brother?"

Third, the household code of the Colossian letter offers the most graphic presentation of κύριος used in ethical admonitions. It reads (Col 3:18-4:1):

> Wives, be subject to your husbands, as is fitting in the Lord (ἐν κυρίῳ). Husbands, love your wives, and do not be harsh with them. Children, obey your parents in everything, for this pleases the Lord (ἐν κυρίῳ). Fathers, do not provoke your children, lest they become discouraged. Slaves, obey in everything those who are your earthly masters, not with eyeservice, as menpleasers, but in singleness of heart, fearing the Lord (φοβούμενοι τὸν κύριον). Whatever your task, work heartily, as serving the Lord (τῷ κυρίῳ) and not men, knowing that from the Lord (ἀπὸ κυρίου) you will receive the inheritance as your reward; you are serving the Lord Christ (τῷ κυρίῳ Χριστῷ δουλεύετε). For the wrongdoer will be paid back for the wrong he has done, and there is no partiality. Masters, treat your slaves justly and fairly, knowing that you also have a Master (κύριον) in heaven.

The demands laid upon these family members, with the exception of the husbands/fathers, all contain a reference to the "Lord" Jesus. Seven times in these verses Paul made reference to Jesus' role as κύριος. He becomes the basis of the wives' submission, the children's obedience, the slaves' service, and the masters' demeanor.

Paul, therefore, used κύριος frequently in ethical instructions to portray the totality of Christian experience. All of life is lived "in the Lord." He exempted no part of a believer's life from Christ's rule. The apostle based these ethical imperatives upon the indicative of God's saving work in Christ. Because God has acted finally and completely in Christ to establish the new age and because believers belong to him, he taught that Christians should live in obedience to him. Typically, Paul utilized the ἐν κυρίῳ formula to express this, although he also found other ways to emphasize that Jesus reigns as Lord in relationships and in the life of the Church.

The Lord's Supper

Related to Paul's use of κύριος in ethical admonitions is his use of it in reference to the Lord's Supper. He mentioned this sacred practice only twice in one of his letters, 1 Corinthians. He termed it κυριακὸν δεῖπνον[155] ("Lord's Supper") in 1 Cor 11:20 and τράπεζα κυρίου ("the table of the Lord") in 1 Cor 10:21. In each case he connected the κύριος title with the observance more than any other christological title.

Having chastised the Corinthians for their abuse of the Lord's Supper (1 Cor 11:17-22), he related to them the tradition as he received it (1 Cor 11:23-25) and presented his understanding of its significance for the life of the churches (11:26). Employing the language of tradition,[156] he affirmed that he received it "from the Lord" (ἀπὸ τοῦ κυρίου). What he meant by "from the Lord" is difficult to ascertain since his version closely resembles the same occasion in the Synoptics (cf. Matt 26:26-30; Mark 14:22-26; and Luke 22:17-20). Inasmuch as he used the language of tradition, one may rule out that he received it as a matter of direct revelation. The best solution seems to be that "from" (ἀπό) designates the earthly Lord Jesus as the source of the account, since these are in fact his words, as Paul understood them. Barrett suggested a "possible compromise" when he wrote: "Paul received the factual tradition by human means, but he received the interpretation of it directly from the Lord."[157]

---

[155]. Κυριακός is used only here and in Rev 1:10 when John spoke of being in the Spirit on the Lord's day (ἐν τῇ κυριακῇ ἡμέρᾳ). Since no corresponding adjective exists in Semitic language, this type of construction is possible only in Greek. There is no reason, however, to agree with Foerster that it arose only on Greek soil since Greek synagogues and churches existed in Palestine. Perhaps a more likely construction would have employed the genitive τοῦ κυρίου. Otherwise see Foerster, "κυριακός," *TDNT*, 3:1095-96.

[156]. See Friedrich Büchsel, "παραδίδωμι," *TDNT*, 2:169-72; also Gerhard Delling, "παραλαμβάνω," *TDNT*, 4:11-14.

[157]. Barrett, *First Corinthians*, 265; Bruce, *Paul*, 283, thought that the source of the tradition was the earthly Jesus who is now identical with the exalted Lord. Otherwise, see Hahn, *Titles*, 87, who claimed that the earthly Jesus was not the source of the tradition. He said (p. 87): "The point is that the authority of the earthly Lord stands behind these eucharistic words, that nevertheless their perpetuation is effected and legitimated by the exalted Lord."

Paul continued by relating the tradition associated with Jesus' final meal with his disciples beginning with the phrase, "the Lord Jesus" (ὁ κύριος Ἰησοῦς), and including the words of institution. In 11:26 he added what seems to be his own interpretation of this custom for the churches: "For as often as you eat this bread and drink the cup, you proclaim the Lord's death until he comes (τὸν θάνατον τοῦ κυρίου καταγγέλλετε ἄχρι οὗ ἔλθῃ)." He understood the Lord's Supper, not only as a commemoration of the past sacrifice (τοῦτο ποιεῖτε εἰς τὴν ἐμὴν ἀνάμνησιν, 11:24), but also as an opportunity to proclaim the gospel in the present situation (καταγγέλλετε). He taught that the church was to engage faithfully in this practice until the future consummation (ἄχρι οὗ ἔλθῃ).

Following this, Paul warned against participating in the Lord's Supper without self-examination. He wrote (11:27-32):

> Whoever, therefore, eats the bread or drinks the cup of the Lord (τὸ ποτήριον τοῦ κυρίου) in an unworthy manner will be guilty of profaning the body and blood of the Lord (τοῦ κυρίου). Let a man examine himself, and so eat of the bread and drink of the cup. For any one who eats and drinks without discerning the body eats and drinks judgment upon himself. That is why many of you are weak and ill, and some have died. But if we judged ourselves truly, we should not be judged. But when we are judged by the Lord (κρινόμενοι δὲ ὑπὸ κυρίου), we are chastened so that we may not be condemned along with the world.

Κύριος is the only christological title present in this passage.

Turning to 1 Cor 10:14-22, a similar pattern emerges with one exception. In 10:16 Paul argued:

> The cup of blessing which we bless, is it not a participation in the blood of Christ (κοινωνία ἐστὶν τοῦ αἵματος τοῦ Χριστοῦ)? The bread which we break, is it not a participation in the body of Christ (κοινωνία τοῦ σώματος τοῦ Χριστοῦ)?

In this text, the cup and the bread portray a clear picture of the Lord's Supper. For Paul, participating in the sacred meal represents the believers' fellowship in *Christ's* blood and body. Only in this passage did he utilize the title "Christ" with Lord's Supper terminology.[158]

[158.] See Kramer, *Christ, Lord, Son*, 162-63, for an explanation of this.

Later, in the same passage, however, Paul reverted back to his preference for κύριος in this context when he wrote (10:21):

> You cannot drink the cup of the Lord (ποτήριον κυρίου πίνειν) and the cup of demons. You cannot partake of the table of the Lord (τραπέζης κυρίου μετέχειν) and the table of demons.

In this warning against idolatry, the cup and table of the Lord stand in antithesis to the cup and table of demons. According to Paul, what pagans sacrifice to their gods, they actually sacrifice to demons. Christians, therefore, can have no part in any sort of pagan worship, for as Paul said: "I do not want you to be partners with demons" (1 Cor 10:20).

Thus it is evident that Paul generally utilized the κύριος predicate in his infrequent references to the Lord's Supper. This fact is all the more significant when one realizes that he customarily employed the title "Christ" in discussions related to the facts of the gospel, particularly the sacrificial death of Jesus.[159] His teachings on baptism, which employ "Christ" almost exclusively, demonstrates this.[160]

[159.] θάνατος relates directly to κύριος only in 1 Cor 11:26 and by extension in Phil 2:8. But the latter may be equally related to the title "Christ" since Paul introduced the Philippian hymn with the phrase (2:5): "Have this mind among yourselves, which is yours in Christ Jesus." In other places, Paul related Jesus' death to the "Son" (Col 1:22; Rom 5:10) and to "Christ" (Phil 3:10; Rom 6:3-11, *passim*). The verbal form (ἀπέθανεν) is reserved almost exclusively for "Christ" (Rom 5:6-8; 6:8, 9, 10; 8:34; 14:9, 15; 1 Cor 8:11; 15:3; 2 Cor 5:14-15; Gal 2:21; Col 2:20), the only exception being the more formal "Lord Jesus Christ" (1 Thess 5:10). Similarly, Paul utilized "Christ" most often with the noun σταυρός (1 Cor 1:17; Gal 6:12; Eph 2:16; Phil 2:8; 3:18; Col 2:14) and with the verb σταυρόω (1 Cor 1:13, 23; 2:2; 2 Cor 13:4; Gal 2:20; 3:1; 5:24). The noun σταυρός refers to "Lord" only in the formal statement (Gal 6:14): "But far be it from me to glory except in the cross of our Lord Jesus Christ (ἐν τῷ σταυρῷ τοῦ κυρίου ἡμῶν Ἰησοῦ Χριστοῦ)." The verbal form occurs only in 1 Cor 2:8: "None of the rulers of this age understood this; for if they had, they would not have crucified the Lord of glory" (οὐκ ἂν τὸν κύριον τῆς δόξης ἐσταύρωσαν). Παραδίδωμι relates to "Lord" in Rom 4:25 and 1 Cor 11:23; typically, it relates to "Christ" or "Son" (e.g., Rom 8:32; Gal 2:20; Eph 5:2, 25). "Blood" (αἷμα) relates to "Lord" only in 1 Cor 11:27. Primarily, it is used in reference to "Christ" (e.g., Rom 3:25; 5:9; 1 Cor 10:16; Eph 1:7; 2:13). Col 1:20 may relate it to "Son" by way of Col 1:13.

[160.] Rom 6:3-4: "Do you not know that all of us who have been baptized into Christ Jesus (ἐβαπτίσθημεν εἰς Χριστὸν Ἰησοῦν) were baptized into his death? We were buried therefore with him by baptism into death, so that as Christ (Χριστός) was raised from the dead by the glory of the Father, we too might walk in newness of life." Also Gal 3:27: "For as many of you as were baptized into Christ have put on Christ" (ὅσοι γὰρ εἰς Χριστὸν ἐβαπτίσθητε, Χριστὸν ἐνεδύσασθε). Note, however, the exception to this in Rom 13:14: "But put on the Lord Jesus Christ (ἐνδύσασθε

Kramer appears to be correct when he said κύριος had "a fixed place in the terminology relating to the Lord's Supper."[161] He failed to account for the evidence of the early Palestinian church, however, when he insisted that this was true because the title κύριος was related to certain cultic meals in Hellenistic religious practices. Evidently, the prayer *maranatha* ("Our Lord, Come!") had become a part of the eucharistic liturgy.[162] If this Aramaic phrase may be traced back to the Palestinian churches and if Paul included it at the end of 1 Corinthians (16:22) because he knew the letter would be read prior to the Lord's Supper observance in that church, it is more likely that the linkage between κύριος and the Lord's Supper began in Palestine.

Nevertheless, another question arises. Since the Lord's Supper commemorated the indicative of God's act in Jesus, particularly his crucifixion, and since Paul primarily utilized "Christ" in such passages, how did κύριος become fixed in his eucharistic liturgy? The answer seems to lie along two lines: (1) ethical and (2) eschatological.

Following Paul's reprimand of the Corinthians for their mishandling of the sacred meal, he warned them generally against eating and drinking in an unworthy manner (ἀναξίως, 11:27). He encouraged them to examine their conduct so they would not profane the body and blood of Christ and thereby fall into judgment. Moreover, he interpreted the Supper as having significance until the *eschaton* (ἄχρι οὗ ἔλθῃ, 11:26). As they celebrated the Lord's Supper, he taught that believers were to anticipate the parousia. When addressing ethical matters,[163] the coming judgment,[164] or the hope of the parousia[165] in other contexts, he showed a preference for the κύριος

τὸν κύριον Ἰησοῦν Χριστόν), and make no provision for the flesh, to gratify its desires." This deviation may be explained from the context, which speaks of the approaching day, known particularly as "the Day of the Lord" in the Old Testament and related primarily to the κύριος title in Paul (1 Cor 1:7-8; 4:5; 5:5; 11:26; 2 Cor 1:14; 1 Thess 2:19; 3:13; 4:15-16; 5:2, 23; 2 Thess 1:7; 2:1-2, 8; 1 Tim 6:14; 2 Tim 1:16-18; 4:8). Philippians (1:6, 10; 2:16, "day of Christ") is the only exception.

[161.] Kramer, *Christ, Lord, Son*, 161; also Eduard Schweizer, *Jesus*, trans. David E. Green (Atlanta: John Knox Press, 1971), 66-67.

[162.] Ibid.

[163.] For a discussion of this and related matters, see above, pp. 69-73.

[164.] E.g., 1 Cor 4:4-5; 5:3-5; 11:32; 1 Thess 4:6; 2 Thess 1:8-10; and 2 Tim 4:8, 14.

[165.] E.g., 1 Cor 1:7-8; 4:5; 5:5; 11:26; 2 Cor 1:14; Phil 3:20; 1 Thess 2:19; 3:13; 4:15-16; 5:2, 23; 2 Thess 1:7; 2:2, 8; 1 Tim 6:14; 2 Tim 1:18; 4:8.

predicate. Therefore, ethical and eschatological considerations altered his normal course of expression so that, when he came to address the indicative of the Lord's Supper tradition, he connected κύριος, not Χριστός, with it.

The Earthly Jesus As Lord

Although Paul understood the resurrection of Jesus to be the foundation of his Lordship,[166] he was also able to speak of the earthly Jesus as Lord. He did this primarily in two ways: (1) by alluding to certain "words of the Lord" which evidently proceeded from Jesus' earthly ministry and (2) by referring to Jesus' brothers as "brothers of the Lord." Each of these deserves brief comment.

In Paul's account of the Lord's Supper, he related:

> the Lord Jesus (ὁ κύριος Ἰησοῦς) on the night when he was delivered up took bread, and when he had given thanks, he broke it, and said: "This is my body which is for you. Do this in remembrance of me."[167]

By "the Lord Jesus" he did not have in mind the exalted Lord, but the earthly, pre-resurrected Jesus. He identified these words specifically as Jesus' and seemed to quote them rather precisely.

When writing on the subject of divorce, Paul alluded to a command which he claimed came from the Lord. He wrote (1 Cor 7:10-11):

> To the married I give charge (παραγγέλλω), not I but the Lord (οὐκ ἐγὼ ἀλλὰ ὁ κύριος), that the wife should not separate from her husband (but if she does, let her remain single or else be reconciled to her husband)— and that the husband should not divorce his wife.

Although his wording varies from the sayings of Jesus on divorce recorded in the Gospels, Paul apparently was conveying the sentiment of what he considered to be an authentic command from Jesus. In fact, this command from the Lord resembles Jesus' words in Mark 10:11-12: "Whoever divorces his wife and marries another, commits adultery against her: and if she divorces her husband and marries another, she commits adultery" (Matt 5:32 par.; cf. Matt 19:9 and Luke 16:8)). The difference in wording may be due to the fact that Jesus' concern was with the seventh commandment, which deals with adultery, while in First Corinthians Paul's concern was with the problem of divorce and remarriage.[168]

---

[166] For a discussion of this see above, pp. 53-59.

[167] 1 Cor 11:23-24, author's translation.

Subsequently, in 1 Corinthians 7, when Paul returned to a subject for which he had received no teaching from the earthly Jesus, he was quick to say that it was from him and not the Lord (τοῖς δὲ λοιποῖς λέγω ἐγὼ οὐχ ὁ κύριος, 7:12). In particular he wrote (7:25): "Now concerning the unmarried, I have no command of the Lord (ἐπιταγὴν κυρίου οὐκ ἔχω), but I give my opinion as one who by the Lord's mercy is trustworthy." Paul had no command from the Lord on the issue of virgins, perhaps because Jesus never addressed it.[169] Yet he did have an opinion which, being an apostle and thereby a caretaker of churches' spiritual health, he felt obliged to share in response to the church's question on the matter.[170]

On another issue in 1 Corinthians, when Paul defended an apostle's right to receive material benefits from his converts, he again alluded to another command from the Lord. Having appealed to common conventions of the day (9:7) and the Old Testament law (9:8-12),[171] he concluded his argument with directives he considered to have come from Jesus. He said (9:14): "In the same way, the Lord commanded (ὁ κύριος διέταξεν) that those who proclaim the gospel should get their living by the gospel." Perhaps he had in mind here the tradition which ultimately gave rise to Luke 10:7,[172] in which Jesus said: "And remain in the same house, eating and drinking what they provide, for the laborer deserves his wages; do not go from house

---

[168.] Fee, *First Corinthians*, 292; David Dungan, *The Sayings of Jesus in the Churches of Paul* (Philadelphia: Fortress, 1971), 139-50, opined that this saying was already known in the churches. According to Dungan, Paul only reminded them of the tradition they already knew.

[169.] Fee, *First Corinthians*, 298.

[170.] That Paul responded to questions asked him by the church is indicated in 1 Cor 7:1: περὶ δὲ ὧν ἐγράψατε.

[171.] Paul quoted Deut 25:4: "You shall not muzzle an ox when it is treading out the grain." Then in typical rabbinic style, arguing from a minor to a major premise, he declared that God's intent did not lie with the ox; rather, "it was written for our sake" (δι' ἡμᾶς γὰρ ἐγράφη).

[172.] Fee, *First Corinthians*, 412-13; *contra*, Dungan, *Sayings of Jesus*, 40-75, who believed Paul had in mind the entire set of mission instructions for the seventy-two (Luke 10:1-12). Earlier (pp. 3-40), Dungan criticized Paul for having disobeyed what amounted to a direct command by Jesus and not receiving material help from the Corinthians. His criticism, however, misses the point. Because one has the right to receive material assistance for his work, does not mean that he must exact it. It was well within Paul's rights to be helped by the Corinthians, as he admits; but he felt he could gain an advantage in ministry by doing otherwise. The command, as Paul saw it, was directed more toward the church than the recipient.

to house." While the wording of the two statements varies, the concept remains the same: those who work for the gospel deserve their just wage. Since Paul customarily alluded to and did not quote a Jesus logion, no need exists to postulate an *agraphon*, or an otherwise lost saying of Jesus. The Gospel of Luke provides sufficient warrant for determining that such a saying was at hand in the sayings tradition, and therefore, as Paul understood, went back ultimately to the earthly Jesus.

Paul also alluded to this same logion in 1 Tim 5:18; and, as in 1 Corinthians 9, he joined it with Deut 25:4. This time, however, he did not relate that it was a word/command from the Lord.

In 1 Thessalonians Paul again referred to a "word of the Lord" on the issue of the parousia. He offered comfort for them with the following words (4:15-17):

> For this we declare to you by the word of the Lord (ἐν λόγῳ κυρίου), that we who are alive, who are left until the coming of the Lord (εἰς τὴν παρουσίαν τοῦ κυρίου), shall not precede those who have fallen asleep. For the Lord himself will descend from heaven with a cry of command, with the archangel's call, and with the sound of the trumpet of God. And the dead in Christ will rise first; then we who are alive, who are left, shall be caught up together with them in the clouds to meet the Lord in the air; and so we shall always be with the Lord.

As with the other "words of the Lord" discussed above, no exact parallel exists in the Gospels. Three possibilities have been suggested which are worthy of attention: (1) Paul alluded to a statement of the risen Lord, which was communicated through charismatic Christian prophets[173]; (2) he referred to a traditional dominical saying preserved only outside the Gospels[174] (as with Acts 20:35); or (3) he summarized Jesus' eschatological teachings.[175]

Scholars have suggested theories (1) and (2) primarily because this logion was not obvious within the known sayings of Jesus.

---

[173]. Kramer, *Christ, Lord, Son*, 159-60.

[174]. Leon Morris, *The First and Second Epistles to the Thessalonians*, NICNT (Grand Rapids: Eerdmans, 1959), 141; and Foerster, *TDNT*, 3:1092

[175]. David Hill, *New Testament Prophecy* (Atlanta: John Knox Press, 1979), 130-31, 166. This also seems to be the position of I. H. Marshall, *1 and 2 Thessalonians*, NCB (Grand Rapids: Eerdmans, 1983), 125-27.

However, if sufficient warrant can be found in the Gospel tradition for this "word of the Lord," there is no need to postulate them.

I. H. Marshall argued that this "word" came originally from Jesus' earthly ministry. He perceived three basic elements to it: (1) the descent of the Lord, (2) the resurrection of the dead, and (3) the rapture of the living.[176] Marshall claimed that these same elements *are found* in the Gospel sources: Matt 24:30-31 refers to the descent of the Lord; Matt 8:11 and 22:23-33 refer to the resurrection of the dead; and Matt 24:30-31 refers to the rapture of the living.[177] Therefore, according to Marshall, Jesus' eschatological teachings in the Gospels provided an adequate basis for Paul's statement that this is a "word of the Lord." Marshall explained Paul's lack of verbal precision upon the basis of his practice of alluding to and not quoting Jesus' words and also his application of the saying in 4:15-17 to the present situation in the Thessalonian church.[178]

Finally, Paul spoke of Jesus' earthly brothers as brothers of the Lord. During his interview with Cephas in Jerusalem three years after his conversion, he claimed to have seen none of the apostles except James, "the brother of the Lord" (τὸν ἀδελφὸν τοῦ κυρίου; Gal 1:19). Elsewhere, writing to defend his rights as an apostle, he asked (1 Cor 9:5): "Do we not have the right to be accompanied by a wife, as the other apostles and the brothers of the Lord (οἱ ἀδελφοὶ τοῦ κυρίου) and Cephas?" In both instances, he understood the "Lord" to be the earthly Jesus and considered these relatives to be "brothers of the Lord."[179]

By alluding to certain commands or words of the Lord and by referring to Jesus' earthly brothers as brothers of the Lord, Paul, who customarily associated the κύριος title with the exalted Christ, also connected it with Jesus' earthly life and ministry. He considered not only the risen Christ "Lord," but also the earthly Jesus. He under-

---

[176.] In 1 Cor 15:52 the same three elements are found stated differently: (a) the last trumpet, (b) the raising of the dead, and (c) the transformation of the living.

[177.] Marshall, *Thessalonians*, 125-27.

[178.] Ibid., 126.

[179.] Hahn, *Titles*, 86-87, believed that the phrase "brothers of the Lord" represented a *technicus terminus* in the early church since Jesus' relatives played such an prominent role in it. This, however, does not seem to be the case, because other than James no other "brother of the Lord" appeared to play a dominant position in the early church. Therefore, it seems best to view these statements as further evidence that Paul could think of the earthly, pre-resurrection Jesus as "Lord."

stood Jesus' earthly authority to be bound up with his authority as exalted Lord; therefore, he made no distinction between the earthly and the exalted κύριος.[180]

Other than the Lord's Supper passage (1 Cor 11:23-25), which appears to be an explicit quotation,[181] Paul only alluded to other dominical sayings. Knowing that he quoted the Old Testament rather loosely at times, it is not inconsistent that he did the same with sayings of the earthly Jesus.[182] This practice does not distract from their authenticity or authority, for Paul's words/commands of the Lord have authority equal to that of the Old Testament. This is evident above all in the sharp distinction he drew between his own apostolic judgment and the "words of the Lord."

This particular point leads to the Jesus-Paul debate, an issue too broad for discussion here. It is likely that Paul was acquainted with some of Jesus' teachings as contained in the Gospels. His contact with Peter (Gal 1:18) at the very least put him in touch with a credible source for those teachings. Accordingly, Paul is the earliest written witness to a sayings tradition.[183]

ΚΥΡΙΟΣ in Paul's Eschatology

No discussion of Paul's use of κύριος would be complete without dealing with his eschatological scheme. Despite relegating it to last in this survey, his doctrine of the "last things" is of central importance in understanding his Christology.[184] As W. D. Davies said: "The belief in the Second Advent was integral to that eschatological faith which Paul shared with the early Church."[185] This belief influences Paul's use of the κύριος predicate in passages which address (1) the Day of the Lord, (2) the coming of the Lord, and (3) the final judgment.

---

[180] This is evident in that the Gospel narratives speak often on ethical and eschatological themes, two themes most often related to the κύριος title by Paul.

[181] The reason for this may be that the Lord's Supper had a fixed, independent form which circulated in the church before Paul; see Joachim Jeremias, *The Eucharistic Words of Jesus*, trans. Norman Perrin (Philadelphia: Fortress, 1966), 101-5.

[182] Fee, *First Corinthians*, 292, n. 10.

[183] On the history of the Jesus-Paul debate see Victor Paul Furnish, "The Jesus-Paul Debate: From Baur to Bultmann," *BJRL* 47 (1965): 342-81.

[184] Schweitzer, *Paul*, 53, thought Paul's eschatology conditioned his whole theology.

[185] Davies, *Paul*, 286.

(1) In the Old Testament the Day of Yahweh (יוֹם יהוה) appears first in Amos 5:18-20:

> Woe to you who desire the day of the Lord!
> Why would you have the day of the Lord?
> It is darkness, and not light;
>   as if a man fled from a lion,
>   and a bear met him;
> or went into the house and leaned
>   with his hand against the wall,
>   and a serpent bit him.
> Is not the day of the Lord darkness, and not light,
>   and gloom with no brightness in it?

It occurs here in Amos without any explanation, suggesting it was already common among the people.[186] Moreover, since the people desired its coming, they must have viewed it positively. Nevertheless, the prophet redirected the concept and claimed it was a day to be feared.

Other Old Testament writers employed this phrase to warn of coming judgment as well as to herald the awaited deliverance.[187] In some cases they used it to speak of an imminent divine manifestation, in others to address beliefs in the final consummation.[188] In general, prior to Jerusalem's fall, the Day of Yahweh had a more negative connotation of judgment and disaster; afterward, it emphasized deliverance and salvation.[189] All in all, the Old Testament "Day of

---

[186] Ernst Jenni, "Day of the Lord," *IDB*, 1:784; Gerhard von Rad, "ἡμέρα," *TDNT*, 2:944, said the concept was not created by the writing prophets. Its origin is unknown.

[187] Isa 2:12-22; Zeph 1:7-10, 14-18; 2:2-3; 3:8; Joel 1:15; 2:31; 3:14-18; Ezek 7:7-12; Zechariah 12-14; Mal 3:2; and 4:1, 5.

[188] George Eldon Ladd, *A Theology of the New Testament* (Grand Rapids: Eerdmans, 1974), 555.

[189] von Rad, *TDNT*, 2:945, remarked: "The fall of Jerusalem and the exile are an important turning-point in prophetic proclamation. After this, prophecy becomes prophecy of salvation and the prophesied day of Yahweh means deliverance, restoration and ultimate salvation for the deeply humiliated people.... Materially, however, there is the change to prophecy of salvation, and in the post-exilic prophets we have full-blooded prophecies of the day of Yahweh which will bring judgment and destruction to the Gentiles but protection (Zech. 12:1ff.), purification (Mal. 3:2), cleansing (Zech. 13:1f.), the endowment of the Spirit (Jl. 3; Zech. 12:10) and paradisean waters (Jl. 4:18; Zech. 14:8) to Jerusalem."

Yahweh" (יום יהוה) formed an important part in the prophets' eschatological outlook.

It is not surprising then that Paul, schooled in his religion from youth, likewise anticipated a Day of the Lord (ἡμέρα κυρίου). For him, however, the "Lord" was Jesus Christ and the "Day of Yahweh" of the Old Testament was the "Day of the Lord Jesus Christ."[190] Primarily, he associated that "Day" with the title κύριος, although in Philippians, he linked it with Χριστός (Phil 1:6, 10; and 2:16). Yet there is no reason to differentiate between Paul's "Day of the Lord" and "Day of Christ,"[191] for he considered them the same.

The "Day of the Lord" according to Paul will come "like a thief in the night" (ὡς κλέπτης ἐν νυκτί, 1 Thess 5:2). For some it will mean sudden destruction (αἰφνίδιος αὐτοῖς ἐφίσταται ὄλεθρος, 1 Thess 5:3) and ultimately eternal devastation (ὄλεθρον αἰώνιον, 2 Thess 1:9) from which there will be no escape (1 Thess 5:3). For others it will issue forth in salvation through the Lord Jesus Christ (σωτηρίας διὰ τοῦ κυρίου ἡμῶν Ἰησοῦ Χριστοῦ, 1 Thess 5:9). That day will be a day of pride in the work accomplished for the gospel (2 Cor 1:14; cf. Phil 2:16) and a day in which God's work in believers' lives will be brought to completion (Phil 1:6). That day will also reveal the Lord Jesus (τὴν ἀποκάλυψιν τοῦ κυρίου ἡμῶν Ἰησοῦ Χριστοῦ, 1 Cor 1:8) and see him glorified among his people (2 Thess 1:10).

Accordingly, the "Day of the Lord" for Paul had ethical ramifications. The imminence of it demanded that believers awaken, remain sober, live uprightly, and seek to be found blameless (1 Cor 1:8; 5:5; 2 Cor 1:14; 1 Thess 5:2-11; Phil 1:6, 10; 2:16).[192]

(2) The "Day of the Lord" will commence with the coming of Jesus. The background for this notion is couched in Old Testament language of theophany in which God comes to judge sin, save the righteous, and establish his Kingdom (Judg 5:4-5; Psalm 18; Ps 68:7-8; Isa 30:27;

---

[190] Paul termed it: (1) "the Day of the Lord" (ἡμέρα κυρίου, 1 Thess 5:2; and ἡ ἡμέρα τοῦ κυρίου, 2 Thess 2:2); (2) "the Day of the Lord Jesus" (τῇ ἡμέρᾳ τοῦ κυρίου Ἰησοῦ, 2 Cor 1:14; cf. 1 Cor 5:5); (3) "the Day of the Lord Jesus Christ" (τῇ ἡμέρᾳ τοῦ κυρίου ἡμῶν Ἰησοῦ Χριστοῦ, 1 Cor 1:8); (4) "the Day of Jesus Christ" (ἡμέρας Χριστοῦ Ἰησοῦ, Phil 1:6); (5) "the Day of Christ" (ἡμέραν Χριστοῦ, Phil 1:10; 2:16); and (6) "that Day" (τῇ ἡμέρᾳ ἐκείνῃ, 2 Thess 1:10; ἐκείνῃ τῇ ἡμέρᾳ, 2 Tim 1:18). Only twice does the New Testament refer to a "Day of God" (2 Pet 3:12; Rev 16:14). Paul never referred to it in this way.

[191] *Contra* J. D. Pentecost, *Things to Come* (Grand Rapids: Dunham, 1958), 229-32, who related the "Day of the Lord" to Israel and the "Day of Christ" to the Church.

[192] Gerhard Delling, "ἡμέρα," *TDNT*, 2:952.

40:3-5, 10-11; Amos 1:2; Hab 3:3-6, 13).[193] Paul expressed Jesus' coming with a variety of terms and images. Most frequently, he employed the term παρουσία, a Greek word meaning, in this context, "arrival" (1 Cor 15:23; 1 Thess 2:19; 3:13; 4:15; 5:23; and 2 Thess 2:1, 8).

Παρουσία was used frequently in Greek literature to refer to the coming of some high-ranking official, often for beneficent reasons. In religious writings it signified a divine epiphany.[194] In Paul it is the "arrival" of the Lord Jesus Christ to fulfill redemptive history.

Another word Paul used for the Second Advent was ἀποκάλυψις ("unveiling" or "revelation"). He stated that Christians await the revelation of the Lord Jesus Christ (ἀπεκδεχομένους τὴν ἀποκάλυψιν τοῦ κυρίου ἡμῶν Ἰησοῦ Χριστοῦ, 1 Cor 1:7). He employed "revelation" here to mean not the impartation of knowledge or the unveiling of a mystery but the coming of God into the world. Historically, Paul understood that this coming took place first in Christ's incarnation, death, and resurrection. He taught that the end of history would see the Second Advent of the "Lord" Jesus, which would "culminate in the cosmic catastrophe" bringing judgment to the wicked and salvation to the faithful.[195] The emphasis behind the term "revelation" lies upon the disclosure of Jesus' present Lordship.[196] When he comes, he who has been hidden shall be revealed in all his glory, power, and majesty.

Paul also described the Lord's coming as an "appearing" (ἐπιφάνεια; e.g., 2 Thess 2:8; 1 Tim 6:14; 2 Tim 4:1, 8; and Tit 2:13). In 2 Thess 2:8 he wrote: "And then the lawless one will be revealed, and the Lord Jesus (ὁ κύριος) will slay him with the breath of his

---

[193.] See Beasley-Murray, *Jesus and the Kingdom*, 3-10, who concluded (p. 10): "The decisive element in the theophany descriptions of the Old Testament, accordingly, is the concept of the coming of God; the descriptions of accompanying phenomena in the natural order are to be viewed as parabolic. The "parables" are not unimportant—they point to the irresistible might of the Lord in his coming, for the resources of creation are his, and nothing in creation can resist his will—but the supremely important matter is that God *comes* into the world, now in the present and (in the teaching of the prophets) in the future, and in his coming he reveals himself."

[194.] Albrecht Oepke, "παρουσία, παρείμι," *TDNT*, 5:860. Schelkle, *Paulus*, 251, wrote: "Das Wort Parusie bezeichnet in der politischen Sprache die Ankunft des Herrschers, in der religiösen die Epiphanie der Gottheit."

[195.] Albrecht Oepke, "ἀποκαλύπτω," *TDNT*, 3:382-83.

[196.] Ladd, *Theology*, 555.

mouth and destroy him by his appearing and his coming (καταργήσει τῇ ἐπιφανείᾳ τῆς παρουσίας αὐτοῦ)." In this text he linked ἐπιφάνεια with παρουσία, both of which refer to the Lord Jesus.[197] While in other places he could connect it with Χριστός (e.g., 2 Tim 4:1; and Tit 2:13), more often he associated it with κύριος (e.g., 2 Thess 2:8; 1 Tim 6:14; and 2 Tim 4:8). In each case he understood the word to have eschatological import, referring to the coming of Jesus. Since he viewed Christ's *first coming* as an eschatological event, he could also refer to it with ἐπιφάνεια in 2 Tim 1:9-10.[198] More often, however, he used it to speak of the Second Coming.

(3) Paul used κύριος not only in connection with the Day of the Lord and Second Coming passages, but he also employed it regularly with regard to eschatological judgment (e.g., 1 Cor 4:4-5; 5:3-5; 11:32; 1 Thess 4:6; 2 Thess 1:5-10; and 2 Tim 4:8, 14). But this is only natural since for Paul παρουσία and judgment belong together.[199] First Corinthians 4:4c-5 provides sufficient warrant:

> It is the Lord (κύριος) who judges me. Therefore do not pronounce judgment before the time, before the Lord comes (ἕως ἂν ἔλθῃ ὁ κύριος), who will bring to light the things now hidden in darkness and will disclose the purposes of the heart. Then every man will receive his commendation from God.

Since he described the "Lord" as coming, Paul understood Jesus to be the referent.[200] He did not portray the judgment in detail here, but he did assert that this judgment would expose the dark secrets of men and reveal their true intentions. Apparently, he borrowed imagery from the Old Testament and other Jewish literature which portrayed God as knowing the secrets of men's hearts.[201] Paul understood that

---

[197]. B, D², K, 88, 1739, 1881, among others omit Ἰησοῦς. It is found, however, in ℵ, A, D*, G, P, Ψ, 33, and 1241. The addition of the word seems less likely since it is clear by the word παρουσία that the Lord Jesus is meant. The omission of it by scribes wishing to bring Paul's quotation in line with Isa 11:4 [LXX] appears more satisfactory. Metzger and his committee retain it in brackets with a (C) rating. Bruce Metzger, *A Textual Commentary on the Greek New Testament* (New York: United Bible Societies, 1975), 636.

[198]. Rudolf Bultmann and Dieter Lührmann, "ἐπιφαίνω, ἐπιφανής, ἐπιφάνεια," *TDNT*, 9:10.

[199]. Kreitzer, *Jesus and God*, 88-90.

[200]. *Contra* Carl Holladay, *The First Letter of Paul to the Corinthians* (Austin, TX: Sweet Publishing Co., 1979), 60, who thought "Lord" means "God" because of its mention in v. 5.

Jesus the κύριος, functioning as Yahweh of the Old Testament, will, at his coming, reveal these thoughts. Such ideas are reminiscent of Jesus' coming as "revelation."

Second Thessalonians 1:5-10 also proves instructive at this point. It suggests that Paul knew of the persecution and suffering which had affected the Thessalonians. To comfort them, he reminded them of the coming judgment:

> This [their steadfastness and faith] is evidence of the righteous judgment of God, that you may be made worthy of the kingdom of God, for which you are suffering—since indeed God deems it just to repay with affliction those who afflict you, and to grant rest with us to you who are afflicted, when the Lord Jesus is revealed from heaven (ἐν τῇ ἀποκαλύψει τοῦ κυρίου Ἰησοῦ ἀπ' οὐρανοῦ) with his mighty angels in flaming fire, inflicting vengeance upon those who do not know God and upon those who do not obey the gospel of our Lord Jesus (τῷ εὐαγγελίῳ τοῦ κυρίου ἡμῶν Ἰησοῦ). They shall suffer the punishment of eternal destruction and exclusion from the presence of the Lord and from the glory of his might (ἀπὸ προσώπου τοῦ κυρίου καὶ ἀπὸ τῆς δόξης τῆς ἰσχύος αὐτοῦ), when he comes on that day to be glorified in his saints, and to be marveled at in all who have believed, because our testimony to you was believed.

Utilizing powerful apocalyptic images of judgment,[202] Paul portrayed the Lord's coming with his mighty angels in flaming fire to execute eternal destruction and to exclude the unrighteous from the Lord's presence. Such language is reminiscent of Old Testament prophetic and apocalyptic passages which depict Yahweh as Ruler and Judge.[203] Here Paul presented the Lord Jesus as the κύριος. Thus for Paul, the Lord Jesus stands as the judge who will correct the injustices suffered by his people at his coming.

Paul's concepts of the "Day of the Lord," the Second Coming, and the judgment appear to form a constellation of related, not distinct,

---

[201.] On Jewish literature depicting God as knowing the secrets of the heart, see Fee, *First Corinthians*, 163, n. 33.

[202.] Marshall, *Thessalonians*, 173-75, may be correct to assume that the judgment in 1:5-6 was already occurring. The point of the passage, however, seems to be final, eschatological judgment.

[203.] Volkmar Herntrich, "κρίνω," *TDNT*, 3:923-33.

ideas for the apostle. Unfortunately, these final events defy systematization, although some have made the attempt.[204] For Paul, they comprise one final, grand event, even as the cross, burial, and resurrection of Jesus form one event in his theology. Furthermore, these concepts are consistent with the prophetic interests of the Old Testament. Paul most likely derived these concepts from the Old Testament, which he considered to be sacred and instructive (2 Tim 3:16). For the purpose of this study, one cannot overlook the significance of the referential shift which has taken place in Paul's writings. He has deliberately applied to Jesus these Old Testament concepts originally reserved for Yahweh. This he did, not on some obscure, secondary theological idea, but on a crucial component of his theology. For a First Century Jew to have believed and written this way is no doubt significant.

Summary

This survey of Paul's use of "Lord" (κύριος) demonstrates a number of facts regarding his use of the title and his doctrine of Christ. (1) He followed the LXX and the contemporary literary practice regarding his use of the title. As with the LXX, he did not draw rigid distinctions between a sacred and secular use. This ambiguity is at times frustrating, nevertheless, to understand clearly how he used it one must take into account other contextual data. (2) He inherited this christological designation from earliest Christianity as evidenced by the Maranatha invocation and the confession, "Jesus is Lord." He used it in the vast majority of cases as a title for Christ, although he also employed it to refer to God in certain Old Testament quotations and to pagan gods. When freely composing the body of his letters, he used κύριος alone; but in the more formal aspects, such as salutations, blessings, and doxologies, he often combined it with other titles.[205] (3) He considered Jesus' Lordship to be cosmic in scope, extending beyond the Church to include "all things." Even when referring to men as "lords," he carefully subsumed all human authority under the authority of the Lord Jesus. (4) He based Jesus' Lordship upon his resurrection and exaltation to the right hand of God. At the same time, however, he also used κύριος to refer to the life and ministry of the earthly Jesus. (5) He

---

[204.] E.g., Schweitzer, *Mysticism of Paul*, 65-68.

[205.] Kramer, *Christ, Lord, Son*, 181.

related κύριος closely to the "Son of God" ascription and frequently used it to underscore the unique relationship between God the Father and the Lord Jesus. This relationship takes on a functional identity between the two which is at times difficult to distinguish. (6) He employed the title most frequently in hortatory sections of his letters, representing the ethical imperative demanded by the gospel. For this reason he understood the title as belonging essentially to the present, although for him the present was tied to the *eschaton*. (7) Due to ethical and eschatological considerations, he utilized κύριος in his infrequent allusions to the Lord's Supper, a meal commemorating the saving events of the gospel. These facts he normally linked with Χριστός. (8) For Paul, κύριος became the christological title par excellence for referring to final things such as (a) the Day of the Lord, (b) the coming of the Lord, and (c) the final judgment.

In each of these contexts Paul used κύριος as a christological title. Yet he knew that many of these functions belonged primarily to Yahweh in the Old Testament. It may be concluded therefore that one reason for Paul's use of κύριος as a christological title was to apply to Jesus concepts and functions originally reserved for Yahweh in the Old Testament. No other christological title could serve to associate Jesus so closely with Yahweh.

The application of Yahweh's functions to Jesus via the κύριος title is of great importance to this study. This factor in Paul's Christology as it relates to Old Testament Yahweh texts forms the next stage of this inquiry.

III. Yahweh Texts in Paul's Letters

Since Paul's quotations of Yahweh texts contained κύριος as the translation for the divine name (יהוה), chapters one and two dealt with κύριος as a christological title in the LXX and Paul's letters. This chapter focuses on these Yahweh texts.

Paul quoted Old Testament Yahweh texts fourteen times primarily in the literary epistles. On occasion he retained these as descriptions of God's person and work. At other times he applied these quotations to Christ. In addition he alluded to Yahweh texts.

Each quotation will be considered in detail by exploring (1) the context of the passage and (2) the quotation itself in light of Paul's doctrine of Christ's Lordship to clarify the referent for each Yahweh text. Allusions will be treated briefly following the quotations.

Yahweh Texts with God As Referent

This section analyzes Old Testament Yahweh texts which have God as their referent. It examines the context and themes under which the apostle maintained these as descriptions of God's person and work.

The Lord and Righteousness—Rom 4:7-8

Context. In Rom 4:1-12 Paul argued that God justifies by his grace[1] all who place faith in Jesus Christ.[2] Whereas in 1:18-3:20 he spoke of man's desperate plight in sin and rebellion against God, in 3:21-31 he presented the antithesis of this situation, the manifestation of God's righteousness[3] apart from the law (3:21).

To bolster his argument, Paul needed scriptural warrant to demonstrate that his doctrine of justification by faith was consistent

---

[1.] Charles H. Cosgrove, "Justification in Paul: A Linguistic and Theological Reflection," *JBL* 106 (1987):666, indicated that the phrase κατὰ χάριν appears to occupy Paul's attention in 4:2-8.

[2.] Ernst Käsemann, "The Faith of Abraham in Romans 4," chap. in *Perspectives on Paul*, trans. Margaret Kohl (Philadelphia: Fortress Press, 1971), 79-80, thought the center of Paul's theology was this doctrine of justification by grace through faith.

[3.] Käsemann, *Romans*, 91.

with how God had worked in the past. He found this in the life of Abraham (Romans 4).[4]

While elements of diatribe may be present in this passage,[5] Paul appears to have constructed his argument upon a midrash of Gen 15:6:

> Opening text: 4:3 (Gen 15:6)
> Exposition of ἐλογίσθη as gift (v. 4, κατὰ χάριν) based upon faith-righteousness (v. 5, λογίζεται ἡ πίστις αὐτοῦ εἰς δικαιοσύνην): 4:4-5
> Supporting text (with key word λογίσηται): 4:6-8 (Ps 32:1)
> Secondary allusion to opening text: 4:9b
> Exposition of ἐπίστευσεν as faith-righteousness (v. 11, τῆς δικαιοσύνης τῆς πίστεως) apart from circumcision (ἀκροβυστία) according to God's grace (v. 16, κατὰ χάριν) and in accord with God's promise to Abraham (vv. 13, 16) extending to all: 4:9-21
> Supporting text: 4:17 (Gen 17:5)
> Supporting text: 4:18 (Gen 15:5)
> Concluding text: 4:22 (allusion to Gen 15:6)
> Application to the new situation in Christ: 4:23-25[6]

[4.] C. F. D. Moule, "Jesus, Judaism, and Paul," in *Tradition and Interpretation in the New Testament: Essays in Honor of E. Earle Ellis*, ed. Gerald F. Hawthorne and Otto Betz (Grand Rapids: Eerdmans, 1987), 44.

[5.] Barrett, *Romans*, 86. For an overview of the history of diatribe see S. K. Stowers, *The Diatribe and Paul's Letter to the Romans*, SBL Dissertation Series, vol. 57 (Missoula, MT: Scholars Press, 1981). Diatribe is a literary or oratory style in which the writer was interrupted by an imaginary opponent who desired to raise some opposition to the argument. Objections frequently took the form of a question or were introduced by ἀλλά or τί οὖν. See Epictetus *Dissertationes* 4.10.5; 1.10.2. Since this device was used commonly in education and public speaking during the time of Paul, he most likely employed it only in an informal way. Present scholarship views it as less fixed than the previous generations of scholars. Stowers, *Diatribe*, 75.

[6.] Dunn, *Unity*, 87-88. E. Earle Ellis, "How the New Testament Uses the Old," chap. in *Prophecy and Hermeneutic in Early Christianity* (Grand Rapids: Eerdmans, 1978), 155, considered this an example of proem midrash. See *Pesiq. R.* 33:7; 44:7; idem, "Exegetical Patterns in 1 Corinthians and Romans," chap. in *Prophecy and Hermeneutic in Early Christianity* (Grand Rapids: Eerdmans, 1978), 217, suggested that 4:1-25 may be a pre-formed exposition serving as the concluding text of Paul's larger midrashic structure (1:17-4:25). He wrote: "This thematic and

Paul added the support of David (Ps 32:1-2),[7] as a type of messianic king, to the key text, Gen 15:6: ἐπίστευσεν δὲ Ἀβραὰμ τῷ θεῷ καὶ ἐλογίσθη αὐτῷ εἰς δικαιοσύνην ("Abraham believed God, and it was reckoned to him as righteousness.") Perhaps he had in mind the rabbinic custom of quoting the prophets and the writings alongside the Torah.[8] Nevertheless, with Ps 32:1-2 he applied the rabbinic principle *Gezera Shawa*, the second of Hillel's exegetical rules, which allowed for the association and interpretation of biblical passages which share a common word, in this case λογίζεσθαι.[9] Thus, the righteousness "reckoned" to Abraham by virtue of his faith (Gen 15:6) is explained as the forgiveness of sins[10] (Ps 32:1-2), since the same word is found there also.[11]

Text. Rom 4:7-8 contains an explicit quotation of Ps 32:1-2 [LXX, 31:1-2]. It reads:

μακάριοι ὧν ἀφέθησαν αἱ ἀνομίαι
καὶ ὧν ἐπεκαλύφθησαν αἱ ἁμαρτίαι·
μακάριος ἀνὴρ οὗ[12] οὐ μὴ λογίσηται κύριος
ἁμαρτίαν.[13]

---

interpretive summary of Old Testament verses, essentially an implicit midrash that interpolates the key-word <u>dikaios</u> into the summary, is used as an authoritative 'text' for the larger exposition."

[7.] Ps 32:1 was cited often in rabbinic literature. See Str-B 3:203-4.

[8.] Käsemann, *Romans*, 113, suggested he may have cited this psalm to accord with the Jewish principle that two witnesses were needed to establish the truth.

[9.] Cranfield, *Romans*, 1:232; and Ellis, "Biblical Interpretation," 699-701.

[10.] While the forgiveness of sins appears central to other New Testament writers, it is nevertheless rare in Paul (e.g., Rom 3:25; 4:7-8; Eph 1:7; and Col 1:14). Typically, Paul used the terms righteousness (δικαιοσύνη) and reconciliation (καταλλαγή). Rudolf Bultmann, "ἀφίημι," *TDNT*, 1:509-12. Barrett, *Romans*, 89, believed ἐπεκαλύφθησαν recalled God establishing Christ as the ἱλαστήριον in 3:25. In general, Paul considered salvation not so much the removal of past guilt, but the liberation from sin's power. See Bultmann, *Theology*, 1:287.

[11.] Ellis, "Biblical Interpretation," 700-701.

[12.] Some manuscripts have ᾧ instead of οὗ, most likely to correspond to the Hebrew לֹו. H. W. Heidland, "λογίζομαι," *TDNT*, 4:292, suggested the distinction between these words is significant. Perhaps the LXX has οὗ to avoid a commercial understanding. Cranfield, *Romans*, 1:234, preferred οὗ to ᾧ based upon (1) better attestation and (2) the principle of the more difficult reading since in 4:3, 4, 6, 9 λογίζεσθαι occurs with the dative.

[13.] "Blessed are those whose iniquities are forgiven, and whose sins are covered; blessed is the man against whom the Lord will not reckon his sin."

It is verbatim with the LXX differing from a literal Hebrew rendering. However, it clearly refers to an Old Testament Yahweh text since the last phrase of the Hebrew reads [32:2]:

אשרי אדם לא יחשב יהוה לו עון ואין ברוחו רמיה[14]

It is introduced with an extended introductory formula based upon the core phrase: καθάπερ καὶ Δαυὶδ λέγει ("So also David says").[15]

Conclusion. Three factors within the context of this passage demonstrate that this Yahweh text refers to God.[16] First, the introductory formula clearly refers to God. It reads:

καθάπερ καὶ Δαυὶδ λέγει τὸν μακαρισμὸν τοῦ ἀνθρώπου ᾧ ὁ θεὸς λογίζεται δικαιοσύνην χωρὶς ἔργων.[17]

Second, the context since the beginning of this new section (3:21) is primarily theocentric. Paul refers to God directly or indirectly over fifteen times from 3:21 to 4:7-8. References to Christ, on the other hand, are few. Third, since Paul normally associated justification with God[18] and since faith-righteousness appears to be the crux of his argument in this midrash, he apparently had God in mind when he referred in Rom 4:8 to κύριος as the one who does not "reckon" sin.

"The Lord of Hosts"—Rom 9:27-29

Context. In Romans 9-11 Paul lamented over the unbelief of his countrymen who rejected the Messiah despite their privileged history and status with God (9:4-5). Nevertheless, he did not think God had

---

[14.] "Blessed is the man to whom the Lord imputes no iniquity, and in whose spirit there is no deceit."

[15.] This is a common introductory formula pattern occurring also as "David says" (Rom 11:9-10), "Moses says" (Rom 10:19), and "Isaiah says" (Rom 10:16, 20; 15:12). Cranfield, *Romans*, 1:233, commented: "By this time the Psalter as a whole was known by his name."

[16.] Foerster, *TDNT*, 3:1087; Lucien Cerfaux, "<<Kyrios>> dans les citations pauliniennes de l'Ancien Testament," chap. in *Receueil Lucien Cerfaux: Etudes d'exégèse et d'histoire religieuse de Monseigneur Cerfaux*, vol. 1 (Gemblux: J. Duculot, 1954), 174-75; J. D. G. Dunn, *Christology in the Making: A New Testament Inquiry into the Origins of the Doctrine of the Incarnation* (Philadelphia: Westminster, 1980), 157-58; and Beker, *Paul*, 102-3.

[17.] "So also David pronounces a blessing upon the man to whom God reckons righteousness apart from works."

[18.] See, e.g., Rom 1:17; 2:13; 3:4, 5, 20, 21, 22, 24, 25, 26, 30; 4:2, 3, 5, 6; 8:30, 33; and 10:3.

rejected his people; on the contrary, he viewed the small number of Jewish Christians as the remnant which would one day issue forth in great renewal for God's people (Romans 11).

When discussing his scheme of salvation history in Romans 9-11, Paul quoted the Old Testament twenty-six times,[19] not as proof-texts for his teachings, but to demonstrate that salvation through Christ fulfills Old Testament ideas concerning God and his promise to bring salvation to all men. For Paul, the people of Messiah Jesus were the true people of God, standing in direct continuity with the Old Testament revelation.[20]

While aspects of Romans 9-11 reflect Stoic diatribe,[21] the overall structure has affinities with rabbinic exegesis. Ellis argued that these chapters are an example of Paul's use of *yelammedenu* midrash. He explained this style of Jewish exposition as a question or problem posed and then answered by biblical exposition. In Romans 9-11, he stated that the questions emerged, not out of scripture, but out of the new situation created when Israel rejected her Messiah.[22]

Rom 9:6-29 appears to be a midrash composed by Paul on the true nature of God's people. The opening text (9:7), a quotation from Gen 21:12, reads: ἐν Ἰσαὰκ κληθήσεταί σοι σπέρμα ("Through Isaac shall your descendants be named"). Paul explained this text (τοῦτ' ἔστιν)[23] affirming that the physical descendants of Abraham are not necessarily heirs to the promise. Subsequent Old Testament texts (Gen 18:10, 14; 25:23; Mal 1:2; *et al*) and commentary support his argument. Isa 1:9, the concluding text (9:29), alludes back to the opening text via the key-word σπέρμα. These final verses form a chiasmus with the following structure:

[19.] For a complete list of these see Ellis, *Paul's Use*, 160-70.

[20.] Ladd, *Theology*, 394-95.

[21.] Longenecker, *Paul*, 56.

[22.] Ellis, "Exegetical Patterns," 218-20. According to Ellis, the questions are not difficult to ascertain. They are: (1) 9:6-29, "Do all those from Israel belong to Israel?" (2) 9:30-10:21, "Why have the Gentiles achieved righteousness and the Jews stumbled?" (3) 11:1-36, "Has God abandoned his people?" While admitting some differences between Pauline and rabbinic exegesis, he nevertheless contended (p. 218): "In spite of the differences the pattern and technique in Romans 9-11 reflect sufficient similarities with the rabbinic discourses to suggest that they arose in a common milieu."

[23.] Τοῦτ' ἔστιν and similar formulas resemble *pesher* (פשר) exegesis found at Qumran. See 4QFlor 1.11-14; CD 7.15-16; 1QpHab 12.6-7. Ellis, "Biblical Interpretation," 695-97.

(v. 24)	ἐξ Ἰουδαίων	a
	ἐξ ἐθνῶν	b
(vv. 25-26)	concerning Gentiles	(b)
(vv. 27-29)	concerning Israel	(a)[24]

Text. Rom 9:27-29 concludes Paul's midrash on the true nature of Israel. It contains two Old Testament Yahweh texts. The first (9:27-28) quotes what appears to be a merged quotation of Hos 2:1 and Isa 10:22. It reads:

ἐὰν ᾖ ὁ ἀριθμὸς τῶν υἱῶν Ἰσραὴλ ὡς ἡ ἄμμος τῆς
 θαλάσσης,
τὸ ὑπόλειμμα σωθήσεται
λόγον γὰρ συντελῶν καὶ συντέμνων ποιήσει
κύριος ἐπὶ τῆς γῆς.[25]

Though it differs from both the LXX and the Hebrew text, it nevertheless has greater affinity with the LXX.[26] It contains κύριος, which alone translates the divine name in combination with two other titles (אדני יהוה צבאות).

Evidently, Paul, inspired by the quotation in 9:26 of Hos 1:10 [LXX, 2:1], continued to borrow from that context the phrase ἐὰν ᾖ ὁ ἀριθμὸς τῶν υἱῶν Ἰσραὴλ ὡς ἡ ἄμμος τῆς θαλάσσης[27] to replace καὶ ἐὰν γένηται ὁ λαὸς Ἰσραὴλ ὡς ἡ ἄμμος τῆς θαλάσσης from Isa 10:22. The similarity between these two are obvious. That Paul

---

[24.] Adapted from Joachim Jeremias, "Chiasmus in den Paulusbriefen," in *Abba: Studien zur neutestamentlichen Theologie und Zeitgeschichte* (Göttingen: Vandenhoeck & Ruprecht, 1966), 283.

[25.] "Though the number of the sons of Israel be as the sand of the sea, only a remnant of them will be saved; for the Lord will execute his sentence upon the earth with rigor and dispatch."

[26.] Metzger, *Textual Commentary*, 523. The Textus Receptus, following later manuscripts, inserts ἐν δικαιοσύνῃ, ὅτι λόγον συντετμημένον after συντέμνων to conform Paul's wording to the exact LXX text (Isa 10:22-23). The absence of these words from other manuscripts could be explained if the scribe passed from συντέμνων to συντετμημένον. Metzger, however, commented: "But it is not credible that Paul, who in ver. 27 does not follow the Septuagint closely, should in ver. 28 have copied verbatim a sentence that is so opaque grammatically." It thus appears Paul's quotation left out these words and that they were added by a later generation of scribes. Other differences are (1) Paul's τὸ ὑπόλειμμα σωθήσεται for the LXX's τὸ κατάλειμμα αὐτῶν σωθήσεται (several early Pauline witnesses, however, have κατάλειμμα), (2) his ἐπὶ τῆς γῆς for the LXX's ἐν τῇ οἰκουμένῃ ὅλῃ, and (3) some LXX manuscripts have ὁ θεός instead of κύριος.

[27.] Paul's quotation differs only slightly from the LXX. Where he has ἐὰν ᾖ, the LXX has καὶ ἦν.

intended to quote Isaiah is evident from the introductory formula: Ἠσαΐας δὲ κράζει ὑπὲρ τοῦ Ἰσραήλ ("and Isaiah cries out concerning Israel").[28] He probably was not without purpose in merging these texts. By substituting ἐὰν ᾖ ὁ ἀριθμὸς τῶν υἱῶν Ἰσραήλ for καὶ ἐὰν γένηται ὁ λαὸς Ἰσραήλ, he contrasted the great number of Jews who rejected Jesus to the relatively small group of Jewish Christians which constituted the true remnant (ὑπόλειμμα). Such text mergers were possible only in the mind of one steeped in the LXX. In associating these texts together, he underscored his belief in the unity of the Old Testament prophetic voice.

This quotation, in both Isaiah and Paul, reflects two key theological ideas: (1) the salvation of a remnant[29] and (2) the swift and thorough execution of divine judgment. Isaiah, the eighth century prophet, predicted that catastrophe would fall upon God's people at the hand of Assyrian soldiers. He understood this coming calamity as God's judgment upon a wicked and perverse people.[30] Nevertheless, he could also envision that a remnant of Israel would survive and would one day be restored to the good fortune and status before God which Israel had enjoyed. He viewed this as a restoration not only to the land or to a way of life or to Jewish customs, but to God.[31] He wrote (Isa 10:21): "A remnant will return, the remnant of Jacob, to the mighty God."

[28.] The introductory formula for Rom 9:27 resembles introductory formulas used in explicit quotations from Qumran. For example, CD 4.7-8 אשר אמר ישעיה ("as Isaiah said"). See also CD 8.14; 19.26-27; 5.8; 1QM 10.1.

[29.] Ronald E. Clements, "'A Remnant Chosen by Grace' (Romans 11:5): The Old Testament Background and Origin of the Remnant Concept," in *Pauline Studies: Essays Presented to Professor F. F. Bruce on His 70th Birthday*, ed. Donald A Hagner and Murray J. Harris (Exeter: Paternoster Press, Ltd., 1980), 110, considered Isa 10:20-23 as a part of a series of interpretations on the child's name Shear-jashub in Isa 7:3. He called this the first real development of the Old Testament remnant concept.

[30.] The language in Rom 9:28 is quite strong. Godet, *Romans*, 366, noted that while λόγον could mean "decree," it is best understood in terms of "reckoning." Gerhard Delling, "συντελέω," *TDNT*, 8:64, listed some of the ways the Hebrew phrase כלה ונחרצה is translated. Its use in Dan 9:27 emphasizes destruction. Gottlob Schrenk, "λεῖμμα," *TDNT*, 4:210, said συντέμνων "denotes stern and pitiless cutting off." Cranfield, *Romans*, 2:502, remarking on the difficult reading of the Hebrew text, nevertheless, stated that the LXX and Paul's rendering of it support the original meaning. For him, the best understanding of the Hebrew is that God completes his sentence finally and decisively.

[31.] F. F. Bruce, *New Testament Development of Old Testament Themes* (Grand Rapids: Eerdmans, 1968), 57-59.

In quoting this Yahweh text, Paul argued that God acted as he always had, that is, through a remnant of faithful believers chosen by his grace. Although most Jews rejected Jesus, Paul viewed the small band of Jewish Christians to be this remnant,[32] thereby giving scriptural warrant for the meagre acceptance of Jesus among his contemporaries. Thus, he reserved the "remnant" concept for Jewish Christians alone.[33] Likewise, he considered the unbelief of his people to be evidence of God's judgment against them.

In Rom 9:29, Paul quoted another Yahweh text virtually verbatim, Isa 1:9.[34] He wrote:

εἰ μὴ κύριος σαβαὼθ ἐγκατέλιπεν ἡμῖν σπέρμα,
ὡς Σόδομα ἂν ἐγενήθημεν καὶ
ὡς Γόμορρα ἂν ὡμοιώθημεν. [35]

He introduced it with the formula: καὶ καθὼς προείρηκεν Ἡσαΐας ("and as Isaiah predicted"). This quotation differs only slightly from the Hebrew, primarily in regard to the use of σπέρμα, which translates two Hebrew words, שריד כמעט ("a few survivors"). He quoted what was originally a Yahweh text as indicated by the words κύριος σαβαώθ, which translates and transliterates respectively the Hebrew, יהוה צבאות. With it he concluded his midrash on the nature of true Israel by referring back to 9:6 with the key-word σπέρμα.

In other combined quotations Paul linked Old Testament texts together by certain key-words.[36] While no clear verbal linkage may appear at first, conceptual linkage may certainly be recognized. The use of ἐγκατέλιπεν and σπέρμα in 9:29 continues the emphasis upon the "remnant." The former word is cognate with λεῖμμα ("remnant"),

---

[32.] Clements, "Remnant," 106-7; and Moule, "Jesus, Judaism, Paul," 47.

[33.] Note the phrase ὑπὲρ τοῦ Ἰσραήλ in 9:27. In Rom 11:1, Paul asked whether God had rejected his people, which, as the reply indicates, he understood to be the Jews. He affirmed that God had not rejected his people. Although Elijah lamented that he alone remained faithful to Yahweh, Paul recalled that even then God had seven thousand men who had not bowed down to Baal. He concluded: "So too at the present time there is a remnant (λεῖμμα), chosen by grace" (Rom 11:5).

[34.] The only difference is the absence of καί in Paul's citation. That Paul could quote the LXX text of Isaiah exactly here yet differ with it considerably in the preceding verses dispels the notion that such differences were due to the availability of a given text when he was composing the letters. See Ellis, *Paul's Use*, 20, n. 5.

[35.] "If the Lord of hosts had not left us children, we would have fared like Sodom and been made like Gomorrah."

[36.] E.g., Rom 9:33 (λίθος); and 15:10-12 (ἔθνη). Ellis *Paul's Use*, 50, 102.

which is expressed in 9:27 by the compound word, ὑπόλειμμα. A similar combination provides the opportunity for conceptual, if not verbal, linkage between an Old Testament quotation and contemporary application in Rom 11:4-5.[37] Σπέρμα, on the other hand, occurs 217 times in the LXX translating the Hebrew root זרע. In approximately half of these, it refers to natural phenomena, agricultural or physiological items. In the remaining places, it is used metaphorically of the family and national life of Israel, often with the notion, "the seed of Abraham." In this case, however, it denotes the remnant,[38] translating שריד, a word not frequently used by Isaiah for the remnant.[39] For the prophet, it meant those who survived Sennacherib's onslaught against Judah (701 B.C.).

In addition to this, both Old Testament quotations (Isa 1:9 and 10:22-23) contain the word κύριος. In the Hebrew יהוה צבאות stands behind each of these, in one expressed (9:29), in the other unexpressed (9:28). Perhaps Paul was familiar with the Hebrew text of Isaiah and was aided in his composition by these similar phrases.

With these two Yahweh texts, Paul indicated that the Lord of Hosts had spared a remnant of Jews who believe in Jesus; otherwise Israel would be utterly destroyed and become a by-word to the nations like Sodom and Gomorrah.[40] He saw Gentiles coming to Christ, while the Jews generally were rejecting him. He did not believe that this confused God's word, rather it confirmed it. Paul, like the prophets

---

[37.] In Rom 11:4 Paul quoted God's reply to the lamenting Elijah: "I have kept (κατέλιπον) for myself seven thousand men who have not bowed the knee to Baal." In the next verse, he interpreted this in light of the new situation: "So too at the present time there is a remnant (λεῖμμα), chosen by grace."

[38.] Gottfried Quell, "σπέρμα," *TDNT*, 7:538.

[39.] The most common word in Isaiah for "remnant" is שאר. Schrenk, *TDNT*, 4:196, mentioned that there are four Old Testament roots for "remnant": (1) שאר (220 times), (2) יתר (103 times), (3) פלט (eighty times), and (4) שרד (twenty-nine times). Accordingly, he thought the prophetic idea of the remnant was fluid, changing according to the historical situation of the prophet. However, he contended it was always reserved for Israel. Paul's interest, he believed, was to demonstrate the fulfilment of the remnant concept in his own time, that is, in light of Jesus (4:205-9). Cranfield, *Romans*, 2:503, suggested Isaiah used שריד instead of his usual word for "remnant" (שאר) because the prophet did not regard the survivors of 701 B.C. to be the holy remnant of Israel. The LXX translators, he argued, used σπέρμα because they thought God's people were the "holy seed" (Isa 6:13; Ezra 9:2). Again, see the discussion in Clements, "Remnant," 106-21.

[40.] Gen 19:24-25.

of old, always delineated between true Israel and those who were simply physical descendants of Abraham.[41]

Therefore, in Rom 9:27-29 Paul took texts which originally referred to one event and brought them into the present. Although they were vague enough to be transferred to the new situation, he retained their general sense. His exegesis thus shares certain similarities with *pesharim* found at Qumran.[42]

Conclusion. From the analysis above, it appears that when Paul quoted these two Old Testament Yahweh texts, he had God in mind.[43] This is demonstrated by the theocentric nature of the passage. While a clear reference to Jesus does not occur in the midrash (9:6-29), θεός does occur eight times.[44] It is also demonstrated by the association of these passages with Israel, the abiding remnant of the Old Testament people of God. Finally, it is indicated by the use of the phrase "Lord of hosts," the special epithet for God associated with the pre-monarchial sanctuary at Shiloh (1 Sam 1:3, 11).[45] Cerfaux said: "Dans une citation d'*Is.*, I.9, κύριος σαβαώθ désigne naturellement Dieu."[46] Thus, God emerges as the clear referent to these Yahweh texts.

"The Mind of the Lord"—Rom 11:34

Context. Moved by the "mystery" (τὸ μυστήριον τοῦτο) of God's present and future dealings with both Jews and Gentiles (11:25),[47] Paul concluded his discussion on God's merciful plan for Israel and the Gentiles with "an eloquent expression of wonder and adoration before the mystery of God's ways, the majesty of His mercy and wisdom"[48] (Rom 11:33-36).

[41.] Cranfield, *Romans*, 2:502.

[42.] Texts found "modernized" in Qumran include: CD 1.13-14; 4.12-18; 6.11-14; 7.15-16; 7.18-21; 8.9-12; 8.14-16; 19:1; 4QFlor 1.2-3; 1.14-16; and 1.16-17. On this term see Joseph A. Fitzmyer, "The Use of Explicit Old Testament Quotations in Qumran Literature and in the New Testament," *NTS* 7 (1961): 297-333.

[43.] Foerster, *TDNT*, 3:1087; and Cerfaux, "Kyrios," 175.

[44.] Rom 9:6, 8, 11, 14, 16, 20, 22, 26.

[45.] B. W. Anderson, "Lord of Hosts," *IDB*, 3:151.

[46.] Cerfaux, "Kyrios," 175.

[47.] Günther Bornkamm, "μυστήριον," *TDNT*, 4:822-23.

[48.] Cranfield, *Romans*, 2:589.

This doxology,[49] which also has hymn-like features,[50] celebrates God's riches, wisdom, and knowledge. According to Eduard Norden[51] it contains nine lines:

> "O the depth of the riches and wisdom and knowledge of God!
> How unsearchable are his judgments
> and how inscrutable his ways!
> For who has known the mind of the Lord,
> or who has been his counselor?
> Or who has given a gift to him
> that he might be repaid?
> For from him and through him and to him are all things.
> To him be glory for ever. Amen."

As a part of its praise and adoration, it quotes two Old Testament texts: (1) Isa 40:13[52] and (2) Job 41:3.[53]

Text. The first of these, Rom 11:34, is an Old Testament Yahweh text as indicated by the phrase "the mind of the Lord" (νοῦν κυρίου), which translates the Hebrew אֶת־רוּחַ יהוה. Literally, this phrase means "the spirit of the Lord." Although some view it only as an allusion[54] or an "echo,"[55] the words and word order correspond so closely to the LXX that it should certainly be considered a quotation.[56]

---

[49]. The final phrase of the passage, "to him be glory for ever. Amen." (αὐτῷ ἡ δόξα εἰς τοὺς αἰῶνας, ἀμήν.), indicates the doxological character.

[50]. Reinhard Deichgräber, *Gotteshymnus und Christushymnus in der frühen Christenheit: Untersuchungen zu Form, Sprache und Stil der frühchristlichen Hymnen* (Göttingen: Vandenhoeck & Ruprecht, 1967), 61-62.

[51]. Eduard Norden, *Agnostos Theos: Untersuchungen zur Formengeschichte religiöser Rede* (Darmstadt: Wissenschaftliche Buchgesellschaft, 1956), 240-43; Günther Bornkamm, *Early Christian Experience*, (New York: Harper & Row, 1979), 106, followed Norden.

[52]. Paul also quoted this text in 1 Cor 2:16, and on this occasion, he applied it to Christ.

[53]. Paul cited from Job in Rom 11:35 and 1 Cor 3:19. In both cases, his citations follow the Hebrew more closely than the LXX. This may simply be due to the fact that he was more familiar with the Hebrew text of this book. See Ellis, "Midrash Pesher," 178.

[54]. Deichgräber, *Gotteshymnus*, 62, wrote: "Es handelt sich nicht um eigentliche Zitate, sondern um Anspielungen."

[55]. F. F. Bruce, *The Epistle of Paul to the Romans*, TNTC (Grand Rapids: Eerdmans,

Yahweh Texts in Paul's Letters

Isa 40:13 [LXX]	Rom 11:34
τίς ἔγνω νοῦν κυρίου,	τίς γὰρ ἔγνω νοῦν κυρίου;
καὶ τίς αὐτοῦ σύμβουλος ἐγένετο,	ἢ τίς σύμβουλος αὐτοῦ ἐγένετο;
ὃς συμβιβᾷ αὐτόν;	

Several differences between Paul's quotation and the LXX may be noticed: (1) the addition of γάρ to introduce the quotation, (2) the change from καί to ἤ in the second line, (3) the reversal of αὐτοῦ and σύμβουλος, and (4) the exclusion by Paul of the final phrase, ὃς συμβιβᾷ αὐτόν. The first difference can easily be accounted for when one considers Paul's habit of using γάρ alone[57] and with other words or phrases[58] in introductory formulas. Differences (2) and (4) are also resolved when one takes into account the three-fold structure throughout the doxology.

In 11:33 Paul celebrated three elements of God's nature:[59] his riches (πλούτου), wisdom (σοφίας), and knowledge (γνώσεως). Following this, he asked three questions taken from the Old Testament which expound and correspond to these attributes. Most likely, he used a chiastic structure:[60]

v. 33	πλούτου	a
	σοφίας	b
	γνώσεως	c
v. 34	Who has known the mind of the Lord?	(c)
	Who has been his counselor?	(b)

1963), 224.

[56.] Cerfaux, "Kyrios," 175, called it a *"citation virtuelle."* See also Cranfield, *Romans*, 2:590; and Ellis, *Paul's Use*, 151.

[57.] Rom 10:13; 1 Cor 2:16; 10:26; and 15:27.

[58.] Rom 4:3; 9:15, 17; 12:9; 13:9; 14:11; 1 Cor 1:19; 3:19; 6:16; 9:9; 2 Cor 6:2; Gal 3:10; 4:27; and 1 Tim 5:18.

[59.] Bornkamm, *Early Christian Experience*, 106, argued against a Greek understanding of "nature" here. He wrote: "Here Paul does not think speculatively in Greek fashion about the nature of God in general. Rather, he thinks historically about God's 'judgments' and 'ways.'" In other words, for Paul, God's historic actions in salvation history inform the categories "riches," "wisdom," and "knowledge."

[60.] Jeremias, "Chiasmus," 284.

> Who has given a gift   (a)
> to him to repay
> him?

Finally, he concluded the doxology with a three-fold statement of praise: "For from him and through him and to him are all things" (ὅτι ἐξ αὐτοῦ καὶ δι' αὐτοῦ καὶ εἰς αὐτὸν τὰ πάντα).[61] Apparently, Paul changed καί to ἤ to establish three separate questions corresponding to riches, wisdom, and knowledge. Likewise, he dropped the final phrase in the LXX quotation from Isa 40:13 to maintain the integrity of the chiastic structure.

Therefore, the only discrepancy between Paul's quotation and the LXX text of Isa 40:13 left unresolved is the reversal of the words, αὐτοῦ and σύμβουλος. The other differences appear to be due to Paul's reorganization of the text to make it "fit" his doxology.

Conclusion. When Paul quoted Isa 40:13 with its phrase νοῦν κυρίου ("mind of the Lord") and placed it within his doxology of praise, he probably had God in mind. This is demonstrated by the theocentric nature of the text. Eleven times in Rom 11:1-32 Paul mentioned God (θεός)[62] as he discussed the new relationship of Israel to God now that the Gentiles had been "grafted in" (Rom 11:17-19). Only once did he allude to Christ, and here not by name or customary title, but as the "Deliverer" (11:26, ὁ ῥυόμενος).[63] The occurrence of θεοῦ in 11:33a and the use of the personal pronoun αὐτοῦ in 11:33b and c, referring back to God (11:33a), naturally carry forward the idea that God is the subject. Thus with this Yahweh text he described the depth of *God's* wisdom and celebrated his sovereignty.

[61.] Because this has similarities with certain statements among Hellenistic writers, some scholars believe Paul borrowed it from Hellenistic sources. They note particularly Marcus Aurelius' soliloquy in *Meditations*, 4.23: "All that is in tune with thee, O Universe, is in tune with me! Nothing that is in due time for thee is too early or too late for me! All that thy seasons bring, O Nature, is fruit for me! All things come from thee, subsist in thee, go back to thee (ἐκ σοῦ πάντα, ἐν σοὶ πάντα, εἰς σὲ πάντα)." See Norden, *Agnostos Theos*, 241-42; also Bultmann, *Theology*, 1:229. While it is possible that Paul chose his words in light of Stoic philosophy, no need exists to believe that he drew from a formula of Hellenistic philosophy to state this verse. These ideas are found in Paul in other places (1 Cor 8:6; Col 1:16, although here it is plainly christocentric). Paul's use of it here lacks Stoic mythical and pantheistic interests. Rather, he affirmed God as the Creator, Sustainer, and Goal of all. Cranfield, *Romans*, 2:591; Barrett, *Romans*, 229; and Beasley-Murray, "Colossians 1:15-20," 173.

[62.] 11:1, 2 (two times), 8, 21, 22 (two times), 23, 29, 30, 32.

[63.] In this verse, Paul quoted Isa 59:20. Kim, *Origin*, 89. Cf. 1 Thess 1:10.

"Praise the Lord, Ye Gentiles"—Rom 15:9-11

Context. Rom 15:7-13 concludes Paul's comments addressed to the "weak" and the "strong" in the Roman church (Rom 14:1-15:13). It begins by repeating the opening exhortation (14:1), "welcome one another" (15:7), directed this time to both weak and strong believers. It also adds the qualifier,[64] καθὼς καὶ ὁ Χριστὸς προσελάβετο ὑμᾶς ("as Christ has welcomed you") and indicates that Christ's action issues forth in God's glory (εἰς δόξαν τοῦ θεοῦ).

In 15:8 Paul, in his usual Jew-first, Greek-second pattern,[65] undergirded the admonition, "welcome one another," and explained Christ's action by noting his role as a servant to the "circumcised." He wrote: λέγω γὰρ Χριστὸν διάκονον γεγενῆσθαι περιτομῆς ὑπὲρ ἀληθείας θεοῦ.[66] By the "circumcised," he meant the Jews "who, especially when described as the 'circumcision', may be regarded as the most awkward and irritating of scrupulous persons."[67] With the perfect tense γεγενῆσθαι, he emphasized that Christ *became* and *remains* the Jews' servant. Appealing to Christ's example, he thereby instructed the Gentiles to welcome them by also becoming their servants. This example, he believed, (1) confirmed the Old Testament promises and (2) established the basis by which the Gentiles might join God's people and glorify him for his merciful gift (15:8, 9).[68]

Beginning in 15:9, Paul gave scriptural warrants for the inclusion of the Gentiles by referring to a series of four Old Testament quotations bound by the key-word ἔθνη ("Gentiles").[69] By invoking the authority of scripture, he argued that the Gentiles will praise God and place their hope in the Jewish Messiah (15:12, "the root of Jesse"). Although it was not typical for Paul, he demonstrated similarities with rabbinic exegesis by quoting from the Law, Prophets, and Writings to support his argument.[70] He began this series of quota-

---

[64.] *Contra* Cranfield, *Romans*, 2:739, who translated καθώς "because."

[65.] See, e.g., Rom 1:16; 2:9, 10; and 1 Cor 1:22-25.

[66.] "For I tell you that Christ became a servant to the circumcised to show God's truthfulness."

[67.] Barrett, *Romans*, 271.

[68.] Beker, *Paul*, 87, believed Paul understood the Old Testament in general to speak of God's promise to create a new people, the church of Jews and Gentiles.

[69.] Ellis, *Paul's Use*, 50, 102, called this a chain quotation or *haraz*. Käsemann, *Romans*, 386, said that for Paul the entrance of the Gentiles was the "decisive eschatological event."

tions with the introductory formula, καθὼς γέγραπται, indicating his intent to refer explicitly to Old Testament teaching on this matter.

Text. Paul's first quotation (15:9) came from Ps 18:49 (LXX, 17:50) and was preserved almost verbatim by the apostle except for the omission of κύριε. In its original context Ps 17:50 [LXX] read:

διὰ τοῦτο ἐξομολογήσομαί σοι ἐν ἔθνεσιν,
κύριε,
καὶ τῷ ὀνόματί σου ψαλῶ[71]

That he quoted what was originally a Yahweh text is confirmed by the Hebrew reading:

על־כן אודך בגוים יהוה
ולשמך אזמרה[72]

But why did Paul eliminate κύριε from the quotation? Was it the result of a memory lapse or did he have a purpose in omitting it? Cranfield suggested that he omitted it because he understood the words to be the Messiah's words of praise.[73] Since the Jewish Messiah could also be called κύριος, the use of the title here would be somewhat confusing. While these appear to be the words of David, the type of messianic king, there is nothing in the context of Paul's quotation to indicate that the Messiah is speaking. Perhaps Paul omitted κύριε because he preferred the verb ὁμολογεῖν (and its cognates) with κύριος to refer to Jesus,[74] and in 15:9 he spoke explicitly of the Gentiles praising *God.* Earlier he had instructed the Roman Christians to confess (ὁμολογήσῃς) Jesus as Lord to be saved.[75] Thus, for clarity of thought, consistency, and perhaps for

---

[70] Ellis, *Paul's Use,* 46, 50, 102, noted that chain quotations in the Talmud normally follow the order: Law, Prophets, and Writings. Paul, in contrast, quoted from the Writings (Ps 18:49 [LXX, 17:50]), Law (Deut 32:43), Writings (Ps 117:1 [LXX, 116:1]), and Prophets (Isa 11:10). Note Gamaliel's use of the three-fold quotation in *b. Sanh.* 90b. Cf. Rom 11:8-9. Longenecker, *Paul,* 59.

[71] "Therefore, I will praise you Lord among the Gentiles, and sing to your name" (author's translation).

[72] "For this I will extol thee, O Lord, among the nations and sing praises to thy name."

[73] Cranfield, *Romans,* 2:745, follows Lagrange, *Romains,* 347.

[74] For a more detailed discussion of the confession, "Jesus is Lord," see above, pp. 50-53. The occurrence of ἐξομολογήσεται in Rom 14:11 can hardly be cited against this, since (1) the referent is clearly God (τῷ θεῷ) and (2) in the context of judgment, it appears to mean confession of sins. See Otto Michel, "ὁμολογέω," *TDNT,* 5:215.

[75] Rom 10:9; cf. 1 Cor 12:3; and Phil 2:9-11.

theological reasons he may have omitted κύριε from this Old Testament Yahweh text.

Following an exact quotation from Deut 32:43 inviting the Gentiles to rejoice with God's people, Paul quoted another Old Testament Yahweh text, which also came from the Psalms (Ps 117:1 [LXX, 116:1]). Having introduced it with καὶ πάλιν ("and again"), he altered slightly[76] the text of the LXX which read:

αἰνεῖτε τὸν κύριον, πάντα τὰ ἔθνη,
ἐπαινέσατε αὐτόν, πάντες οἱ λαοί[77]

He wrote:

αἰνεῖτε, πάντα τὰ ἔθνη, τὸν κύριον
καὶ ἐπαινεσάτωσαν αὐτὸν πάντες οἱ λαοί[78]

Since κύριον in the LXX corresponds to the divine name in the Hebrew, he again quoted a Yahweh text.

The two key words in this quotation are ἔθνη and λαοί. In the LXX ἔθνη typically means the world outside Israel (= Gentiles)[79] and λαός the people of God (= Israel).[80] They are paralleled here to indicate that in this verse they are understood as synonyms.[81] In Paul λαός occurs eleven times and only here in the plural. In the previous verse (15:10), it is contrasted to ἔθνη and refers to the Jews as the Gentiles are invited to join God's people (μετὰ τοῦ λαοῦ αὐτοῦ) in rejoicing. Thus, Paul used this quotation, along with the others, to demonstrate that the Old Testament summoned all nations and

---

[76.] Käsemann, *Romans*, 386, noted several differences, including (1) in the first line Paul placed the address prior to the object, (2) in the second line he added the connective, καί, and (3) he changed the second-person imperative ἐπαινέσατε to the third-person ἐπαινεσάτωσαν. Some manuscripts, all comparatively late, have ἐπαινέσατε, while earlier, better witnesses contain ἐπαινεσάτωσαν. Since copyists often tried to "improve" texts by bringing them into conformity with other manuscripts, the latter appears to be the best reading.

[77.] "Praise the Lord, all nations, praise him, all peoples" (author's translation).

[78.] "Praise the Lord, all Gentiles, and let all the peoples praise him."

[79.] Hermann Strathmann, "λαός," *TDNT*, 4:50.

[80.] Ibid., 32. Strathmann said λαός in the LXX is "a specific term for a specific people, namely, Israel." It usually translated the Hebrew עם.

[81.] K. L. Schmidt, "ἔθνος," *TDNT*, 2:369; Cranfield, *Romans*, 2:746, noted that λαοί here translates the rare Hebrew term האמים, which occurs only three times in the Old Testament (Gen 25:16, referring to the sons of Ishmael; Num 25:15, referring to Midianites; Ps 117:1).

all peoples to praise God.[82] He did not include Israel since he expected his nation to be praising God already.

Conclusion. As has already been suggested, Paul's use of these Yahweh texts points directly to God as indicated by two factors.[83] (1) The straight-forward statement in 15:9 that Christ became a servant to the Jews "in order that the Gentiles might glorify God for his mercy" (τὰ δὲ ἔθνη ὑπὲρ ἐλέους δόξασαι τὸν θεόν) signifies a theocentric meaning to these Yahweh texts. As evidenced by the introductory formula, καθὼς γέγραπται, these four scripture quotations guarantee the correctness of Paul's assertion. (2) The blessing appended to Paul's discussion, which has the "God of hope" as its subject (15:13), further demonstrates that God is the referent.

It is interesting to note that the context of both these verses and Rom 9:27-29, where Paul also retains κύριος for God, concerns Israel as the people of God and the inclusion of the Gentiles into God's saving plan.

"The Lord Knows the Thoughts of the Wise"—1 Cor 3:20

Context. Paul brought his discussion on the nature of true wisdom, an argument he began in 1:18, to conclusion in 1 Cor 3:18-23. According to Earle Ellis,[84] the apostle argued his point utilizing a common midrashic structure:

1:18-31	Midrash
2:1-5	Application
2:6-16	Midrash
3:1-17	Application
3:18-20	Concluding texts

In the following chapter he applied the results of his argument and scriptural exposition to the situation in the Corinthian congregation.[85] Apparently rivals had rallied around certain leaders and boasted of pneumatic experiences which they interpreted to be marks

---

[82.] Such universalism is widespread in the Old Testament, particularly in the prophets. See Isa 25:6, 7; 26:2; 45:18-25; 55:4-7; Jer 12:16; 16:19; Ezra 47:22; Zeph 3:9; Zech 2:10-11; 9:7; Ps 67:5; 117:1; and 148:11-13.

[83.] Cerfaux, "Kyrios," 175-76.

[84.] Ellis, *Prophecy*, 213-16. In 3:21-4:21 he believed Paul applied the midrash beyond the concluding texts.

[85.] In addition to this, Paul alluded to the situation in 1 Cor 6:5; 8:1-3; 10:15; 12:8; and 13:8-12.

of maturity and wisdom. Actually, however, Paul claimed that their experiences had resulted only in human and fleshly wisdom, which was more characteristic of this age than the age to come.[86]

In 1 Corinthians 3 Paul challenged their opinion concerning their leaders, affirming that their faith and growth were due ultimately to God and not men (1 Cor 3:5-9). On the other hand, in 3:10-15 he underscored their responsibility in how they built upon the foundation, Jesus Christ. He affirmed that one may build with lasting materials (χρυσόν, ἄργυρον, λίθους τιμίους) or with shoddy materials (ξύλα, χόρτον, καλάμην); nevertheless, the true nature of the work will be revealed on "the Day" (ἡ ἡμέρα)[87] when it is tested by fire.[88] Some, he said, would build and receive a reward (μισθόν). Others would have their work burn up but would themselves be saved. Clearly, Paul had in mind eschatological judgment.

Paul continued the emphasis upon judgment, this time combined with temple of God (ναὸς θεοῦ) imagery, in 3:16-17.[89] While some would build with shoddy materials and thereby lose their reward, he believed others were determined to destroy the church by their schismatic attitudes and practices. These, he warned, would suffer eternal destruction from the hand of God (3:17: φθερεῖ τοῦτον ὁ θεός).[90]

In view of the threat of eternal destruction or loss of future reward, Paul warned again[91] of the dangers inherent in worldly wisdom, particularly that of self-deception.[92] These trouble-makers should not be deceived, he acknowledged, because if they continue[93] in their

---

[86] Bornkamm, *Paul*, 71; and Ellis, *Prophecy*, 61, 69, 113.

[87] On the Day of Yahweh in the Old Testament see Isa 2:12; Jer 46:10; and Amos 5:18.

[88] Some important Old Testament texts associate fire with "the Day": Joel 2:3, 30; Mal 4:1; and Isa 66:15; cf. 2 Thess 1:7.

[89] Cf. 2 Cor 6:16; and Eph 2:21.

[90] The clear sense is eschatological destruction. See Fee, *First Corinthians*, 147-49.

[91] Ibid., 152. Fee argued that there is nothing new in 3:18; it is only a restatement of the previous argument in 1:18-3:4.

[92] The present, imperative verb ἐξαπατάτω indicates that this is in fact already happening. Similar warnings against self-deception are found in 1 Cor 6:9; 15:33; Gal 6:3,7. Cf. Munck, *Paul*, 164, 167.

[93] Εἰ ("if") begins a first class conditional construction which assumes the condition to be true.

pursuit of worldly wisdom, they would stand before God in judgment. He wrote (3:18): "If any one among you thinks that he is wise in this age, let him become a fool that he may become wise."[94] As Conzelmann noted, this is no call to intellectual suicide or to praise foolishness and irrationality; rather, it is a summons to faith in the word of the cross.[95] Their wisdom is only for this age (3:18, ἐν τῷ αἰῶνι τούτῳ), an age which is passing away (1:20, 27-29; 2:6, 8). In the new economy, however, the cross and resurrection stand as the inauguration of the new age. Paul encouraged them to abandon worldly wisdom, embrace the folly of the cross, and thereby be made wise.[96]

Text. In 3:19-20 Paul presented the rationale (γάρ) for his previous statement from his argument (3:19a) and from scripture (3:19b-20). In 1:18-25 he established that God's wisdom, embodied in the word of the cross, amounted to foolishness in the eyes of the world. In 3:19a he set up the opposite contention, which is equally true, that this world's wisdom is foolishness in God's eyes (παρὰ τῷ θεῷ). To reinforce this argument, he appealed to two Old Testament texts, Job 5:13 and Ps 94:11 (LXX, 93:11), joined together by the key-word "wise."

Having begun with an introductory formula,[97] γέγραπται γάρ, Paul quoted Job 5:13:[98] ὁ δρασσόμενος τοὺς σοφοὺς ἐν τῇ πανουργίᾳ αὐτῶν (1 Cor 3:19: "He catches the wise in their craftiness"). The language here presents the image of the hunt in which the hunter (God) used the cunning of the prey (the so-called "wise")

[94.] 1 Cor 3:18; a similar formula (εἴ τις δοκεῖ . . .) is found in 8:2; 11:16; and 14:37. In each case it appears to convey a position held by some rival party. Paul used such terminology to force them to consider his point of view.

[95.] Hans Conzelmann, *First Corinthians*, Hermeneia, trans. James W. Leitch (Philadelphia: Fortress, 1975), 79-81.

[96.] Barrett, *First Corinthians*, 94; and Fee, *First Corinthians*, 151. Μωρὸς γενέσθω . . . γένηται σοφός appears to form a chiastic expression.

[97.] A similar introductory formula is found in Qumran, כי כתיב ("for it was written"), in CD 11.20.

[98.] This quotation appears to be the only explicit quotation of Job in the New Testament (cf. Rom 11:35). Since this citation appears closer to the Hebrew text than the LXX (Ellis, *Paul's Use*, 151), either it represents Paul's own translation from the Hebrew or a different Greek manuscript tradition with which Paul was familiar. Cf. R. P. C. Hanson, "St. Paul's Quotations of the Book of Job," *Theology* 53 (1950): 250-53.

to capture them. The capture is reminiscent of the judgment described in 3:12-17.

Paul added further scriptural support to his exhortation when he quoted Ps 94:11 (LXX, Ps 93:11). Employing καὶ πάλιν to connect these texts, he wrote (3:20): κύριος γινώσκει τοὺς διαλογισμοὺς τῶν σοφῶν ὅτι εἰσὶν μάταιοι ("The Lord knows that the thoughts of the wise are futile"). Paul's quotation differed only slightly from the LXX which reads: κύριος γινώσκει τοὺς διαλογισμοὺς τῶν ἀνθρώπων ὅτι εἰσὶν μάταιοι.[99] The Hebrew text indicates that Paul quoted a Yahweh text:

[100]יהוה ידע מחשבות אדם כי-המה הבל

The only difference between Paul's quotation and the LXX lies in the substitution of σοφῶν for ἀνθρώπων.[101] Some suggest that this results from the fact that he quoted from memory.[102] Others imply that Paul quoted from a *florilegium*.[103] Probably, however, 1 Cor 3:20 contains Paul's deliberate adaptation of the Old Testament as a part of a *pesher*-type exegesis to the present context, which denegrates human wisdom.[104] Since 1:18, "wisdom" has been Paul's theme. He has expressed frequently that God's wisdom stands in sharp contrast to man's wisdom, which is folly in God's sight. It is thus only natural for Paul to adjust the Old Testament quotation to fit his previous argument, especially since he upholds the integrity of the original Psalm.[105]

---

[99] Ps 93:11, LXX: "The Lord knows that the thoughts of men are futile."

[100] Ps 94:11, HT: "Yahweh knows the thoughts of man that they are a breath" (author's translation).

[101] Some later manuscripts have replaced σοφῶν with ἀνθρώπων, most likely to bring Paul's text into conformity with the LXX. Bruce M. Metzger, *The Text of the New Testament: Its Transmission, Corruption, and Restoration*, 2d ed. (New York: Oxford University Press, 1968), 197-98, remarked that copyists often did this.

[102] E.g., Munck, *Paul*, 146.

[103] Lucien Cerfaux, "Vestiges d'un florilège dans I Cor. 1.18-3.24?" *Revue d'historie ecclesiastique* 27 (1931): 521-34, believed that in 1:18-3:24 Paul used a *florilegium* of Old Testament quotations which had its source in his rabbinic training in Jerusalem in which he was consistently warned against Greek wisdom; idem, "Kyrios," 176. See, however, the refutation by Munck (*Paul*, 145-46).

[104] Ellis, *Paul's Use*, 14-15, 144-45; idem, *Prophecy*, 177, 195-96; and Fee, *First Corinthians*, 152, n. 8.

[105] A. M. Harmon, "Aspects of Paul's Use of the Psalms," *Westminster Theological Journal* 32 (1969): 22, noted that Paul had in mind not just the verse in isolation

The word διαλογισμός occurs in the New Testament often connoting evil thoughts (Matt 15:19; Luke 5:22; 6:8; 9:47; and Rom 1:21). It carries the same meaning in the LXX (Ps 55:5; 93:11; Isa 59:7; and Jer 4:14).[106] However, the important aspect here is not evil motive, but God's verdict that these thoughts are μάταιοι.

Μάταιος means "vain," "futile," "without result," "empty," or "fruitless."[107] It connotes deception—note the exhortation in 3:18 against self-deception—that is, appearing to be something, it is actually nothing.[108] Thus, the verse discloses the deception inherent within human wisdom. It appears impressive, eloquent, and important; but all the while God knows that it is in fact an empty shell. This again ties in with the judgment motif in 3:12-15. Μάταιος is reminiscent of the works which will be burned up at the coming judgment. They have an appearance, but no lasting value.

Conclusion. It is difficult to determine whether Paul had in mind God or the Lord Jesus when he quoted this Old Testament Yahweh text. When examining instances of κύριος found in the vicinity of 1 Cor 3:20, one notices that in each case they refer to Christ.[109] However, other factors may indicate that κύριος here means θεός: (1) the argument since 1 Cor 1:18 centers around the wisdom of God (σοφία θεοῦ), (2) θεός occurs frequently in chapter three,[110] (3) the clear reference to the wisdom of this world as foolishness with God (μωρία παρὰ τῷ θεῷ) in 3:19, and (4) the subordination passage in 3:23 which acknowledges, ὑμεῖς δὲ Χριστοῦ, Χριστὸς δὲ θεοῦ. These

---

but the entire Psalm; for while Paul contrasted divine and human wisdom, the Psalm contrasted the ways of God and the ways of man. This may be underscored above all by Ps 93:8 (LXX): σύνετε δή, ἄφρονες ἐν τῷ λαῷ, καί, μωροί, ποτὲ φρονήσατε. The writer appealed to the senseless (ἄφρονες) and the fools (μωροί) and encouraged them to think (φρονήσατε).

[106.] Cf. Gottlob Schrenk, "διαλογισμός," *TDNT*, 2:96-98.

[107.] Otto Bauernfeind, "μάταιος," *TDNT*, 4:519-22; and Morris, *1 Corinthians*, 72.

[108.] Beauty as μάταιος (Prov 31:30); man's strength and ability as μάταιος (Ps 61:9 [LXX]; 59:11 [LXX]; Isa 28:29; 33:11); other gods as μάταιος (Hos 5:11; Isa 2:20; 30:15; Ezek 8:10). Cf. *P.Oxy.* 1.58.20; and Philo *Som* 1.244.

[109.] 1 Cor 3:5, καὶ ἑκάστῳ ὡς ὁ κύριος ἔδωκεν: Paul's expressions about apostleship with the κύριος predicate usually refer to Jesus (1 Cor 9:1-2; 2 Cor 10:8; 13:10). 1 Cor 4:4, ὁ δὲ ἀνακρίνων με κύριός ἐστιν, along with 4:5, ἕως ἂν ἔλθῃ ὁ κύριος: Paul normally spoke of the Lord's coming and judgment with Jesus in mind. See pp. 82-88.

[110.] θεός occurs in 3:6, 7, 9 (three times), 10, 16 (two times), 17 (two times), 19, 23. References to Christ are fewer, 3:1, 5, 11, 23 (two times).

factors indicate that Paul quoted this Old Testament text with God in mind.[111]

"The Lord Almighty"—2 Cor 6:18

Context. The relationship of 2 Cor 6:14-7:1 to the rest of the letter has long been a subject of debate. Its unusual concentration of features not characteristic of Paul,[112] similarities with Qumran's teachings,[113] and lack of use in the surrounding context have caused many scholars to question both its authorship and present location.[114]

If 2 Cor 6:14-7:1 represents a non-Pauline fragment, one may question its place in a discussion of Paul's use of Old Testament Yahweh texts. Nevertheless, the question remains unresolved and the possibility of resolution is slim. Therefore, it is included in this discussion.

The passage forms a complete unit of thought; therefore, appeal to a wider context is unnecessary. Its structure consists of the following:

(6:14a)   an exhortation addressed to believers not to associate closely with non- believers[115]

[111.] Cerfaux, "Kyrios," 176; Dunn, *Christology*, 158; and Foerster, *TDNT*, 3:1087.

[112.] These include (1) Pauline *hapax legomena* (e.g., ἑτεροζυγοῦντες, μετοχή, συμφώνησις, Βελιάρ, συγκατάθεσις, μολυσμοῦ), (2) the unusual introductory and concluding formulas to the scriptural quotations, and (3) the ethical admonition for believers to separate from unbelievers appears to contradict similar teaching elsewhere (particularly 1 Cor 5:10; 7:12-16).

[113.] For example, (1) the concern of Qumran doctrine to separate from the world (1QS 5.13-17; 9.8-9; CD 6.14-18), (2) the use of "Belial" for Satan (1QM 1.1, 5, 13; 13.2, 4; 11QMelch 1.26), (3) the "light" and "darkness" dualism (1QS 1.9-11; 2.16-17; 3.3, 13, 19-20, 24-25; 1QM 1.1, 3, 9; 13.5-6; 4QFlor 1.9), and (4) the importance of 2 Sam 7:14-16 for Qumran (4QFlor 1.11). Joseph A. Fitzmyer, *Essays on the Semitic Background of the New Testament* (London: Geoffrey Chapman, 1971), 205-17, considered the affinities so significant that he concluded that Christians reworked an existing Essene teaching.

[114.] Among those who consider Paul the author of this passage are Gordon Fee, "II Corinthians vi.14-vii.1 and Food Offered to Idols," *NTS* 23 (1977): 147; Barrett, *2 Corinthians*, 196-97; Bruce, *Corinthians*, 213-16; Margaret E. Thrall, "The Problem of II Cor. vi.14-vii.1 in Some Recent Discussion," *NTS* 24 (1977): 144-48; Walter Schmithals, "Die Korintherbriefe als Briefsammlung," *ZNW* 64 (1973): 282-86, who argued that it, along with other Pauline fragments, belonged to Paul's previous letter (1 Cor 5:9-11). For some options regarding location see Furnish, *II Corinthians*, 371-83.

(6:14b-16a)   a series of rhetorical questions
(6:16b)   a declaration giving the basis for the exhortation
(6:16c-18)   a catena of scriptural quotations and allusions
(7:1)   a final appeal for believers to cleanse themselves based upon the "promises" of scripture

In each case the rhetorical questions[116] and the scriptural appeals reinforce the initial admonition.

Since the present interest involves Paul's use of Yahweh texts, features which do not impact upon this aspect of the passage will not be treated. What is determinative here is that this passage is an ethical plea for Christians to avoid relationships which would lead away from Christ to iniquity, unbelief, and idolatry.[117]

Text. Paul concluded the series of rhetorical questions by asking (6:16a): "What agreement has the temple of God (ναῷ θεοῦ) with idols?" Prompted evidently by this question, he declared (6:16b): ἡμεῖς γὰρ ναὸς θεοῦ ἐσμεν ζῶντος ("For we are the temple of the living God").[118] In the following verses he explained from scripture[119] some implications involved with God's temple.

---

[115]. This appears to be the meaning of ἀπίστοις. However Hans Dieter Betz, "2 Cor 6:14-7:1: An Anti-Pauline Fragment?" *JBL* 92 (1973): 89-90, considered the "unbelievers" to be Gentile Christians who refused to obey the Jewish law. On the possible meanings of the exhortation, see Barrett, *2 Corinthians*, 196; and Furnish, *II Corinthians*, 372.

[116]. Cf. Sir 13:1-3, 17-18, which also uses rhetorical questioning to emphasize the danger of associating with rich and arrogant men. Cf. also Rom 2:3-4, 21-23.

[117]. The juxtaposition of the various elements in the rhetorical questions presents a broad view of what believers were to avoid: iniquity, darkness, Belial, unbelievers, and idols. From this it is difficult to ascertain completely the force of the admonition.

[118]. Paul used the temple of God imagery elsewhere to describe the church. In 1 Cor 3:16-17 he stated: "Do you not know that you are God's temple and that God's Spirit dwells in you? If any one destroys God's temple, God will destroy him. For God's temple is holy, and that temple you are."

[119]. (1) 6:16 quotes Lev 26:11-12 tempered perhaps by Ezek 37:27; (2) 6:17 quotes Isa 52:11-12; and (3) 6:18 quotes 2 Sam 7:14 [LXX, 2 Kgdm 7:14]. In each case Paul's quotation varies greatly from the LXX and the Hebrew text. See Ellis, *Paul's Use*, 150-51, 178-79.

Unlike other combined quotations in Paul's letters, 2 Cor 6:16c-18 contains three quotation formulas: (1) at the beginning, καθὼς εἶπεν ὁ θεός ("as God said"),[120] (2) in the middle, λέγει κύριος ("says the Lord"), and (3) at the conclusion, λέγει κύριος παντοκράτωρ ("says the Lord Almighty"). Each quotation formula stresses the seriousness of the exhortation; however, only the final formula is organically connected with the text it relates. Therefore, since the latter contains the κύριος predicate, it represents the focus of this section.

Using καί to join this final quotation to the rest of the testimonia, Paul cited 2 Sam 7:14,[121] perhaps due to its connection with the construction of the temple. He wrote: καὶ ἔσομαι ὑμῖν εἰς πατέρα καὶ ὑμεῖς ἔσεσθέ μοι εἰς υἱοὺς καὶ θυγατέρας, λέγει κύριος παντοκράτωρ ("'and I will be a father to you, and you shall be my sons and daughters,' says the Lord Almighty"). The text from which he quoted likely read: ἐγὼ ἔσομαι αὐτῷ εἰς πατέρα, καὶ αὐτὸς ἔσται μοι εἰς υἱόν ("I will be a father to him, and he will be a son to me").[122]

Several differences are immediately apparent: (1) the omission of ἐγώ, (2) the change from αὐτῷ to ὑμῖν, (3) the change from αὐτὸς ἔσται to ὑμεῖς ἔσεσθε, and (4) the change from εἰς υἱόν to εἰς υἱοὺς καὶ θυγατέρας. In the original context, God promised David that he would be a father to his son, Solomon, as he ruled the nation and built the temple. In the present context, the author expanded the promise of God's Fatherhood to include the entire believing community (cf. Rev 21:7; Heb 1:5).[123] Updating the text in this way accounts completely for alterations made to the original.

Paul concluded the quotation with the formula, λέγει κύριος παντοκράτωρ. Since it occurs in this form no other place in Paul[124] and since it is present in the immediate context of the final quotation (in 2 Sam 7:8), it is likely that the author derived this concluding

---

[120.] This introductory formula is not paralleled in Paul's letters, but it is found in Qumran (CD 6.13; 8.9).

[121.] The same text is interpreted messianically in 4QFlor 1.11.

[122.] 2 Sam 7:14 [LXX], author's translation.

[123.] Perhaps "sons" has been expanded to include "daughters" according to Isa 43:6: "I will say to the north, Give up, and to the south, Do not withhold; bring my sons from afar and my daughters from the end of the earth."

[124.] In the New Testament it is found only here and in Revelation (1:8; 4:8; 11:17; 15:3; 16:7, 17; 19:6, 15; and 21:22).

formula from a Greek text[125] of 2 Samuel 7.[126] This, therefore, makes it an integral part of the quotation and not merely some unconnected formula.

Conclusion. When Paul concluded the series of quotations with λέγει κύριος παντοκράτωρ and thereby appealed to the Yahweh text originally in 2 Sam 7:8, he clearly had God in mind.[127] This conclusion is based upon the following evidence: (1) the introductory formula which reads "as God said," (2) the reference to God in the first quotation (6:16c) taken from Lev 26:11, and (3) the father-image prevalent in 6:18.[128]

Summary

It is hardly unusual that Paul, a Jew schooled in his faith from childhood, would quote Old Testament Yahweh texts and apply them to God. It is also a fact not without christological significance.

Since Paul did not hesitate to apply Old Testament Yahweh texts to Jesus as well as to God, he apparently understood that an underlying unity existed between them which transcended function to encompass aspects of nature, being, name, and essence. On the other hand, since he did not refer all Yahweh texts to Jesus and in some contexts retained these as descriptions of God, he also envisioned a distinction between them. It is thus impossible to say he fully identified or distinguished them. Furthermore, it is improper to claim, as Robin Scroggs has done, that Paul never identfied Christ with God in any substantial way.[129]

This investigation reveals that Paul referred Yahweh texts to God in the following contexts: (1) justification and faith-righteousness (Rom 4:7-8), (2) divine wisdom and sovereignty (Rom 11:34; 1 Cor 3:20), (3) the Fatherhood of God (2 Cor 6:18), and particularly (4) the

---

[125.] The HT of 2 Sam 7:8 reads אמר יהוה צבאות.

[126.] *Contra* Joachim Gnilka, "2 Cor 6:14-7:1 in the Light of the Qumran Texts and the Testaments of the Twelve Patriarchs," in *Paul and Qumran: Studies in New Testament Exegesis*, ed. Jerome Murphy-O'Connor (London: Chapman, 1968), 53, who considered it a "spontaneous creation" by the writer.

[127.] Foerster, *TDNT*, 3:1087; and Cerfaux, "Kyrios," 177.

[128.] Interestingly, the emphasis in Paul is not God's Fatherhood of all but God's Fatherhood of Jesus. See A. W. Wainwright, *The Trinity in the New Testament* (London: S.P.C.K., 1962), 41-50. On the relationship between God as Father and the Lord Jesus Christ see pp. 63-69.

[129.] Scroggs, *Christology*, 52.

relationship of Jews and Gentiles to God's saving plan in Christ as the true people of God (Rom 9:27, 29; 15:9, 11).

Yahweh Texts with Christ As Referent

Attention must now be focused upon instances in which Paul quoted Old Testament Yahweh texts and applied them to Christ via the κύριος predicate. The question arises, however: Did Paul know that the κύριος texts were, in Hebrew, Yahweh texts? Since Paul never addressed this question directly, no definitive answer may be given. Such a question, of course, is contingent upon his acquaintance with the Hebrew texts. In Phil 3:5 Paul claimed that he was a "Hebrew born of Hebrews." One may interpret this statement to mean that he was familiar with the Hebrew language and, given first-century educational opportunities for Jewish boys, possibly even the Hebrew scriptures. Also although Paul's quotations demonstrate an affinity generally with the LXX, some quotations bear a greater resemblance to the Hebrew text.[130] These two factors indicate that Paul may well have been acquainted with the Hebrew scriptures, but it does not necessarily follow that he knew that his κύριος texts were Yahweh texts. Nevertheless, other factors in Paul's letters indicate that he did. (1) Although κύριος is primarily a christological title in Paul's letters, he made God the referent to several κύριος texts as demonstrated in the first part of this chapter. (2) One phrase in the Philippian hymn (2:9) proclaims that at the exaltation God bestowed upon Jesus "the name which is above every name" (τὸ ὄνομα τὸ ὑπὲρ πᾶν ὄνομα). Since an allusion to an Old Testament Yahweh text follows this phrase (from Isa 45:23) and since the confession "Jesus Christ is Lord" (κύριος Ἰησοῦς Χριστός) climaxes the hymn, it is likely that "the name which is above every name" (= κύριος) refers to Yahweh, the unspeakable name of the Old Testament God.[131] (3) In 2 Tim 2:19 Paul appears to "correct" the LXX with his quotation of Num 16:5.

Num 16:5 [HT]: וידע יהוה את-אשר-לו
Num 16:5 [LXX]: ἔγνω ὁ θεὸς τοὺς ὄντας αὐτοῦ
2 Tim 2:19: ἔγνω ὁ κύριος τοὺς ὄντας αὐτοῦ

[130.] Rom 11:35 [Job 41:4]; 1 Cor 3:19 [Job 5:12-13]; 2 Cor 8:15 [Exod 16:18]; 2 Tim 2:19 [Num 16:5].

[131.] Hurtado, *One God*, 97. See also Fitzmyer, *A Wandering Aramean*, 119-23.

While the LXX renders יהוה with θεός, Paul's quotation in 2 Tim 2:19 demonstrates affinity with the HT by translating יהוה with κύριος. This suggests not only that Paul was familiar with the HT but also that he knew κύριος to be a more adequate translation of יהוה than θεός. These instances within Paul's letters intimate, therefore, that he knew the correlation between the divine name (יהוה) and κύριος in the LXX passages he quoted.

"Calling upon the Name of the Lord"—Rom 10:13

Context. In Romans 9-11, a passage dedicated to the status of Israel in God's plan in light of the inclusion of the Gentiles, Paul contrasted righteousness based on faith (9:30, ἐκ πίστεως) with righteousness based on the law (9:31, εἰς νόμον; 9:32, ἐξ ἔργων).[132] Throughout these verses he quoted frequently from the Old Testament to demonstrate that faith-righteousness is taught therein. Since Rom 10:13 is a crucial text in this discussion, a thorough examination of the context is in order to discover the overall meaning of the passage.

In Rom 10:8 Paul cited Deut 30:14 on the accessibility of the "word" (τὸ ῥῆμα): "the word is near you, in your mouth and in your heart" (author's translation). He explained this text in a manner characteristic of Qumran exegesis: "(τοῦτ' ἔστιν) that is, the word of faith which we preach."[133] In 10:9-12 he described the content of this word of faith in terms of Jesus' Lordship and resurrection, two potent Pauline emphases.

Despite the opinion of some, the ὅτι-clause which begins 10:9 cannot be classified either as causal or recitative.[134] Paul is both describing the content of his preaching[135] and explaining further the

---

[132]. Jacque Dupont, "'Le Seigneur de tous' (Ac 10:6; Rm 10:12): Arrière-fond scripturaire d'une formule christologique," in *Tradition and Interpretation in the New Testament: Essays in Honor of E. Earle Ellis*, ed. Gerald F. Hawthorne and Otto Betz (Grand Rapids: Eerdmans, 1987), 229-30.

[133]. 1QpHab 5.6-8; 6.8; 7.3-5; 10.2-4; and 12.2-10. See James D. G. Dunn, "'Righteousness from the Law' and 'Righteousness from Faith': Paul's Interpretation of Scripture in Romans 10:1-10," in *Tradition and Interpretation in the New Testament: Essays in Honor of E. Earle Ellis*, ed. Gerald F. Hawthorne and Otto Betz (Grand Rapids: Eerdmans, 1987), 216-18.

[134]. *Contra* Käsemann, *Romans*, 291, who classified it recitative; also *contra* Cranfield, *Romans*, 2:26, who classified it causal, although he admitted the other possibility.

[135]. William Sanday and Arthur C. Headlam, *A Critical and Exegetical*

Deut 30:14 citation. This is clearly seen when he picks up the phrases "in your mouth" and "in your heart" in 10:9 in the exact order they appear in the Old Testament text.[136] Paul wrote: "If you confess with your mouth (ἐν τῷ στόματί σου) 'Jesus is Lord' and believe in your heart (ἐν τῇ καρδίᾳ σου) that God raised him from the dead, you shall be saved" (Rom 10:9, author's translation).

The confession "Jesus is Lord" (κύριον Ἰησοῦν), employed by Paul here and elsewhere,[137] was rather well-fixed within early Christianity. It arose not in light of persecution[138] but most likely to meet liturgical needs in the churches,[139] perhaps in baptism[140] or worship.[141]

Paul used this confession here and with a slightly different word order in 2 Cor 4:5 tying it closely to his preaching and the believer's response. In Rom 10:9 he affirmed that salvation is promised to those who "confess" (ὁμολογήσῃς) with their mouths "Jesus is Lord." Yet, in 1 Cor 12:3 he maintained that "no one can say (εἰπεῖν) 'Jesus is Lord' except by the Holy Spirit." Likewise, in Phil 2:11, he proclaimed that at the parousia every tongue will "confess (ἐξομολογήσηται) that Jesus Christ is Lord, to the glory of God the Father." In each of these cases, he acknowledged that the expression is something "said" or "confessed."

Evidently, this spoken expression formed the foundation of Paul's evangelistic proclamation and the expected response a believer would make to that message. It probably emerged "from the earliest stratum of Christian conviction."[142]

Commentary on the Epistle to the Romans, ICC (New York: Charles Scribner's Sons, 1920), 290, understood the subject of the "word of faith" to be the person of Christ and the resurrection.

[136.] Lagrange, *Romains*, 258, commenting that Paul followed the order of the Mosaic text, said: "c'est la raison donné par tous." Otherwise see Käsemann, *Romans*, 290.

[137.] 1 Cor 12:3; 2 Cor 4:5; Phil 2:11; Col 2:6; 3:24 (τῷ κυρίῳ Χριστῷ).

[138.] *Contra* Cullmann, *Earliest Christian Confessions*, 28-29, who understood the confession in light of the *anathema* in 1 Cor 12:3.

[139.] Lagrange, *Romains*, 253; and Käsemann, *Romans*, 291.

[140.] Cranfield, *Romans*, 2:527; and Bultmann, *Theology*, 1:81, 312.

[141.] Käsemann, *Romans*, 291. Whether it represented an acclamation of the Church or a confession is not germane to this discussion; however, acclamation implies confession. For a discussion on the differences between acclamation and confession, see Goppelt, *Theology*, 2:80.

Parallel to the confession of Jesus' Lordship in Rom 10:9 is the belief in the resurrection, as indicated by the phrase "that God raised him from the dead."[143] As demonstrated above,[144] the resurrection formed a key component in Paul's κύριος Christology. Therefore, in 10:9 Paul taught that those who confess his Lordship in the context of believing in the resurrection will be saved.

In 10:10 Paul reversed the order of the verbs as found in 10:9 to form a chiastic structure (ὁμολογήσῃς . . . πιστεύσῃς . . . πιστεύεται . . . ὁμολογεῖται)[145] and returned to his theme that righteousness by faith is superior to righteousness based on works.[146] The key-word therefore is faith (πιστεύεται), for Paul is defending a righteousness based on faith. This is confirmed by the Old Testament text, containing the word "faith," which Paul cited in 10:11 (Isa 28:16).[147]

With this quotation he supported the maxim in 10:10 that faith leads to righteousness.[148] He introduced the citation with an introductory formula, "for the scripture says" (λέγει γὰρ ἡ γραφή), and returned to a passage he quoted earlier in 9:33 in the same context. This time, however, he added πᾶς ("everyone") as his own interpretive commentary (midrash pesher) contributing to his concept of the universality of the gospel.[149]

[142.] Longenecker, *Christology*, 127; cf. Kramer, *Christ, Lord, Son*, 65.

[143.] This phrase also includes the message of Christ crucified (Gal 3:1; 1 Cor 1:23; 15:3-5). Käsemann, *Romans*, 291. The aorist indicative verb, ἤγειρεν, indicates the unique, once-for-all act. Cranfield, *Romans*, 2:530.

[144.] See pp. 53-59.

[145.] A. T. Robertson, *A Grammar of the Greek New Testament in the Light of Historical Research*, 2d ed. (New York: Hodder & Stoughton, 1915), 392, 820, suggested that the change from a second-person active verb form to an impersonal third-person passive form may state these truths effectively in terms of a principle.

[146.] Käsemann, *Romans*, 291, believed the word δικαιοσύνη indicates eschatological justification since salvation for Paul is primarily future. He went on to say that the real issue is not individual faith but the confession of the believing community. However, is not the dichotomy between universality and individuality more imagined than real? Paul could not conceive of one without the other.

[147.] Note the explanatory use of γάρ. Cranfield, *Romans*, 2:531.

[148.] Ellis, *Paul's Use*, 164-65. "Scripture" (γραφή) may indicate not only the content of a particular passage, but also the unified voice of scripture as a whole (p. 21).

[149.] Ibid., 14-15, 139; idem, *Prophecy*, 152-53, 174; see also Dupont, "'Le Seigneur de tous,'" 229-30. Cranfield, *Romans*, 2:531, said the addition of πᾶς "makes explicit

The context of the quoted passage (Isa 28:16) is the stone image found frequently in the New Testament,[150] usually with christological import. It reads: הַמַּאֲמִין לֹא יָחִישׁ.[151] When translators rendered it in Greek, they added ἐπ' αὐτῷ in an effort to make the meaning more explicit and altered the verbal idea with the Greek καταισχυνθῇ ("to be disappointed").[152]

Paul cited the LXX, changing the verb tense to accomodate his eschatological outlook.[153] In 9:33 he quoted the same text with αὐτῷ referring to Christ. It seems likely that it should refer to him here as well.[154] Nevertheless, by it Paul indicated that those who believe in Christ will not suffer disappointment at the parousia, the implication being that those who depend upon works-righteousness will.

In 10:12 Paul expounded the universality implicit in the word "everyone" (πᾶς, 10:11). He stated: "For there is no distinction between Jew and Greek; the same Lord is Lord of all and bestows his riches upon all who call upon him" (cf. Rom 3:22, 29; and Gal 3:28). Again, he returned to the κύριος predicate referred to earlier in the confession of 10:9 with the phrase: ὁ γὰρ αὐτὸς κύριος πάντων ("the same Lord is Lord of all"). Since κύριος refers to Jesus in 10:9, he probably had Jesus in mind here also.[155]

Paul described the κύριος as bestowing riches upon all who call on him. He frequently spoke of divine "riches" which come to the faithful.[156] The important phrase here, however, for the present discussion is "all who call upon him" (πάντας τοὺς ἐπικαλουμένους αὐτόν).

The verb ἐπικαλέω was well established in Greek literature for invoking a god in prayer.[157] It is found in the LXX with a similar

---

what is implicit in his understanding of the verse."

[150.] Matt 21:42; Luke 20:17; Eph 2:20; 2 Tim 2:19; and 1 Pet 2:4.

[151.] "He who believes will not be in haste."

[152.] In the active and middle voices this verb carries the idea "to put to shame"; in the passive, however, it means "to be disappointed." BAGD, "καταισχύνω," 410.

[153.] From aorist, passive, subjunctive form, καταισχυνθῇ, to a future, passive, indicative form, καταισχυνθήσεται.

[154.] Kreitzer, *Jesus and God*, 124; and Cranfield, *Romans*, 2:531.

[155.] Cranfield, *Romans*, 2:531; and Murray, *Romans*, 2:55.

[156.] See, e.g., Rom 2:4; 9:23; Phil 4:19; Eph 2:4, 7; 3:8. Käsemann, *Romans*, 292, thought "riches" refer to God's eschatological grace.

meaning as petitioners call upon Yahweh.[158] In the New Testament it is used in reference to Christ, not God.[159] Although it can be understood to include elements of worship, adoration, and obedience, it primarily signified prayer. Evidently, it indicates that Paul thought believers should offer prayers to the Lord Jesus who would respond by bestowing on them divine riches.[160]

Text. The last quotation in this chain,[161] which is at the same time an Old Testament Yahweh text, occurs in 10:13. It reads: πᾶς γὰρ ὃς ἂν ἐπικαλέσηται τὸ ὄνομα κυρίου σωθήσεται ("For 'every one who calls upon the name of the Lord will be saved'"). It summarizes Paul's argument in 10:9-12, for it contains elements of universality (πᾶς), Christology (κύριος), soteriology (σωθήσεται), and invocation (ἐπικαλέσηται). This final idea, found in 10:12, sparked Paul's use of Joel 2:32 here, for in Rom 10:12 and 10:13 it appears as a key-word.

Originally, Joel 2:32 promised deliverance for a remnant of Israel prior to the onset of the eschatological Day of the Lord (יוֹם יהוה). It suggested that the remnant would come not only from Jerusalem, but also from among loyal Diaspora Jews. Some have thought that its writer would have been astonished by Paul's application of it in his Roman letter;[162] nevertheless, in light of God's recent act in Christ, which tore down the wall of hostility (τὸ μεσότοιχον τοῦ φραγμοῦ, Eph 2:14) and established "one new man" (ἕνα καινὸν ἄνθρωπον, Eph 2:15), Paul understood it to teach the inclusion of the believing Gentiles along with believing Jews. Therefore, he could say without hesitation, upon the basis of scripture, that everyone, both Jew and Gentile, who calls upon the name of the Lord Jesus will be saved.

Paul introduced the quotation from Joel 2:32 [LXX, Joel 3:5] with the particle, γάρ.[163] He quoted "virtually verbatim"[164] the LXX, which rendered the Hebrew[165] rather precisely. He omitted only two

---

[157.] K. L. Schmidt, "ἐπικαλέω," *TDNT*, 3:496-500.

[158.] Gen 13:4; 21:33; 26:25; Ps 78:6; 79:18; 104:1; 118:4; Isa 64:6; Jer 10:25; Zeph 3:9; Zech 13:9; and Joel 2:32.

[159.] Rom 10:12; 1 Cor 1:2; Acts 2:21; 9:14, 21; 22:16; and 2 Tim 2:22.

[160.] *Contra* Käsemann, *Romans*, 292, who denied that prayers were offered to Jesus in early Christianity. He related the word primarily to preaching and confession (thereby worship).

[161.] Ellis, *Paul's Use*, 186.

[162.] John M. P. Smith, William Hayes Ward, and J. Brewer, *A Critical and Exegetical Commentary on Micah, Zephaniah, Nahum, Habakkuk, Obadiah and Joel*, ICC (New York: Charles Scribner's Sons, 1911), 124-25.

words, καὶ ἔσται ("and it shall be").[166] This suggests that Paul saw "the Day" as having already dawned in the new age inaugurated by Jesus' death and resurrection. In contrast the Old Testament writer still awaited it.

Conclusion. Several important factors indicate that Paul applied this Old Testament Yahweh text to Jesus.[167] (1) Whereas the bulk of Romans 9-11 is theocentric, this portion of Paul's argument is primarily christocentric as indicated by his christological use of the Old Testament. In 9:33 he quoted Isa 28:16, alluding also to Isa 8:14, on the scandal associated with the "stone." The Jews, he said, had stumbled over the stumbling stone, whom he depicted as Christ.

From the context of Isa 8:14, it is clear that Yahweh (יהוה) is "the stone of stumbling" (λίθον προσκόμματος). Having forecast the doom that will come upon Israel by God's hand, Isaiah wrote (8:13-15):

> But the Lord of hosts, him you shall regard as holy; let him be your fear, and let him be your dread. And he will become a sanctuary, and a stone of offence, and a rock of stumbling to both houses of Israel, a trap and a snare to the inhabitants of Jerusalem. And many shall stumble thereon; they shall fall and be broken; they shall be snared and taken.

When Paul quoted these words, he applied them to Christ,[168] whom he referred to elsewhere as a stumbling block to the Jews,[169] and thereby identified him with Yahweh. He quoted Isa 28:16 again—this time, however, with no reference to Isa 8:14—in 10:11 with the same christological intent, for he had just stated that those who believe (πιστεύσῃς) that God raised Jesus from the dead will be saved.

[163.] Ellis, *Paul's Use*, 164-65, called it the introductory formula for this text.

[164.] Ibid., 151, 187; and Cerfaux, "Kyrios," 179.

[165.] The Hebrew reads (3:5): והיה כל אשר־יקרא בשם יהוה ימלט ("and it shall be that all who call upon the name of the Lord shall be delivered"—author's translation).

[166.] Note the parallel in Acts 2:21.

[167.] Cerfaux, "Kyrios," 179; and Kreitzer, *Jesus and God*, 114, 124.

[168.] Kreitzer, *Jesus and God*, 114, 124.

[169.] 1 Cor 1:23: ἡμεῖς δὲ κηρύσσομεν Χριστὸν ἐσταυρωμένον, Ἰουδαίοις μὲν σκάνδαλον, ἔθνεσιν δὲ μωρίαν.

Likewise, in 10:6-7 Paul took another Old Testament text (Deut 30:12, 14) and explained it in terms of Christ.[170] He wrote:

> But the righteousness based on faith says, Do not say in your heart, "Who will ascend into heaven?" (that is [τοῦτ' ἔστιν], to bring Christ down) or "Who will descend into the abyss?" (that is [τοῦτ' ἔστιν], to bring Christ up from the dead).

While these verses originally referred to the Law, Paul redirected them to refer to Christ, who is the end of the Law (10:4).

(2) In addition to the christocentric nature of Paul's discussion, clear references to the resurrection also suggest that κύριος in 10:13 refers to Christ. As stated above, Paul explained Deut 30:12-14 in christological terms. To the question, "Who will descend into the abyss?" he explained "that is to bring Christ up from the dead" (τοῦτ' ἔστιν Χριστὸν ἐκ νεκρῶν ἀναγαγεῖν). Likewise, he expressed the content of his preaching in terms of a christological confession and belief in the resurrection (10:9). As indicated earlier,[171] he thought that the title κύριος now belonged to Christ upon the basis of the resurrection (Phil 2:9-11). It therefore seems probable that this emphasis on the resurrection facilitated the application of this Old Testament Yahweh text to Jesus.

(3) The relationship of these verses to eschatological salvation also suggests this. It was proposed earlier that Paul altered the scripture texts he expounded in conformity to his eschatological position. He related salvation ultimately to the *eschaton* as indicated by the future tense verbs σωθήσῃ (10:9), καταισχυνθήσεται (10:11), and σωθήσεται (10:13).[172] In chapter two it was indicated that Paul related his doctrine of last things to the person of Jesus Christ above all with the κύριος title. Since the quotation originally had to do with the eschatological "Day of the Lord" and since for Paul that "Day" had become the "Day of the Lord Jesus Christ," it is therefore likely that eschatological considerations caused the apostle to refer this Yahweh text to Jesus.

(4) Further evidence that Paul applied the κύριος predicate in Rom 10:13 to the Lord Jesus lay in the christological confession in 10:9. He characterized his preaching and the believers' response with

---

[170] On the difficulty of Paul's understanding of this text see Dunn, "Rom 10:1-10," 216-28.

[171] See the discussion above, pp. 53-59.

[172] Kim, *Origin*, 286-88.

the confession, "Jesus is Lord" (κύριον Ἰησοῦν). He then went on to quote Joel 2:32 [LXX, 3:5], a text which contains the κύριος predicate. It seems likely, therefore, that he understood Jesus to be the κύριος, not only of the Christian confession, but also of Joel 2:32. The implication of Paul's application of this Yahweh text to Jesus is significant for it suggests that he identified Jesus with Yahweh.

How Paul was able to make this identification and yet remain a monotheist must be dealt with later. Nevertheless, in light of the christocentric focus of Rom 9:33-10:13, its emphasis upon the resurrection, its relation to Paul's eschatology, and the confession that "Jesus is Lord," there can be little doubt that in quoting Joel 2:32 Paul referred this Old Testament Yahweh text to the Lord Jesus Christ.

"Every Knee Shall Bow"—Rom 14:11

Context. Paul turned the discussion from the coming of the Day of the Lord (Rom 13:11-14) to exhortations addressed to the "weak" and the "strong" of the Roman church to welcome and not disparage one another (Rom 14:1-15:13). Though he had no personal knowledge of the situation in Rome, he either heard or suspected that the factious spirit so prevalent at Corinth (1 Corinthians 8-10) was disturbing the Roman community as well.[173] He identified the would-be "weak" Christians as scrupulous persons who distinguished one day from another (14:5) and abstained from eating meat or drinking wine (14:2, 21). The strong, on the other hand, had no such rules or regulations.

Whereas some assume that in these verses Paul referred to "the mutual disparagement of Jew and Gentile,"[174] a theme already espoused in Romans 9-11, others see Paul speaking only in the most general terms.[175] Nevertheless, Paul concluded this section by repeating the opening exhortation, Διὸ προσλαμβάνεσθε ἀλλήλους ("Therefore, welcome one another"), along with a statement regarding the "circumcised" and Old Testament proofs of God's work among the Gentiles. This indicates a close connection between the Jew and Gentile problem once again.

[173.] Käsemann, *Romans*, 364-65.

[174.] Barrett, *Romans*, 255-57; and Kim, *Origin*, 310. This appears to fit the argument except for the abstinence from wine, which was not a Jewish custom.

[175.] Wayne A. Meeks, "Judgment and the Brother: Romans 14:1-15:13," in *Tradition and Interpretation in the New Testament: Essays in Honor of E. Earle Ellis*, ed. Gerald W. Hawthorne and Otto Betz (Grand Rapids: Eerdmans, 1987), 290.

Having encouraged the strong (evidently) to welcome the weak in faith (14:1),[176] Paul disavowed the kind of judging which often takes place in religious communities among those who do and do not adhere to given moral regulations (14:1-4). Accordingly, he believed both groups acted in their own minds in genuine honor and service to the Lord (14:5-6). He continued in 14:8 saying: "if we live, we live to the Lord, and if we die, we die to the Lord; so then, whether we live or whether we die, we are the Lord's (τοῦ κυρίου ἐσμέν)." Clearly he thought Christians should not engage in judging one another since all they do, they do to their Lord to whom they belong. Whereas Paul typically connected "belongingness" to the title "Christ," he associated it here with κύριος.[177]

Paul identified the κύριος to whom believers belong as Christ in a verse expressing the purpose (εἰς τοῦτο γὰρ . . . ἵνα) of his death and resurrection. He wrote (14:9): εἰς τοῦτο γὰρ Χριστὸς ἀπέθανεν καὶ ἔζησεν, ἵνα καὶ νεκρῶν καὶ ζώντων κυριεύσῃ ("For to this end Christ died and lived again, that he might be Lord both of the dead and of the living").[178] Paul typically spoke of Jesus' resurrection utilizing other verbs which more clearly denote "raising" such as ἀνέστη (1 Thess 4:14) or ἐγήγερται (1 Cor 15:3; cf. 2 Cor 5:14-15). Here, however, he replaced his customary expressions for resurrection with ἔζησεν.[179]

While it may not be evident at first why he made such an alteration, nevertheless the location of ἔζησεν after ἀπέθανεν can only refer to Jesus' resurrected life.[180] Moreover, if one takes this verb as an ingressive aorist, it denotes a specific act and may be translated "came to life."[181]

---

[176] Whereas in 14:1 he placed the burden of welcoming upon the strong, in 15:7 he made it a reciprocal responsibility.

[177] Rom 1:6; Romans 6; 1 Cor 3:23; 6:12-20 (both "Christ" and "Lord"); 7:22-24; 15:23; 2 Cor 10:7; Gal 3:29; 5:24. E. P. Sanders, *Paul and Palestinian Judaism* (Philadelphia: Fortress, 1977), 461; and Furnish, *Theology and Ethics*, 179.

[178] The phrasing of this text, namely, Jesus died and rose again to be Lord of the living and the dead, is reminiscent of Paul's reference to him as "the firstborn from the dead" (πρωτότοκος ἐκ τῶν νεκρῶν) in Col 1:18.

[179] This departure from Paul's normal manner of expression caused great consternation among copyists in later centuries. Influenced perhaps by 1 Thess 4:14, some added ἀνέστη to the already compound verb; others replaced ἔζησεν with ἀνέστη to render the meaning more precise. Metzger, *Textual Commentary*, 531.

[180] Cranfield, *Romans*, 2:707.

Perhaps Paul altered his pattern to create a chiastic structure and compare the believer's life and death with Christ's death and life after the resurrection in 14:8b and 9a:

8b ζῶμεν . . . ἀποθνῄσκωμεν
9a ἀπέθανεν . . . ἔζησεν

Another reason for this change may be that he desired to link this verse to the Old Testament quotation in 14:11, which included the key-word ζῶ, as will be discussed below. In any case, Paul believed that Christ died and came to life again so that he might be established as Lord (κυριεύσῃ) over the dead and the living (νεκρῶν καὶ ζώντων).[182]

Against the background of Christ's ruling as Lord (14:7-9), Paul returned to the issue at hand, namely, the tendency of one to pass judgment on another. In good rhetorical style he asked two questions: the first directed to the weak, the second to the strong.[183] He followed these questions with an appeal to the coming judgment of God:

> Why do you pass judgment on your brother? Or you, why do you despise your brother? For we shall all stand before the judgment seat of God.[184]

[181.] Käsemann, *Romans*, 372.

[182.] On this text Bruce, *Romans*, 246, wrote: "By virtue of His death He is Lord of the dead; by virtue of His resurrection He is Lord of the living." Such a distinction skews the true picture of Paul's teaching. He viewed Christ's death and resurrection not as separate happenings, but as one great eschatological event which inaugurates the Kingdom of Christ (Col 1:13). Barrett, *Romans*, 260, argued correctly that Paul was not interested in making a theological distinction between the two events; he was interested primarily in "rhetorical balance." Paul understood Jesus' death to possess power only because of its sequel. Thus, only as these two events stand together do they possess salvific power and efficacy. Beker, *Paul*, 199.

[183.] Cranfield, *Romans*, 2:709, noted that this reverses the order of 14:3.

[184.] Some see in Paul's words similarities to Jesus' statements in Matt 7:1 (e.g., Davies, *Paul*, 138; and Longenecker, *Paul*, 189). However, since such expressions were common in Judaism, this need not be the case. See Furnish, *Theology and Ethics*, 57-58. Gerald F. Hawthorne, "The Role of Christian Prophets in the Gospel Tradition," in *Tradition and Interpretation in the New Testament: Essays in Honor of E. Earle Ellis*, ed. Gerald F. Hawthorne and Otto Betz (Grand Rapids: Eerdmans, 1987), 126, turned the argument around and suggested that Paul, a Christian prophet who expressed the words of the risen Lord, may have been the source for material traditionally associated with Jesus' earthly ministry.

Stated in this way, Paul intimated that judging one another was inconceiveable in light of the fact that all will stand before God's judgment seat (τῷ βήματι τοῦ θεοῦ).[185]

Text. Paul offered scriptural support for his statement in 14:10 that all must appear before the judgment seat of God. He introduced the quotation with γέγραπται γάρ, a formula which bears similarities to introductory formulas for explicit quotations at Qumran.[186] Quoting primarily from Isa 45:23, he wrote (14:11):

ζῶ ἐγώ, λέγει κύριος, ὅτι ἐμοὶ κάμψει πᾶν γόνυ καὶ πᾶσα γλῶσσα ἐξομολογήσεται τῷ θεῷ

"As I live, says the Lord, every knee shall bow to me and every tongue shall confess to God" (author's translation)

The Greek text from which he drew probably read:

κατ' ἐμαυτοῦ ὀμνύω . . . ὅτι ἐμοὶ κάμψει πᾶν γόνυ καὶ ἐξομολογήσεται[187] πᾶσα γλῶσσα τῷ θεῷ

"I swear by myself . . . every knee shall bow to me and every tongue shall confess to God" (author's translation)

The Hebrew text reads:

כי־לי תכרע כל־ברך תשבע כל־לשון

Two differences between Paul's quotation and the Greek rendering may be noticed: (1) the substitution of ζῶ ἐγώ, λέγει κύριος for κατ' ἐμαυτοῦ ὀμνύω and (2) the reversal of the verb and subject from ἐξομολογήσεται πᾶσα γλῶσσα to πᾶσα γλῶσσα ἐξομολογήσεται. Each will be briefly considered.

Why did Paul substitute ζῶ ἐγώ, λέγει κύριος for κατ' ἐμαυτοῦ ὀμνύω? Cranfield suggested that since Paul quoted from memory, he inadvertently substituted one formula, which was more familiar, for

---

[185.] Käsemann, *Romans*, 372. The term βῆμα ("judgment seat") occurs twice in Paul with reference to eschatological judgment: (1) with reference to God in Rom 14:10 and (2) with reference to Christ in 2 Cor 5:10. There is, however, no substantial difference for the apostle. The original reading θεοῦ is supported by the best witnesses. Evidently some copyists rather early substituted Χριστοῦ for θεοῦ due to the influence of 2 Cor 5:10. Metzger, *Textual Commentary*, 531.

[186.] CD 11.20; כי כתוב "for it was written."

[187.] While some manuscripts read ὀμεῖται πᾶσα γλῶσσα τὸν θεόν (including B and the Majority text) instead of ἐξομολογήσεται πᾶσα γλῶσσα τῷ θεῷ (A Q), Paul's use of similar wording in Phil 2:11 suggests that his manuscripts of the Greek OT contained the latter. However, Ellis, *Prophecy*, 178, suggested that a Targum may be the source of the rendering "confess" (ὀμεῖται).

the other.[188] But could there not have been theological reasons for the alteration? Does not Paul's ability to quote verbatim and his tendency to alter texts in other places with theological intent militate against a mere slip of the memory here?[189]

Perhaps Paul consciously replaced the oath-like phrase, κατ' ἐμαυτοῦ ὀμνύω ("By myself I have sworn"), of Isa 45:23 with the similar, ζῶ ἐγώ, λέγει κύριος ("as I live, says the Lord"), derived from Isa 49:18 or elsewhere,[190] "with the clear intention of identifying 'the Lord' in the quotation with the Lord Christ who 'lived again' . . . and is the Lord both of the dead and the living (verse 9)."[191] Thus, Paul may have merged these quotations so that κύριος in the phrase ζῶ ἐγώ, λέγει κύριος ([HT] חי-אני נאם-יהוה) would be identified with Christ who died and "lived again" (ἔζησεν) and reigns as Lord over the realm of the living and the dead. This hypothesis accounts for the unusual use of ἔζησεν to refer to the resurrection as well as for the substitution of one oath for the other.

The second difference between Paul's quotation and the LXX may also reinforce this theory. It concerns the reversal of the verb and subject from ἐξομολογήσεται πᾶσα γλῶσσα to πᾶσα γλῶσσα ἐξομολογήσεται. It may reflect Paul's proclivity towards chiasmus:

κάμψει	a
πᾶν γόνυ	b
πᾶσα γλῶσσα	(b)
ἐξομολογήσεται	(a)

Moreover, perhaps it also reveals Paul's attempt to disrupt the parallelism which would naturally identify both phrases with God (τῷ θεῷ) in the second line. It would therefore indicate that Paul

---

[188.] Cranfield, *Romans*, 2:710; Ellis, *Paul's Use*, 109, noted that there are four λέγει κύριος quotations in Paul (Rom 12:9; 14:11; 1 Cor 14:21; and 2 Cor 6:16ff.). In each case the phrase appears to be an important component to the quotation and may have already been present in the text when it was quoted by the writer. Ellis opined that these may indicate the work of early Christian prophets. Idem, "Λέγει κύριος Quotations in the New Testament," chap. in *Prophecy and Hermeneutics in Early Christianity* (Grand Rapids: Eerdmans, 1978), 182-87; also idem, "The Role of Christian Prophets in Acts," chap. in *Prophecy and Hermeneutics in Early Christianity* (Grand Rapids: Eerdmans, 1978), 137.

[189.] Ellis, *Paul's Use*, 14-15, 114-49.

[190.] E.g., Num 14:28; Jer 22:24; Ezek 5:11.

[191.] Matthew Black, *Romans*, NCB (Greenwood, SC: Attic Press, 1973), 167; idem, "Christological Use," 8.

meant for the first phrase to be associated with Christ (i.e., the bowing of the knee) and the second with God (i.e., confession).

Paul's argument would then proceed as follows. Stop disputing and judging one another; rather receive one another. Everyone, whether he adheres to certain rules and regulations or not, is governed by his own mind. He eats and observes special days in honor of the Lord Jesus, giving thanks to God. If he lives, he lives to the Lord Jesus; if he dies, he dies to the Lord Jesus—all because he belongs to the Lord Jesus. This is why Christ died and lived again, to be Lord of the living and the dead. Stop judging and despising your brother (who also belongs to the Lord), because all of us shall stand before the judgment seat of God. Remember what the scripture says: "As I live again, says the Lord Jesus, every knee shall bow to me and every tongue shall confess[192] (within the context of the judgment seat) to God". Each one shall give an account of himself.[193] Paul thus had a two-fold argument against judging and despising one's brother: (1) belongingness to the Lord Jesus Christ and (2) knowledge that the judgment seat of God awaits each believer.

Conclusion. In addition to the clear identification of Christ as Lord in 14:9 and the verbal linkage between ζῶ (14:11) and ἔζησεν (14:9), several other reasons may be given to support the thesis that Paul applied the first line of this Yahweh text to Jesus via the κύριος predicate.

(1) In the Philippian hymn (2:6-11), Paul referred the same Old Testament text (Isa 45:23) to Jesus who is also identified there as κύριος. He wrote: "that at the name of Jesus *every knee should bow*, in heaven and on earth and under the earth, and *every tongue confess*

---

[192]. Black, "Christological Use," 8, argued that ἐξομολογήσεται should be translated "every tongue shall *praise* God." It is difficult to see how such a translation would fit into the judgment seat motif. It does, however, accord well with the idea of previous verses that believers observe (or do not observe) days and eat (or abstain from eating) in honor of the Lord (κυρίῳ) and give thanks to God (εὐχαριστεῖ τῷ θεῷ). Otto Michel, "ὁμολογέω," *TDNT*, 5:215, opined that the word "denotes the eschatological confession of sins which each must make before the judgment throne of God." Käsemann, *Romans*, 373, believed it means the acclamation that takes place in worship. As in the Old Testament, it means worshipers acknowledge God as Judge and Lord.

[193]. Good manuscripts (B F G 1739 1881) omit τῷ θεῷ. Nestle-Aland (26th edition) places it within brackets, revealing some uncertainty. It is easy to see why a copyist would add the words had they been originally absent, i.e., to clarify the referent of the verb. On the other hand, since τῷ θεῷ ends 14:11, it would be easy to see how a copyist might omit the same words at the end of 14:12. Metzger, *Textual Commentary*, 531-32.

that Jesus Christ is Lord to the glory of God the Father" (Phil 2:10-11). A more complete analysis of this text will be given later.

(2) Since Paul, as demonstrated earlier,[194] linked the resurrection above all with the christological title κύριος, the close association of this text with the resurrection may also confirm that Paul meant κύριος in the quotation to be understood as Jesus. He mentioned the resurrection directly in 14:9 (ἔζησεν). If the interpretation of the passage above is correct, then he mentioned it indirectly in the altered part of the quotation (ζῶ ἐγώ, λέγει κύριος).

(3) It was noted earlier that Paul used κύριος as a christological designation in ethical admonitions.[195] He traced this emphasis to his belief that Jesus presently reigns as Lord, a doctrine expressed in this passage by the phrase: ἵνα καὶ νεκρῶν καὶ ζώντων κυριεύσῃ ("that he might be Lord both of the dead and of the living"). He associated it also to a Christian's belonging to him, a theme also stated in this passage through the words: τοῦ κυρίου ἐσμέν ("we are the Lord's"). Since this passage had definite ethical import for the life of the Roman church and since κύριος was Paul's christological designation par excellence in ethical matters, it is reasonable to assume that he understood κύριος in the Yahweh text of 14:11 to be referring to Christ.

(4) Related to this is the fact, noted above,[196] that Paul used the κύριος predicate with reference to Christ particularly in view of the last things. Prior to this discussion against believers judging one another (14:1-15:13), he referred to the coming of the Day of the Lord (13:11-14)—understood to be the Lord Jesus Christ. He warned against behavior unbecoming to a Christian (13:12-13), which included quarreling and jealousy (μὴ ἔριδι καὶ ζήλῳ). Furthermore, he encouraged believers to put on the *Lord Jesus Christ*, making no effort to gratify fleshly desires. The connection between these ethical discussions should be considered. They are related, not separate. It is apparent that he grounded his appeal to receive and not judge or disparage one another upon the basis of the Lord's return. Since he comes again, Paul taught that Christians should welcome and not despise one another. Thus, it appears that Paul wrote Rom 14:1-15:13 with the expectation that Jesus would soon return.

[194.] See above, pp. 53-59.

[195.] See above, pp. 69-74.

[196.] See above, pp. 83-88.

This accords well with the appeal he made to eschatological judgment in 14:10-12. It also indicates that he treated fairly the context of Isa 45:23, since therein the Old Testament writer depicted the nations coming to bow before Yahweh in eschatological adoration.[197]

Taken individually, one of these arguments may not convince that Rom 14:11 is a Yahweh text which Paul applied to the Lord Jesus. But in concert with one another, (1) the clear statement of Christ's Lordship in 14:9, (2) the way Paul theologically altered the text, including the verbal linkage between ζῶ in 14:11 and ἔζησεν in 14:9, (3) the application of Isa 45:23 to Christ in Phil 2:11, (4) the ethical import of Paul's entire discussion, (5) the association of this passage with resurrection, and (6) judgment, indicate that this is in fact what Paul has done.[198]

"Boast in the Lord"—1 Cor 1:31 and 2 Cor 10:17

In both 1 Cor 1:31 and 2 Cor 10:17 Paul quoted an abbreviated version of Jer 9:24. On each occasion he appears to have applied this Yahweh text to Christ. Each will be considered in detail.

1 Cor 1:31

Context. Prompted by a report from Chloe's people that divisions existed in the Corinthian congregation (1:11), Paul addressed this problem in the beginning of 1 Corinthians (1:10-4:21). Encouraging them to agree and to do away with dissension, he confronted a church divided evidently around the teaching of certain outstanding personalities who served as rallying points for the different factions.[199]

---

[197] Ellis, *Paul's Use*, 124, called Paul's quotation in 14:11 "a definite eschatological quotation." Käsemann, *Romans*, 373. Kreitzer, *Jesus and God*, 107.

[198] *Contra* Cranfield, *Romans*, 2:710; also Cerfaux, "Kyrios," 176, who based his argument primarily upon (1) the parallelism of the quotation and (2) the use of the introductory formula. Against (1), it appears that Paul has consciously disrupted the parallelism to redirect the quotation as indicated above. Against (2), it seems Cerfaux begins with the premise that κύριος citations with an introductory formula refer to God while those without refer to Christ. While this may be true in some cases, it need not be true here and in 1 Cor 1:31, another Yahweh text which Paul applied to Christ.

[199] Although the exact nature of the problem in Corinth is difficult to ascertain, it appears to revolve around the term σοφία (wisdom). R. A. Horsley, "Wisdom of Word or Words of Wisdom in Corinth," *CBQ* 39 (1977): 232, suggesting it involved the style and the content of Apollos' ministry, wrote: "Through the latter's [Apollos'] ministry some of the Corinthians apparently had come to regard the (Christian) gospel as wisdom, the leaders as teachers of wisdom, and themselves as wise. This

Paul addressed the problem by appealing to the nature of the gospel, which he characterized as ὁ λόγος ὁ τοῦ σταυροῦ ("the word of the cross," 1:18) and Χριστὸν ἐσταυρωμένον ("Christ crucified," 1:23). The true gospel, he believed, contradicted human wisdom while at the same time establishing the wisdom of God. In rabbinic fashion he structured his argument around Old Testament texts and application. Ellis[200] posited the following structure:

1:18-31	Midrash
2:1-5	Application
2:6-16	Midrash
3:1-17	Application
3:18-20	Concluding texts

The section of his argument under consideration here (1:18-31) appears to be a proem midrash:

Opening text: 1:19 (Isa 29:14)
Exposition, with an allusion to Isa 19:11-12, on σοφία. God has rendered worldy wisdom (σοφία) foolishness and established his own wisdom (σοφία) in "Christ crucified." Christ is the wisdom (σοφία) and power of God. God has chosen the foolish, weak, and ignoble things to put to shame the wise, strong, and seemingly important things—by standards of worldly wisdom—so that no one may be able to boast (καυχήσηται) before God. Believers are "in

---

wisdom was, to be sure, 'like that of the Greeks,' a mixture of philosophy, religion and rhetoric. But this was understood by Apollos and others as Sophia, the Divine Teaching to be contemplated in Scriptures. Indeed Sophia had been understood for generations as the real focus and substance of Jewish religion by Hellenistic Jews such as Philo, and this *sophia* included eloquent speech as an important facet." Otherwise, Gordon Fee, *First Corinthians*, 49, saw the problem arising from Hellenistic influences in the church. He thought the key to understanding it involves contemporary itinerant philosophers, particularly sophists, who magnified rhetoric to the exclusion of content. The Corinthian church, he believed, viewed Paul, Apollos, and Peter as representatives of this movement and "their new-found faith as an expression of *sophia*—the divine *sophia*, to be sure, but *sophia* nonetheless." He considered this sufficient warrant for the division in the church.

[200.] Ellis, *Prophecy*, 214. The application sections, he observed, are evident by (1) the shift to past tense (2:1; 3:1), (2) personal and Corinthian references, (3) the absence of Old Testament citations, and (4) similar introductory language in 2:1 and 3:1.

Christ Jesus," who became wisdom for us: 1:19-30

Concluding text: 1:31 (Jer 9:24), with καυχᾶσθαι, the key word which connects the closing text with the exposition (1:29)[201]

With two references to the cross (1:18, 23) and two references to Christ as the wisdom of God[202] (1:24, 30), this exposition represents an outstanding effort in christological exegesis.

Paul referred to Christ as the "wisdom of God" in 1:24 and 1:30. In the former he combined it with the phrase, θεοῦ δύναμιν ("the power of God"), which is reminiscent of a similar phrase in Rom 1:16 describing the gospel. In the latter he altered it slightly to read: ὃς ἐγενήθη σοφία ἡμῖν ἀπὸ θεοῦ ("who has become wisdom for us from God"). In connection with this notion he portrayed the Christian life "in Christ Jesus" (ἐν Χριστῷ Ἰησοῦ). As demonstrated in chapter two, Paul used the "in Christ" formula to represent the indicative of the gospel, in particular Christ's death and resurrection as it inaugurated the new age. His use of it here thus connects it with previous verses which emphasize "Christ crucified" and the "word of the cross."[203]

[201.] Adapted from Ellis, *Prophecy*, 213, who believed good reasons exist for considering 1:18-31 a pre-formed midrash incorporated by Paul into his discussion. See also V. P. Branick, "Source and Redaction Analysis of 1 Corinthans 1-3," *JBL* 101 (1982), 251-69, who saw a midrashic pattern in this section, but said it fails to fit the context of the discussion. K. Bailey, "Recovering the Poetic Structure of I Cor. i.17-ii.2: A Study in Text and Commentary," *NovT* 17 (1975), 265-96, posited a thirteen-part chiastic structure for this section. Branick, "1 Corinthians 1-3," 257-58, however contended that Bailey's reconstruction forces Paul into a structure too rigid to be credible.

[202.] On Paul's Wisdom Christology see Dunn, *Christology*, 163-76; Ellis, *Prophecy*, 45-62; Hurtado, *One God*, 41-50; Davies, *Paul*, 163-76; and Kim, *Origin*, 115-26, 258. Although scholars are divided over the origin of the concept, Paul's heritage in Judaism appears to provide the most likely source. Jewish writers personified "Wisdom" as mediator between God and man, both in matters of salvation and creation (Prov 8:22-31; Wis 7:22-8:1; 9:1-7; Job 28:23-27; and Sir 24:3-12).

[203.] Paul further described "wisdom" employing three other metaphors: δικαιοσύνη (righteousness), ἁγιασμός (holiness or sanctification), and ἀπολύτρωσις (redemption). While "righteousness" often has ethical import, its use here suggests more forensic and therefore eschatological significance. In the end God will acquit those who are found in Christ. "Holiness" also carries ethical meaning, but here it emphasizes God's act of setting apart and establishing a people. "Redemption" is used widely in Paul as a metaphor depicting salvation (e.g., Rom 3:24; Col 1:14). Paul's explanation of Christ as divine wisdom in this passage thus has tremendous soteriological implications.

Text. Taking his cue from 1:28-29, which explains how God has put an end to boasting in human wisdom, Paul demonstrated the only true basis for boasting in 1:31 when he appealed to Jer 9:24 (LXX, 9:23). He introduced the citation with the formula, καθὼς γέγραπται ("as it is written"). He wrote (1 Cor 1:31): ὁ καυχώμενος ἐν κυρίῳ καυχάσθω ("Let the one who boasts, boast in the Lord."). Despite the use of an introductory formula, his quotation differs significantly from the LXX which reads:

ἀλλ' ἢ ἐν τούτῳ καυχάσθω ὁ καυχώμενος, συνίειν καὶ γινώσκειν ὅτι ἐγώ εἰμι κύριος ποιῶν ἔλεος καὶ κρίμα καὶ δικαιοσύνην ἐπὶ τῆς γῆς, ὅτι ἐν τούτοις τὸ θέλημά μου, λέγει κύριος.[204]

In 2 Cor 10:17 Paul quoted the same verse with the exact wording without an introductory formula. This may indicate that Paul's form of the Old Testament text existed as a standard abbreviation of the text and was not just an *ad hoc* rendering.[205]

Ἐν τούτῳ in the LXX version of Jer 9:23 is a prepositional phrase which, with the demonstrative pronoun, stands in the place of the rest of the text and gives the basis for boasting. Jeremiah taught that one should therefore boast only as he knows who the Lord (Yahweh) is and that he, by virtue of his will, exercises mercy, justice, and righteousness on the earth. Paul truncated this with the phrase ἐν κυρίῳ. Although the form of the quotation varies greatly, his use of it lies close to Jeremiah's intent.[206] This becomes increasingly evident when one considers v. 30 which describes Christ as God's wisdom for us, understood as righteousness, holiness, and redemption.

[204.] Jer 9:23, LXX: "But let the one who boasts, boast in this, that he understands and knows that I am the Lord, practicing mercy and justice and righteousness upon the earth, for my delight is in these things, says the Lord" (author's translation).

[205.] Cerfaux, "Kyrios," 183, postulated the existence of a florilegium. Ellis, *Paul's Use*, 22, noted that Jer 9:24 is quoted both with and without an introductory formula (1 Cor 1:31; 2 Cor 10:17) as is Hab 2:4 (Rom 1:17; Gal 3:11). The free rendering of Jer 9:24 indicates that the use of the introductory formula has little to do with the explicitness of a quotation. Cf. Munck, *Paul*, 145, who insinuated that the wording is Paul's.

[206.] Fee, *First Corinthians*, 87. Paul probably was acquainted with passages which speak of boasting "in God" (Ps 44:9 [43:9]; 56:10 [55:11]; Deut 10:21), "in the Lord" (Ps 56:10 [55:11]; 34:3 [33:3]). Cf. Sir 9:16; 10:22; 25:6. On Paul's use of Jer 9:23-24 see Josef Schreiner, "Jeremia 9,22.23 als Hintergrund des paulinischen 'Sich-Rühmens,'" in *Neues Testament und Kirche*, ed. J. Gnilka (Freiburg: Herder, 1974), 530-42.

Conclusion. As indicated by his description of Christ's work in 1:30, Paul quoted this Yahweh text (κύριος in LXX, יהוה in the Hebrew text) and applied it to Christ.[207] Arguing christologically in previous verses against human σοφία, he claimed that Christ had become God's σοφία in relation to man ("but to those who are called, both Jews and Greeks, Christ the power of God and the wisdom of God" in 1:24; ἡμῖν in 1:30). Thus, man's boasting before God (1:29) cannot be established upon the basis of worldly wisdom, power or birth, but only "in the Lord," that is, in what Christ accomplished through the cross (1:18, 23) for the salvation of man (1:30).

Paul spoke of boasting (καυχᾶσθαι) often as the basic attitude of the Jew toward their privileged status before God. He set it in contrast to the attitude of faith.[208] In Phil 3:3 he insisted that those who believe in Christ are the true circumcision. It is they, he wrote, who serve God in the spirit and who boast in Christ Jesus (καυχώμενοι ἐν Χριστῷ Ἰησοῦ) since they place no confidence in their flesh. In Gal 6:14 he wrote: "but far be it from me to glory (καυχᾶσθαι) except in the cross of our Lord Jesus Christ" (ἐν τῷ σταυρῷ τοῦ κυρίου ἡμῶν Ἰησοῦ Χριστοῦ). While Paul did speak of boasting in God, he did so primarily in a perjorative sense,[209] except in Rom 5:11 where he again linked it with Christ and salvation. He wrote (Rom 5:11): καυχώμενοι ἐν τῷ θεῷ διὰ τοῦ κυρίου ἡμῶν Ἰησοῦ Χριστοῦ δι' οὗ νῦν τὴν καταλλαγὴν ἐλάβομεν ("boasting in God through our Lord Jesus Christ through whom now we have received reconciliation").

With the exception then of Paul's use of καυχᾶσθαι in contrast to faith[210] and his use of it to describe his apostolic ministry,[211] he employed καυχᾶσθαι in the context of Christ's work which effected man's salvation. Thus, when he wrote in 1 Cor 1:31, "let the one who

---

[207]. Cerfaux, "Kyrios," 183; Bousset, *Kyrios Christos*, 149-50; Fee, *First Corinthians*, 87, argued that in Paul, the "Lord" is Christ "unless the context clearly rules otherwise." *Contra* Foerster, TDNT, 3:1087, who said κύριος refers to God.

[208]. Rom 2:17, 23; 3:27; 4:2; 1 Cor 1:29; 3:21; 4:7; Gal 6:4, 13; Eph 2:9. Rudolf Bultmann, "καυχάομαι," *TDNT*, 3:648, wrote: "For Paul καυχᾶσθαι discloses the basic attitude of the Jew to be one of self-confidence which seeks glory before God and which relies upon itself."

[209]. Rom 2:17; and 1 Cor 1:29.

[210]. Rom 2:17, 23; 3:27; 4:2; 1 Cor 1:29; 3:21; 4:7; Gal 6:4, 13; and Eph 2:9.

[211]. Rom 5:3; 15:17; 1 Cor 9:15-16; 15:31; 2 Cor 1:12-14; 5:12; 7:4, 14; 8:24; 9:2-4; 10:8, 13, 15, 16; 11:10, 16-18, 30; 12:1, 5, 6, 9; Phil 1:26; 2:16; and 2 Thess 1:4.

boasts, boast in the Lord," he applied this Old Testament Yahweh text to Jesus, whom he understood to be the "wisdom of God."

2 Cor 10:17

Context. In 2 Corinthians 10[212] Paul appealed to the Corinthians to be obedient (10:1-6) in light of certain antagonists who had arrived (11:4) from Palestine.[213] Although they had a Jewish heritage (11:22) and portrayed themselves as apostles and ministers of Christ (11:13, 23), he considered them false apostles (11:13) and sarcastically referred to them as "super-apostles" (11:5; 12:11; ὑπερλίαν ἀποστόλων).[214] But despite the amount of space Paul dedicated to his refutation, it is difficult to reconstruct an entirely coherent picture of these opponents due to his sarcasm and combative style. Nevertheless, their attacks upon Paul's apostolate appear to be his primary concern.[215]

Text. Prompted by his opponents' self-commendation and boasting, Paul quoted once again Jer 9:24 [LXX, 9:23]:[216] ὁ δὲ καυχώμενος

[212.] The relationship of 2 Corinthians 10-13 to the rest of the letter has long been a source of debate. The transition from the rather peaceful tone of 2 Corinthians 1-9 to the terse and combative style of chs. 10-13 has caused scholars to imagine a number of possibilities. The concern of this section is nonetheless unaffected by various theories of composition and redaction. See the discussion and bibliography in Furnish, *2 Corinthians*, 35-48, 459; cf. Beker, *Paul*, 294-96.

[213.] Ellis, *Prophecy*, 105, argued upon the basis of the claim that they are "apostles of Christ" (11:13) that they were from Palestine. He contended this phrase referred only to those who were commissioned directly by the Risen Lord and were perhaps acquainted with him during his earthly ministry. Cf. 1 Cor 9:1; and 15:8-9.

[214.] Wayne A. Meeks, *The First Urban Christians: The Social World of the Apostle Paul* (New Haven: Yale University Press, 1983), 41; Ellis, *Prophecy*, 102. Contra Barrett, "Christianity at Corinth," chap. in *Essays on Paul* (Philadelphia: Westminster, 1982), 20-21; and Ralph P. Martin, "The Opponents of Paul in 2 Corinthians: An Old Issue Revisited," in *Tradition and Interpretation in the New Testament: Essays in Honor of E. Earle Ellis*, ed. Gerald F. Hawthorne and Otto Betz (Grand Rapids: Eerdmans, 1987), 285.

[215.] The opponents criticized Paul for worldliness (10:2) and denegrated his relationship to Christ (10:7). They accused him of lacking rhetorical skill and impressive bodily presence (10:10). They purposed to infiltrate Paul's field and upset his territory, all the while boasting of their accomplishments (10:13-18). They found fault with his insistence on working without accepting financial aid from the Corinthians (11:5-15); and perhaps they took advantage of the people's generosity (12:11-13). Ellis, *Prophecy*, 104, noted that they, like Paul, claimed to be πνευμάτικοι who experienced visions and had special revelations from God. As far as Paul was concerned, these opponents placed his ministry and the future of the gospel's move west in jeopardy (10:13-16).

ἐν κυρίῳ καυχάσθω ("Let the one who boasts, boast in the Lord").[217] In contrast to his quotation of the same text in 1 Cor 1:31, he did not use an introductory formula; nevertheless, he probably did intend it as an explicit quotation.[218]

Conclusion. Little in the context reveals whether Paul had in mind God or the Lord Jesus when he quoted this Old Testament Yahweh text. Perhaps 10:18 provides the only key. It affirms: "For it is not the man who commends himself that is accepted, but the man whom the Lord commends (ἀλλὰ ὃν ὁ κύριος συνίστησιν)." This statement gives a polemical twist to the quotation by indicating that although Paul's opponents commend themselves and boast in their work, the Lord's commendation is all that matters. Since the issue at hand is Paul's apostolic authority and jurisdiction in Corinth, he likely has this in mind here. Elsewhere, Paul associated his apostolic calling and authority to the title κύριος as it refers to Jesus (1 Cor 9:1; 2 Cor 10:8; 13:10).[219] This, along with the fact that (1) he used the same text (Jer 9:24) to refer to Christ in 1 Cor 1:31 and (2) he typically employed the term καυχᾶσθαι in regard to Christ's work of salvation,[220] indicates that he understood Jesus to be the κύριος in 10:17 as well.[221]

"The Mind of the Lord"—1 Cor 2:16

Context. Paul continued his emphasis on true wisdom in 1 Corinthians 2. Speaking of his own ministry in Corinth, he made no claim

---

[216.] Furnish, *II Corinthians*, 474, called it a "free adaptation of a LXX text," probably Jer 9:24, although the LXX version of 1 Sam 2:10 is almost identical. Paul elsewhere demonstrated the importance for him of Jeremiah 9 (Rom 2:29; 1 Cor 1:31).

[217.] 2 Cor 10:17, author's translation.

[218.] Many New Testament passages quote the Old Testament explicitly without an introductory formula, e.g., Matt 7:23; Luke 8:16; Mark 10:6-8; Rom 10:18; 2 Cor 13:1; Eph 5:31; Gal 3:11; Heb 10:37-38. Cf. CD 6.3 quotes Num 21:13 without an introductory formula. On the differences between Paul's quotation and Jer 9:24 [LXX, 9:23] see above, pp. 134-35.

[219.] See Rom 1:1; 1 Cor 1:1, 17; 2 Cor 1:1; Gal 1:1; Philem 1; Phil 1:1; Col 1:1; Eph 1:1; 1 Thess 2:6; 1 Tim 1:1, 12; 2:7; 2 Tim 1:1, 11; and Tit 1:1.

[220.] See above, pp. 133-36.

[221.] Cerfaux, "Kyrios," 184; Bousset, *Kyrios Christos*, 149-50; Bultmann, *Theology*, 1:124; Furnish, *II Corinthians*, 474; *contra* Alfred Plummer, *A Critical and Exegetical Commentary on the Second Epistle of St Paul to the Corinthians*, ICC (Edinburgh: T. & T. Clark, 1915), 290.

to eloquence or worldly wisdom (ἦλθον οὐ καθ' ὑπεροχὴν λόγου ἢ σοφίας, 2:1); rather, he preached only "Jesus Christ and him crucified" (εἰ μὴ Ἰησοῦν Χριστὸν καὶ τοῦτον ἐσταυρωμένον, 2:2). Yet, demonstrations of God's Spirit and power accompanied his message; this fact, he felt, should draw the Corinthians away from those who espouse human wisdom over the cross (2:5).

The structure of Paul's argument in 1 Cor 2:6-16 is somewhat difficult to ascertain. Ellis suggested that these verses represent a pre-formed midrash adopted by Paul:

> Theme and initial texts (Isa 64:4; 65:16): 2:6-9
> Exposition linked to the initial and final texts by key
>   words ἄνθρωπος, ἰδεῖν, γινώσκειν: 2:10-15
> Final texts and application (Isa 40:13): 2:16[222]

While this appears at first to be a suitable thesis, the Old Testament texts which Paul cited do not appear to be the basis of his argument as one would expect in a midrash. Rather, they seem only to support his contention that God's Wisdom, once hidden, has now been revealed by the Spirit. It has been also suggested that Paul utilized a chiastic structure:

a	6a
b	6b
(b)	7-9
(a)	10-16[223]

This suggestion offers a more satisfactory scheme of the passage with the exception of 2:7, which belongs more to the theme in a than b. The structure of this section, therefore, apparently has few recognizable features and appears to be part of Paul's *ad hoc* argument supported by occasional Old Testament quotations.

Text. At the conclusion of this section (2:16), Paul quoted Isa 40:13, another Old Testament Yahweh text. He introduced the citation with the simple conjunction γάρ[224] and wrote (2:16): τίς γὰρ ἔγνω νοῦν κυρίου, ὃς συμβιβάσει αὐτόν ("For who has known the

---

[222]. Adapted from Ellis, *Prophecy*, 156. See also pp. 25-26 and 59-60.

[223]. Peter Stuhlmacher, "The Hermeneutical Significance of 1 Cor 2:6-16," in *Tradition and Interpretation in the New Testament: Essays in Honor of E. Earle Ellis*, ed. Gerald F. Hawthorne and Otto Betz (Grand Rapids: Eerdmans, 1987), 333.

[224]. Γάρ occurs alone (Rom 10:13; 11:34; 1 Cor 10:26; 15:27) and in combination with other words or phrases (Rom 4:3; 9:15, 17; 12:9; 13:9; 14:11; 1 Cor 1:19; 3:19; 6:16; 9:9; 2 Cor 6:2; Gal 3:10; 4:27; 1 Tim 5:18) in Pauline introductory formulas.

mind of the Lord so as to instruct him?'").²²⁵ In Rom 11:34 he cited the same text with a slightly different emphasis:

τίς γὰρ ἔγνω νοῦν κυρίου;
ἢ τίς σύμβουλος αὐτοῦ ἐγένετο; ²²⁶

In both cases he abbreviated the form of the quotation from the LXX which read:

τίς ἔγνω νοῦν κυρίου	(1)
καὶ τίς αὐτοῦ σύμβουλος ἐγένετο,	(2)
ὃς συμβιβᾷ αὐτόν; ²²⁷	(3)

Whereas in Rom 11:34, he included lines (1) and (2), in 1 Cor 2:16, he included lines (1) and (3). Why he deleted (3) in Rom 11:34 has already been discussed.²²⁸ It appears he omitted line (2) in 1 Cor 2:16 because it failed to meet his purpose, which was to contrast God's revelation of wisdom by the Spirit to the natural man's inability to recognize and discern spiritual realities.²²⁹ The natural man (ψυχικὸς ἄνθρωπος, 2:14) can no more penetrate God's mind to instruct him than he can hope to grasp spiritual things without divine endowment (τὰ ὑπὸ τοῦ θεοῦ χαρισθέντα ἡμῖν, 2:12). Thus, when Paul asked the rhetorical question, "Who has known the mind of the Lord so as to instruct him?" the answer comes back, on a human level, "No one." "But," he replied, "we have the mind of Christ."²³⁰

Since Paul quoted this text at the end of a discussion on the Spirit's role in revelation and wisdom, either he had in mind the Hebrew text,²³¹ which contains the phrase רוּחַ יהוה (Spirit of Yahweh), or he

---

[225] Robertson, *Grammar*, 724, noted that the relative ὅς "denotes a consecutive idea, 'so as to'."

[226] Rom 11:34: "'For who has known the mind of the Lord, or who has been his counselor?'"

[227] Isa 40:13, LXX: "For who has known the mind of the Lord and who has become his counselor so as to instruct him?" (author's translation).

[228] See above, pp. 101-102.

[229] Gerhard Delling, "συμβιβάζω," *TDNT*, 7:765-66, reasoned that Paul's abbreviation "sharpens the statement."

[230] Despite some witnesses which contain νοῦν κυρίου, earlier and more diverse support goes to the reading νοῦν Χριστοῦ. It also appears to be the more difficult reading. Howard, "Tetragram," 80, opted for the reading κυρίου (= "we have the mind of the Lord") because he assumed the tetragrammaton appeared originally in the *lemma* and κυρίου would be an acceptable word to comment on יהוה but not Χριστοῦ. His thesis falls, however, with the paucity of early attestation.

considered νοῦς (mind), in this case, to be synonymous with πνεῦμα (spirit).[232] Paul, more than any other New Testament writer, used the term νοῦς and his use of it here is clearly determined by the context.[233] He claimed that the Spirit had revealed to believers God's hidden wisdom contained in the message of Christ's crucifixion (2:10). This Spirit enables them, he argued, to understand their spiritual gifts and to discern spiritual things (2:12, 15). But he also said that the natural man has never received these gifts nor the ability to understand them (2:14), because they are only spiritually discerned. Thus Paul presented the hermeneutical key to "the mind of the Lord" in his doctrine of God's revelatory πνεῦμα.

Paul's comment on the Old Testament verse in 2:16b underscores this fact. It contains δέ, used here as an adversative,[234] to contrast the natural with the spiritual man. While the natural man does not have the Spirit (= Lord's mind), believers (ἡμεῖς)[235] have the mind of Christ (cf. Rom 8:9; Phil 2:5). To have the mind of Christ means reciprocally that they have the Spirit and thereby have been let in on the divine mystery.[236]

Conclusion. There appears to be little dissent that Paul took Isa 40:13, an Old Testament Yahweh text, and applied it to Jesus as κύριος.[237] This is demonstrated primarily by Paul's remark following the quotation: "But we have the mind of Christ." Kreitzer explained:

> He [Paul] goes on to further amplify this reference, and christologically redirect it, by emphasizing that the

---

[231.] Robin Scroggs, "Paul: ΣΟΦΟΣ and ΠΝΕΥΜΑΤΙΚΟΣ," *NTS* 14 (1967/68): 53-54.

[232.] Davies, *Paul*, 182, n. 6; Hermann Hanse, "ἔχω," *TDNT*, 2:820-22; Johannes Behm, "νοῦς," *TDNT*, 4:958, noted that Hellenistic mysticism equated νοῦς and πνεῦμα also. Kim, *Origin*, 86, n. 1, remarked that only in Isa 40:13 does the LXX translate רוח with νοῦς, elsewhere it uses πνεῦμα.

[233.] Behm, *TDNT*, 4:958.

[234.] Fee, *First Corinthians*, 119.

[235.] *Contra* Munck, *Paul*, 157, who understood "we" to refer to mature Christians (preachers ?) over against spiritual babes.

[236.] Kim, *Origin*, 86, n. 1.

[237.] Dissenting opinions include Foerster, *TDNT*, 3:1087; and Delling, *TDNT*, 7:765-66. Those who consider κύριος here to refer to Christ are Cerfaux, "Kyrios," 184; Bousset, *Kyrios Christos*, 149-50; Bultmann, *Theology*, 1:124; Kreitzer, *Jesus and God*, 19, 224, n. 8; Munck, *Paul*, 157; Hanse, *TDNT*, 2:820; and Stuhlmacher, "1 Cor 2:6-16," 338.

Christian has 'the mind of Christ' (ἡμεῖς δὲ νοῦν Χριστοῦ ἔχομεν). Of course, such redirection involves a shifting of the focus of concentration from God to Christ and serves as an example of the way in which theocentrism and christocentrism are interwoven in a complex pattern within many of the Old Testament quotations and allusions occurring within the New Testament documents.[238]

It is not a little significant that Paul used Isa 40:13 in Rom 11:34 as a theocentric text, while in 1 Cor 2:16, when addressing the Spirit's role in the life of a believer, he referred it to Christ (cf. 2 Cor 3:16-18). This illustrates Paul's flexibility in utilizing these Old Testament texts and his ambiguity in delineating strictly between the Lord Jesus and God the Father.

"The Earth Is the Lord's"—1 Cor 10:26

Context. First Corinthians 10:26 forms part of the conclusion of Paul's response to a question posed by the Corinthians concerning food sacrificed to idols (8:1, περὶ δὲ τῶν εἰδωλοθύτων; 8:4, περὶ τῆς βρώσεως οὖν τῶν εἰδωλοθύτων). The amount of space devoted to this topic indicates the seriousness of the matter for the apostle; yet the exact nature of the question is impossible to reconstruct with certainty from his argument.[239]

In 8:1-13 and 10:23-11:1 it appears that Paul is concerned with the act of eating food sacrificed to idols and the subsequent affect upon the "weak." In 10:1-22, however, his concern centers upon eating this food within the context of pagan worship. Yet 8:10 suggests that the latter is for him the deeper, more pressing question.

He agreed in general with the premise of the "strong,"[240] that is "an idol has no real existence" and "there is no God but one" (8:4). But he also warned that one man's liberty is another's stumbling

---

[238] Kreitzer, *Jesus and God*, 19.

[239] Schmithals, "Korintherbriefe," 263-88, noting the ambiguity in 1 Cor 8:1-11:1, thought 8:1-13 and 10:23-11:1 belonged to a separate letter from 10:1-22. C. K. Barrett, "Things Sacrificed to Idols," chap. in *Essays on Paul* (Philadelphia: Westminster Press, 1982), 40-59, offers a helpful discussion of the background.

[240] The weak and the strong appear to reflect a Jewish Christian/Gentile Christian tension: ἀπρόσκοποι καὶ Ἰουδαίοις γίνεσθε καὶ Ἕλλησιν καὶ τῇ ἐκκλησίᾳ τοῦ θεοῦ (10:32). See Ellis, *Prophecy*, 121. Otherwise see Meeks, *First Urban Christians*, 98-99, who saw the issue arising as a result of socio-economic tensions with the "strong" being the affluent and the "weak" being the poor.

block and thus freedom must be curtailed for the sake of others (8:7-13). He illustrated this principle by his own example and argued that, as an apostle, he had rights but did not have to use them (9:1-27). Appealing to the Lord's Supper as one's participation in Christ's sacrifice and in the "one body" (10:17, ἓν σῶμα), he warned against sharing in pagan cultic rites, because "what pagans sacrifice they offer to demons and not to God" (10:20).[241] Thus, for Paul, drinking the cup of demons and eating idol meat at their table amounted to partnership with demons (10:20, κοινωνοὺς τῶν δαιμονίων).

As he concluded his response, Paul returned once again to his previous posture and indicated that at home (10:25-26) or at a neighbor's (10:27-29)[242] one should eat what is sold at the market or served to him without questioning. Thus, in 8:1-11:1 it is apparent that he addressed two separate issues: (1) eating idol meat in private and (2) eating idol meat within the context of pagan worship.[243] Moreover, as he had done earlier, in this closing section (10:23-11:1) he alternated between two concerns: (1) personal freedom and (2) the good of others.[244] For Paul, both must be kept in balance.

Taking up a slogan which was evidently popular among certain Corinthian libertines (πάντα ἔξεστιν = "all things are lawful"),[245] Paul qualified their claim in light of his concern for others (10:23). All things may be lawful, he said, but all things will not benefit others[246] (οὐ πάντα συμφέρει) nor will they build up the church (οὐ πάντα οἰκοδομεῖ). For Paul, personal liberty must never disregard

---

[241.] On the Jewish attitude toward pagan gods see Str-B 3:48-60.

[242.] *Contra* Deissmann, *Light*, 351, n. 2, who thought 10:27 did not represent a meal in a private residence.

[243.] Some Corinthians evidently maintained they had a right to continue going to these cultic meals. Such meals were common in antiquity, accounting for a major source of religious and social engagements. Native Corinthians participated in these all their lives and perhaps continued to do so even after their conversion. See W. L. Willis, *Idol Meat in Corinth: The Pauline Argument in 1 Corinthians 8 and 10*, SBLDS 68 (Chico, CA: Scholars Press, 1985), 8-64.

[244.] Fee, *First Corinthians*, 478.

[245.] Cf. 1 Cor 6:12. F. F. Bruce, *1 and 2 Corinthians*, NCB (Grand Rapids: Eerdmans, 1971), 62, 97.

[246.] *Contra* R. St. John Parry, *The First Epistle of Paul the Apostle to the Corinthians*, 2d ed (Cambridge: University Press, 1926), 153, who considered the phrase to refer to the person who exercises liberty. This interpretation misses the context of the verses. Also, when Paul wanted to indicate a personal reference, he qualified it with μοι (e.g., 1 Cor 6:12).

the welfare of a fellow believer. He said: "Let no one seek his own good, but the good of his neighbor" (1 Cor 10:24).

For the "weak," pursuing the good of one's neighbor means eating whatever is sold in the market (ἐν μακέλλῳ) without raising a question for the sake of one's conscience (either his or the other man's). Regarding this Barrett remarked:

> Paul is nowhere more un-Jewish than in this μηδὲν ἀνακρίνοντες. His whole life as a Pharisee had been essentially one of ἀνάκρισις, not least into foods.[247]

Barrett's point, no doubt, is true, for Jews exercised extreme caution in regard to diet to avoid violating the law (see, e.g., Acts 10:9-23; 11:2-3; 4 Macc 5:2; *b.Hul.* 13b.; *m.Abod.Zar.* 2.3; and *t.Abod.Zar.* 4.6). Paul's exhortation, then, represents a liberalizing of his Jewish concerns for food; yet, even this he is able to verify from scripture.

Text. 1 Cor 10:26 contains Paul's citation of an Old Testament Yahweh text from Ps 24:1 (LXX, 23:1). It reads: τοῦ κυρίου γὰρ ἡ γῆ καὶ τὸ πλήρωμα αὐτῆς ("For 'the earth is the Lord's, and everything in it'"). With the exception of γάρ, which serves to introduce the quotation,[248] it reproduces verbatim the text of the LXX. The Hebrew upon which it is based reads: ליהוה הארץ ומלואה ("The earth is the Lord's and the fulness thereof").

Paul gave scriptural support for his "liberal" stance toward eating idol meat with this quotation of Ps 24:1, a text quoted often by Jewish teachers to indicate that a blessing should be said before a meal (e.g., *b.Ber.* 35a; *t.Ber.* 4.1). Perhaps his remark in 10:30 ("if I partake with thankfulness, why am I denounced because of that for which I give thanks?") suggests that he had in mind here as well a reference to "giving thanks" before a meal. At all events, he argued that since the Lord[249] created and owns the earth and everything in it,[250] all food is therefore clean.[251]

[247.] Barrett, "Things Sacrificed," 49; Fee, *First Corinthians*, 482, agreed, with the exception of Paul's view of circumcision.

[248.] Eduard Lohse, "Zu I Cor 10.26, 31," *ZNW* 47 (1956): 277-80, suggested that γάρ represents an introductory formula such as the more common γέγραπται γάρ. At the very least it provides the scriptural reason behind his stance in 10:25.

[249.] Archibald Robertson and Alfred Plummer, *A Critical and Exegetical Commentary on the First Epistle of St Paul to the Corinthians*, ICC (Edinburgh: T. & T. Clark, 1911), 220, remarked that τοῦ κυρίου lies in the emphatic position.

[250.] Gerhard Delling, "πλήρωμα," *TDNT*, 6:302, considered πλήρωμα to mean "contents" or that which fills the earth.

Conclusion. By "Lord" did Paul mean God the Father or the Lord Jesus? Certainly Judaism considered Yahweh the Creator of all; this is a fundamental theme of the Old Testament.[252] Bo Reicke wrote: "The firm conviction that the God of Israel is the Creator and Ruler of all things, all peoples, and all history is one of the constitutive ideas of the OT."[253] That Psalm 24 had a firm place in a creation motif is indicated by the heading given it (LXX, 23:1): Ψαλμὸς τῷ Δαυιδ τῆς μιᾶς σαββάτων.[254] Its use on the first day of the week, the day ascribed traditionally to creation, demonstrates it had strong ties to ideas of creation in Jewish theology.

Nevertheless, this does not prove that Paul had God in mind when he quoted this verse.[255] In fact, the weight of the evidence demonstrates that he applied this text and these concepts to the Lord Jesus.[256] Several factors indicate this.

(1) The discussion in 8:1-11:1 deals with problems arising in everyday life in Corinth. Paul instructed them to seek the good of others first, to avoid idolatry, and to eat food without questioning. As demonstrated above,[257] when Paul dealt with ethical matters, he characteristically appealed to the Lordship of Jesus and often utilized the κύριος predicate to assist in emphasizing his point.

(2) Throughout this discussion the christological use of κύριος dominates.[258] In a passage which refers to the Lord's Supper (10:14-22), he stated (10:21): οὐ δύνασθε ποτήριον κυρίου πίνειν καὶ ποτήριον δαιμονίων, οὐ δύνασθε τραπέζης κυρίου μετέχειν καὶ τραπέζης δαιμονίων ("You cannot drink the cup of the Lord and the cup of demons. You cannot partake of the table of the Lord and the table of demons."). Earlier in the same passage he alluded to "the

---

[251.] Cf. Mark 7:19, καθαρίζων πάντα τὰ βρώματα; Acts 10:15, ἃ ὁ θεὸς ἐκαθάρισεν, σὺ μὴ κοίνου.

[252.] Genesis 1-2; Deut 10:14; Job 38-41; Psalm 8; Ps 24:1; and Psalm 104.

[253.] Reicke, *TDNT*, 5:890.

[254.] Barrett, "Things Sacrificed," 52.

[255.] *Contra* Foerster, *TDNT*, 3:1087; Cerfaux, "Kyrios," 176, wrote: "Le <<Seigneur>> qui a créé la terre et en est le maitre, c'est Deiu. Paul ne peut penser autrement."

[256.] Kramer, *Christ, Lord, Son*, 156.

[257.] See the discussion above, pp. 69-74.

[258.] 1 Cor 8:6; 9:1, 5, 14; 10:21. He used Χριστός in 10:4, 16; 11:1.

cup of blessing" as participation in the blood of Christ (10:16). Likewise, he called the bread participation in the body of Christ (10:16). Thus, there can be little doubt that κύριος in the phrases "the cup of the Lord" and "the table of the Lord" in 10:21 refers to Christ.[259]

(3) Perhaps the most significant evidence that κύριος in this Yahweh text refers to Christ regards the structure of Paul's argument on eating idol meat. He began in 8:4 by affirming that "an idol has no real existence" and "there is no God but one." He then quoted a pre-formed Christian tradition[260] in 8:6:

> "Yet for us there is one God, the Father,
>   from whom are all things and
>   for whom we exist,
> and one Lord, Jesus Christ,
>   through whom are all things and
>   through whom we exist."

This confession is a uniquely Christian formulation.[261] It presents Jesus Christ as the "one Lord" who serves as mediator in creation (δι' οὗ τὰ πάντα) and redemption (ἡμεῖς δι' αὐτοῦ).[262]

Scholars differ over Paul's purpose in quoting the confession here. Some believe he intended to capitalize upon the confession's creation motif.[263] Others think soteriological concerns dominate his mind.[264] But should one draw strict lines of demarcation on this issue? Are not cosmology and soteriology substantially related in scripture?[265] Indeed, they are and 1 Cor 8:6 presents a good case in point. Never-

---

[259] For a more complete discussion of κύριος in Lord's Supper passages, see pp. 74-78.

[260] John C. Gibbs, *Creation and Redemption* (Leiden: E. J. Brill, 1971), 59; Dunn, *Christology*, 179; Cullmann, *Christology*, 2, concluded that the earliest formulas connect Christ with creation.

[261] Conzelmann, *1 Corinthians*, 144. Fred B. Craddock, *The Pre-existence of Christ in the New Testament* (Nashville: Abingdon Press, 1968), 92, understood this confession to be the result of Hellenistic influences. Others, however, consider the Jewish wisdom tradition to be its immediate background, including: A. Feuillet, *Le Christ Sagesse de Dieu d'après les épitres pauliniennes* (Paris: Librairie Lecoffre, 1966), 59-85; also Gibbs, *Creation*, 72; and Moule, *Origin*, 43.

[262] Cullmann, *Christology*, 247-48; and Gibbs, *Creation*, 60-61.

[263] E.g., Gibbs, *Creation*, 62-63.

[264] Jerome Murphy-O'Connor, "1 Cor 8:6: Cosmology or Soteriology?" *RB* 85 (1978): 260-66.

[265] Reicke, *TDNT*, 5:886-96.

theless, the creation motif does come to mind for Paul once again in the closing verses of this discussion (10:26); and it may be his primary reason for quoting Ps 24:1 here.

Consequently, in introducing this topic, Paul (1) denounced rival gods and (2) quoted a pre-formed christological confession which affirmed the One God and One Lord Jesus as the source of all things (τὰ πάντα). Likewise, at the end of his discussion, he (1) denounced idols and pagan sacrifices as offerings to demons (10:19-22) and (2) quoted scriptural tradition (Ps 24:1) which acknowledged *the Lord* as Creator of all things (τὸ πλήρωμα αὐτῆς, 10:26). Since the pre-formed christological confession extolled Jesus the κύριος as active in creation, it is also likely that Paul considered Jesus the κύριος of Ps 24:1 (cf. Col 1:15-17).

Therefore, (1) ethical considerations, (2) other occurrences of κύριος in the context, and (3) the structure of Paul's entire discussion—particularly with reference to creation—indicate that Paul applied Ps 24:1, an Old Testament Yahweh text, to the Lord Jesus.

"The Lord Knows Those Who Are His"—2 Tim 2:19

Context. In 2 Tim 2:1-2, Paul exhorted Timothy to entrust unto faithful men (παράθου πιστοῖς ἀνθρώποις) what he had learned from the apostle with the hope that these would pass on the deposit of truth (παραθήκην, 1:12, 14) to others. Paul warned the young man that this task would require that he endure suffering, avoid worldly entanglements, and labor hard at his divinely appointed task (2:2-7).[266] He summarized this "gospel" in 2:8-13 and encouraged Timothy to remember Jesus Christ who came from David's line (ἐκ σπέρματος Δαυίδ) and was raised from the dead (cf. Rom 1:3-4). Utilizing a faithful saying (πιστὸς ὁ λόγος), he concluded the personal exhortation to Timothy with the promise of Christ's faithfulness and future victory for those who suffer and endure (2:11-13).

Turning to issues which influenced the church, Paul instructed Timothy to remind his people of these things[267] and to avoid verbal disputes (λογομαχεῖν)[268] which lead nowhere (2:14). Apparently he

---

[266.] The promise, "the Lord will grant you understanding in everything" (2:7), refers primarily to Timothy's task of overseeing the Ephesian church and implies that, as Paul was commissioned by the Lord, so was Timothy.

[267.] Ταῦτα probably refers both to the Christian message deposited by Paul (1:12, 14; 2:2) and to the truth inherent in the faithful saying, i.e., the demand of Christian suffering and endurance and the promise of life, future victory, and Christ's faithfulness. See Kelly, *Pastoral Epistles*, 182; also Barrett, *Pastoral Epistles*, 105.

knew that heretical teachers like Hymenaeus and Philetus were troubling some of the faithful and had "shot wide of the truth" (περὶ τὴν ἀλήθειαν ἠστόχησαν; cf. 1 Tim 1:6; 6:21) by claiming that the resurrection had already taken place.[269] In contrast to the heretics who were disrupting the congregation, he claimed that God's firm foundation has been established and continues to stand (2:19).[270]

Text. Paul characterized God's firm foundation as bearing an inscription which consists of two quotations, the first being an almost literal citation of Num 16:5 and the second being a quotation of unknown origin,[271] yet having some affinity with certain Old Testament texts.[272] In the former, which is an Old Testament Yahweh text, he wrote: ἔγνω κύριος τοὺς ὄντας αὐτοῦ ("The Lord knows those who are his"). Interestingly, the LXX reads differently: ἔγνω ὁ θεὸς τοὺς ὄντας αὐτοῦ. It translates יהוה in the Hebrew text by ὁ θεός.[273] Nevertheless, Paul appears to demonstrate an awareness of the Hebrew original with his translation of κύριος.

With these quotations Paul comforted Timothy, a man whose church was plagued with false teachers and those of wavering faith. In effect Paul assured him that all will be well with his congregation because the Lord knows those who truly belong to him.[274] The second

---

[268.] See 1 Tim 1:4, 7; 6:4, 20; 2 Tim 2:16; 3:7; Tit 3:9. Dibelius and Conzelmann, *Pastoral Epistles*, 111.

[269.] Barrett, *Pastoral Epistles*, 105; C. F. Evans, *Resurrection and the New Testament* (London: SCM Press, 1970), 4, underscored how quickly the resurrection moved to the center-stage in dialogue with Paul's "orthodox" position.

[270.] Walter Grundmann, "στήκω, ἵστημι," *TDNT*, 7:651, noted that ἕστηκεν here denotes that which endures and is not susceptible to change. In contrast to the faith of the congregation which is susceptible to change, the foundation thus stands and cannot be moved. See BAGD, "ἀνατρέπω," 62.

[271.] Lock, *Pastoral Epistles*, 101, suggested that both texts quote the Old Testament and have reference to the rebellion of Korah (Numbers 16). But, he said, they may have been modified by certain sayings of the Lord (Matt 7:23; Luke 13:27) and have been part of an early gospel or a collection of otherwise unknown Christian sayings. Dibelius and Conzelmann, *Pastoral Epistles*, 112, considered a Christian poem the most likely origin. Kelly, *Pastoral Epistles*, 186, argued against a poetic structure and suggested that each is a proverb packed with scriptural allusions which Paul's readers would recognize. C. F. D. Moule, *The Birth of the New Testament*, 3d ed. (San Francisco: Harper & Row, 1982), 120, opined that 2:19 may be a "reverse reminiscence" of Jesus' words in Matt 7:21-23. While the language at points is certainly similar, not enough affinity exists to say that they are related.

[272.] Num 16:26; Isa 26:13; 52:11; and Ps 6:8.

[273.] Num 16:5 (HT): וידע יהוה את-אשר-לו.

part of the inscription instructed those who name the Lord's name to depart from "iniquity," understood not as sin but as opposition to the truth[275] (cf. Rom 2:8; 1 Cor 13:6; 2 Thess 2:10, 12). This interpretation is borne out particularly in 2:18 when Paul charged Hymenaeus and Philetus with shooting wide of the truth. Thus, Paul encouraged the faithful believers to withdraw from these men who propogate error.[276]

Conclusion. At first glance, it may appear that Paul had God in mind when he quoted this text, particularly because of the way he prefaced the quotation with the phrase: ὁ μέντοι στερεὸς θεμέλιος τοῦ θεοῦ ἕστηκεν ("But God's firm foundation stands").[277] Yet a more detailed analysis of the context and Paul's thought reveals that on this occasion he again applied this Yahweh text to Christ.[278]

(1) Accordingly, one must first grasp the meaning behind the phrase, "God's firm foundation," which is perhaps the main reason to interpret this Yahweh text theocentrically. Several possibilities emerge. This foundation (θεμέλιος) may be either (a) Christ alone (Rom 15:20; 1 Cor 3:11), (b) the apostles and prophets of the Church with Christ as the cornerstone (Eph 2:20), (c) the truth of the gospel, (d) the church as a whole (cf. 1 Tim 3:15), or (e) the genuine Ephesian Christians.[279] While each of these ideas has some merit, the christo-

---

[274.] Too much is often made of the thought of election in this passage. Certainly God's elective love and grace is a fundamental theme of the Old Testament (Gen 18:19; Exod 33:12; Amos 3:2; Hos 11:12; 13:5; Jer 1:5; Ps 1:6; 36:18 [LXX]). However, Num 16:5 betrays little, if any, evidence of this. Korah and his rebellious companions are members of God's elect people, yet their true character is revealed when they oppose Moses. The emphasis is thus less on election and more upon God's insight into man's heart and character (cf. 1 Cor 8:3; Gal 4:9). *Contra* Rudolf Bultmann, "γινώσκω," *TDNT*, 1:706.

[275.] Gottlob Schrenk, "ἀδικία," *TDNT*, 1:156.

[276.] Barrett, *Pastoral Epistles*, 106-107.

[277.] Other possible evidence for a theocentric emphasis of this Yahweh text is (1) the phrase ἐνώπιον τοῦ θεοῦ in 2:14 and (2) the admonition to hasten to present yourself to God in 2:15. With regard to the former, many good manuscripts also contain κυρίου (A D Ψ 048); nevertheless, in light of the use of the same phrase in 1 Tim 5:4, 21; 2 Tim 4:1, the most likely reading is "before God." See Metzger, *Textual Commentary*, 647.

[278.] Otherwise see Foerster, *TDNT*, 3:1087.

[279.] Lock, *Pastoral Epistles*, 100; Kelly, *Pastoral Epistles*, 186, understood θεμέλιος to be the genuine Ephesian Christians since (1) Paul contrasted the sure foundation with the unstable heretics and (2) he mentioned an inscription engraved upon the foundation which refers to God's elect people. But one could well ask, if Paul considered the faith of some in Ephesus to be upset (ἀνατρέπουσιν), could he then

logical understanding of θεμέλιος has much to commend it [280] for three reasons. (1) It appears elsewhere in Paul (Rom 15:20; 1 Cor 3:11; cf. Eph 2:20). (2) It acknowledges Christ as the content of the gospel's truth and the reason for the Church's existence, thus giving a rationale for the rest of the possibilities. (3) If κύριος in 2:19 refers to Christ, as will be argued below, then it takes into account the content of the inscription (τὴν σφραγίδα ταύτην).[281] These factors suggest that the firm foundation established by God refers to Christ as the content of the gospel and the basis for the Church's existence.[282]

(2) Also instructive in this regard is the phrase, ὁ ὀνομάζων τὸ ὄνομα κυρίου ("the one who names the name of the Lord") which occurs in the second half of the inscription. The Greek word ὀνομάζω occurs nine times in the New Testament,[283] three of which are relevant to the case here. In Acts 19:13 Luke related the story of Sceva's sons who, evidently under Paul's example, sought to cast out demons by naming the name of the Lord Jesus (ὀνομάζειν . . . τὸ ὄνομα τοῦ κυρίου Ἰησοῦ). In Rom 15:20 Paul told his future friends that his ambition was not to preach the gospel where Christ had already been named (ὅπου ὠνομάσθη Χριστός) and thus build on another's foundation. In Eph 1:21 he celebrated God's work through Christ since God raised him from the dead and seated him at the right hand far above every ruler, authority, power, dominion, and every name that is named (παντὸς ὀνόματος ὀνομαζομένου). One must also not forget Phil 2:9-11, which declares that God has given him the name above every name, probably referring to the title κύριος. This evidence, taken together, appears to demonstrate that Paul employed the concept "naming the name of the Lord" with the Lord Jesus. If he has the Lord Jesus in mind in the second quotation, he probably had him in mind in the first.

---

considered the faith of some in Ephesus to be upset (ἀνατρέπουσιν), could he then call them "God's firm foundation"?

[280.] Schmidt, *TDNT*, 3:63-64.

[281.] Gottfried Fitzer, "σφραγίς κτλ.," *TDNT*, 7:948, indicated that σφραγίς is used metaphorically here to mean "inscription"; so also Barrett, *Pastoral Epistles*, 106-107.

[282.] *Contra* Dibelius and Conzelmann, *Pastoral Epistles*, 112; also Georg Bertram, "στερεός," *TDNT*, 7:612-13, who considered God the foundation. Further evidence may be passages which refer to Christ and contain related words such as λίθος (Rom 9:32-33) and πέτρα (1 Cor 10:4).

[283.] Luke 6:13, 14; Acts 19:13; Rom 15:20; 1 Cor 5:11; Eph 1:21; 3:15; 5:3; and 2 Tim 2:19.

(3) In addition, the quotation, "The Lord knows those who are his," indicates a sense of belongingness. Chapter two indicated that Paul often related belongingness to Jesus, particularly with the title Χριστός.[284] Although the christological title is different, since other evidence points in the same direction, one may well take the sense of belongingness here to refer again to Christ as Lord (cf. Rom 14:8).

To summarize, (1) the christological significance of the foundation, (2) Paul's use of ὀνομάζω with reference to Jesus' Lordship, and (3) his practice of associating belongingness to Christ indicate a christocentric meaning to the Old Testament Yahweh text quoted in 2 Tim 2:19.[285] Thus, in the context of false teachings regarding the resurrection, Paul applied to Christ this passage which originally was reserved for Yahweh.

Allusions to Yahweh Texts in Paul's Writings[286]

Allusions in 1 Corinthians and the Thessalonian Letters

When Paul warned the Corinthians to avoid pagan ritual meals, he may have alluded to an Old Testament Yahweh text in 1 Cor 10:21 with the phrase, "the table of the Lord" (τραπέζης κυρίου).[287] According to the context, the phrase referred clearly to the Lord's Supper.[288] The allusion came from Mal 1:7, 12 (τράπεζα κυρίου), a passage in which the Lord condemned the priests for defiling the altar (also called "the table of the Lord" = שֻׁלְחַן יהוה) by sacrificing thereon

---

[284.] See above pp. 69-74.

[285.] One may also add certain contextual factors. In 2:7, Paul promised that the κύριος, apparently referring to the Lord Jesus, will grant Timothy understanding of his divinely appointed task (cf. 2:24, δοῦλον κυρίου). With a faithful saying (2:12), Paul assured Christians that they will reign with him (συμβασιλεύσομεν) who also suffered and lived again. Christians ought to pursue righteousness, faith, love, and peace with those who call upon the name of the Lord (τὸν κύριον). Elsewhere, Paul used similar language to refer to the Lord Jesus (Rom 10:13; 1 Cor 1:2).

[286.] As with the quotations, this section is confined to allusions where κύριος translates the divine name. Rom 2:6, alluding to Ps 61:13 [LXX] ([HT] 62:13; [ET] 62:12), does not apply since אדני stands behind the LXX κύριε (cf. 2 Tim 4:14). Likewise 2 Cor 8:21 alludes to Prov 3:4 which renders אלהים with κύριος.

[287.] Ellis, *Paul's Use*, 153.

[288.] 1 Cor 10:16-17. Kramer, *Christ, Lord, Son*, 158, may be correct when he suggested the phrase included the entire service of the Lord's Supper. However, his comment that the Lord's Supper had a developed liturgy by this time is less certain.

blind and crippled animals. Such offerings were in no way acceptable to Yahweh. Equally unacceptable to the Lord, according to Paul, was the participation in pagan cultic rites by believers who thought they were immune to their influence.

Paul's expression ("the table of the Lord") was not inspired by those pagan cultic meals, for there is apparently no evidence that pagan feasts employed such terminology.[289] Rather, it was inspired by the phrase received through Jewish tradition.[290] "The table of the Lord" in Paul (= Lord's Supper) is associated with "the table of the Lord" in Malachi (= altar) above all by the image of sacrifice, for Paul concluded his account of the Lord's supper with the interpretation: "For as often as you eat this bread and drink this cup, you proclaim the Lord's death until he comes" (1 Cor 11:26; cf. 10:20). Since this clearly refers to Jesus, Paul has applied the phrase, τραπέζης κυρίου, to the Lord Christ.[291]

In the following verse (1 Cor 10:22), Paul again alluded to a Yahweh text with the question: "Shall we provoke the Lord to jealousy?" (ἢ παραζηλοῦμεν τὸν κύριον;). It may refer loosely to God's statement in Deut 32:21: "They have stirred me to jealousy with what is no god" ([LXX] αὐτοὶ παρεζήλωσάν με ἐπ' οὐ θεῷ). It came from a section of the Torah which rehearsed God's care for his people (Deut 32:1-14) and recalled their idolatry and subsequent rejection by God (Deut 32:15-26).

Although Deut 32:21 does not contain a reference to the divine name, Deut 32:19 indicates that it is Yahweh (יהוה) who spoke. Paul appears to have been aware of this and manufactured this truncated allusion much as he did the quotation in 1 Cor 1:31 and 2 Cor 10:17.

While verbal affinity at first appears to be slight, when one compares other verses in the immediate context of both sections, the allusion is made manifest.

    1 Cor 10:20   θύουσιν δαιμονίοις καὶ οὐ θεῷ
    Deut 32:17   ἔθυσαν δαιμονίοις καὶ οὐ θεῷ

Since the verbal affinity between these texts is significant and both warn against idolatry,[292] it appears Paul did intend an allusion.

[289.] Goppelt, *TDNT*, 8:213-14.

[290.] Cerfaux, "Kyrios," 185.

[291.] Ibid.

[292.] First Corinthians 10 draws heavily from Israel's experience in the wilderness to warn against participation in idol worship. This further reinforces the allusion

Furthermore, since the immediate context presents Christ as Lord, he could not mean otherwise here. First Corinthians 10:22, therefore, provides another example in which Paul applied to Christ an allusion to an Old Testament Yahweh text.[293]

In 1 Thess 2:17-3:10 Paul shared his desire to visit with the Thessalonian church again and gave thanks for Timothy's report of their steadfastness. He concluded this section of his letter with a prayer that God the Father and the Lord Jesus Christ would direct his way to them and cause them to abound more and more in love. In the closing words of this prayer he appears to allude[294] to Zech 14:5, which declared: ἥξει κύριος (HT = יהוה) ὁ θεός μου, καὶ πάντες οἱ ἅγιοι μετ' αὐτοῦ ("The Lord, my God, will come and all the holy ones with him"—author's translation). Departing from the exact wording, Paul wrote (1 Thess 3:13): ἐν τῇ παρουσίᾳ τοῦ κυρίου ἡμῶν Ἰησοῦ μετὰ πάντων τῶν ἁγίων αὐτοῦ ("at the coming of our Lord Jesus with all his holy ones"—author's translation). Although the phraseology is different, the conceptual linkage is unmistakable, since both passages expect that (1) the Lord will appear and (2) he will be accompanied by his "holy ones," understood in both texts as angels.[295]

With this allusion Paul referred to a passage that described, in language typical of Old Testament theopanies, the destruction which awaited Israel's enemies and the blessings which God's people would enjoy at the dawning of the Day of the Lord (Zechariah 12-14).[296] He adapted it to the new eschatological situation in Christ[297] and prayed

---

here. Fee, *First Corinthians*, 473-74, noted that the argument in 10:22 comes full circle from the beginning of the chapter.

[293]. Cerfaux, "Kyrios," 183.

[294]. Kreitzer, *Jesus and God*, 117-18; Ernest Best, *A Commentary on the First and Second Epistles to the Thessalonians*, Black's New Testament Commentaries (London: Adam and Charles Black, 1972), 152-53, called it a quotation; Marshall, *Thessalonians*, 102-3, referred to it as an "echo."

[295]. Contra James E. Frame, *A Critical and Exegetical Commentary on the Epistles of St. Paul to the Thessalonians*, ICC (Edinburgh: T. & T. Clark, 1912), 139, who, following the prevailing New Testament sense, thought they were believers. Angels are associated with judgment in the Old Testament (Dan 7:18) as well as in the New Testament (Mark 8:38; 13:27). Cf. Matt 25:31; and Jude 14. See Best, *Thessalonians*, 152-53; Marshall, *Thessalonians*, 102-3. Morris, *Thessalonians*, 114-15, understood "his holy ones" here to mean both angels and departed saints.

[296]. Zech 14:5 also impacts the meaning of 1 Thess 4:14 and 2 Thess 1:7-10.

[297]. E. S. Steele, "The Use of Jewish Scriptures in 1 Thessalonians," *BTB* 14 (1984):

that the Lord Jesus would present the Thessalonian believers blameless before God at the parousia. Whereas Zechariah said, "the Lord my God comes," Paul declared, "our Lord Jesus comes." The application of this Yahweh text to Christ is again dramatic.

Similarly, in the paraenetic section following the prayer, Paul encouraged the Thessalonian Christians to pursue lives pleasing to the Lord and warned specifically against sexual immorality (πορνεία, 4:3). He alluded to an Old Testament concept, which found clear expression in Ps 94:1[298] ([LXX, 93:1]: ὁ θεὸς ἐκδικήσεων κύριος = [HT] אל־נקמות יהוה), thereby giving the basis for his injunction: "because the Lord is an avenger (ἔκδικος κύριος) in all these things, as we solemnly forewarned you" (4:6). Paul thus admonished the Thessalonians to remain sexually pure else the Lord himself would judge their sin and pay them back for overstepping the bounds. The "Lord" about whom Paul spoke is no doubt Jesus; otherwise the specific reference to God in 4:7 is unnecessary. This is indicated further by the phrases "in the Lord Jesus" (4:1) and "through the Lord Jesus" (4:2), which often accompanied Paul's ethical instructions. Marshall may be correct when he stated that Paul cited Ps 94:1 and deliberately omitted ὁ θεός so that the text could be applied to Jesus.[299]

The forewarning (προείπαμεν) which Paul mentioned in 4:6 probably referred to his teaching ministry on his first visit to Thessalonica.[300] Since it is connected with a scriptural allusion, one may conclude that at least some of what Paul taught his new churches came from the Hebrew scriptures. Moreover, it may be reasonably assumed that Paul applied to Jesus Yahweh texts, not only in written correspondences, but also in personal instruction. Acts suggests that such instruction took place first in the synagogues.

Prior to writing 2 Thessalonians Paul had heard that the church was facing persecution and tribulation. He addressed this at the beginning of his letter and offered comfort in light of Christ's coming and the eschatological judgment (1:4-12). He promised that God (1:5) would repay those who afflicted them and provide rest for the faithful "when the Lord Jesus is revealed from heaven with his mighty angels

---

14. See 1 Thess 2:19; 4:15; 5:23; 2 Thess 2:1; and 1 Cor 15:23.

298. See also Deut 32:35. For vengeance in Paul see Rom 12:19; 13:4; and 2 Tim 1:8.

299. Marshall, *Thessalonians*, 112.

300. Frame, *Thessalonians*, 152-53; Best, *Thessalonians*, 166.

in flaming fire, inflicting vengeance upon those who do not know God and upon those who do not obey the gospel of the Lord Jesus" (1:7-8).[301]

The language of these verses recalls Old Testament prophetic and apocalyptic passages, and several allusions to Yahweh texts are evident. Paul stated that Christ will come "in flaming fire" (ἐν πυρὶ φλογός) to "inflict vengeance" (διδόντος ἐκδίκησιν), an allusion[302] to Isa 66:15 [LXX] which declares that Yahweh comes as fire (κύριος ὡς πῦρ ἥξει) to inflict vengeance (ἀποδοῦναι ἐν θυμῷ ἐκδίκησιν) and rebuke "in flames of fire" (ἐν φλογὶ πυρός).[303] Whereas in 1:5 Paul clearly referred to God as judge, in 1:7-8 he placed the role of executing divine justice upon the coming Lord Jesus.

Paul continued the judgment theme in 1:9, where he promised that the persecutors of the Thessalonians will suffer eternal destruction (ὄλεθρον αἰώνιον) and exclusion "from the presence of the Lord and from the glory of his might" (ἀπὸ προσώπου τοῦ κυρίου καὶ ἀπὸ τῆς δόξης τῆς ἰσχύος αὐτοῦ). This allusion, which repeats the LXX nearly verbatim, comes from a recurring refrain in Isaiah 2,[304] a chapter dealing with the Day of the Lord. The application of this text to Christ via the κύριος predicate is clear and all the more significant in light of the strong monotheistic tone of the passage. In Isa 2:11, 17, for example, the writer declared that "Yahweh alone will be exalted on that day" (καὶ ὑψωθήσεται κύριος μόνος ἐν τῇ ἡμέρᾳ ἐκείνῃ). While aspects of 2 Thess 1:8 may reflect other Old Testa-

---

[301] There may be a subtle identification of the persecutors here. Perhaps "those who do not know God" (τοῖς μὴ εἰδόσιν θεόν) refer to Gentiles and "those who do not obey the gospel" (τοῖς μὴ ὑπακούουσιν τῷ εὐαγγελίῳ) refer to Jews. See Marshall, *Thessalonians*, 177-78.

[302] de Lacey, "'One Lord,'" 197; and Ellis, *Paul's Use*, 154.

[303] Fire often accompanies Old Testament theophanies (Exod 3:2; 19:18; Deut 5:4; Dan 7:9).

[304] Isa 2:10, 19, 21: ἀπὸ προσώπου τοῦ φόβου κυρίου, καὶ ἀπὸ τῆς δόξης τῆς ἰσχύος αὐτοῦ. Paul quoted this refrain verbatim with the exception of the word φόβου. It should be relegated to an allusion, however, since it is not a complete thought but only part of a whole. Cerfaux, "Kyrios," 178, believed Paul eliminated φόβου so that the text could be applied to Christ. It is unclear, however, if Christ comes with fire to execute divine judgment, which is certainly a fearful prospect, why Paul would feel the need to eliminate it. Best, *Thessalonians*, 264, offered a more plausible explanation when he suggested that Paul omitted it to strengthen the parallelism of the phrase.

ment texts,[305] the purpose here is to notice that Paul has applied to Jesus words which the Old Testament reserves for Yahweh.[306]

Paul concluded this section with a prayer which, in the final injunction, included the phrase (1:12): ὅπως ἐνδοξασθῇ τοῦ ὄνομα τοῦ κυρίου ἡμῶν Ἰησοῦ ἐν ὑμῖν ("so that the name of our Lord Jesus may be glorified in you"). This appears to be an allusion[307] to Isa 66:5 which says: ἵνα τὸ ὄνομα κυρίου δοξασθῇ ("so that the name of the Lord [= יהוה] may be glorified").

The probability of an allusion is strengthened by the fact that Paul referred to Isa 66:15 in 2 Thess 1:8. From a hermeneutical standpoint it provides evidence that Isaiah 66 was important for Paul as he composed 2 Thess 1:5-12.[308] Furthermore, it gives credence to Dodd's idea that, when Paul quoted from the Old Testament, he had in mind the complete context and not just isolated scripture fragments.[309] From a christological standpoint it indicates that the association between Jesus and Yahweh was not limited to function, since "name" in Hebrew thought signifies much of what may be called "nature" or "person."[310] Certainly, this passage presents another example of the application of Yahweh texts to Christ and implies his identification with Yahweh's nature and power.

---

[305] On this see D. E. H. Whiteley, *The Theology of St. Paul* (Philadelphia: Fortress, 1972), 106-7.

[306] Ibid. See also Kreitzer, *Jesus and God*, 120; and de Lacey, "'One Lord,'" 197.

[307] Ibid. Whiteley called it "a loose quotation, at best"; Kreitzer, *Jesus and God*, 119-20.

[308] Cerfaux, "Kyrios," 178, suggested that Paul may have been the one to collect the descriptive elements of the parousia. But he also left open the possibility that he was inspired by extant apocalypses.

[309] C. H. Dodd, *According to the Scriptures: The Substructure of New Testament Theology* (London: Nisbet & Co., 1952), 126.

[310] Whiteley, *Theology*, 107. This fact is strengthened by the benedictory ending to chapter one: κατὰ τὴν χάριν τοῦ θεοῦ ἡμῶν καὶ κυρίου Ἰησοῦ Χριστοῦ ("according to the grace of our God and the Lord Jesus Christ"). The article τοῦ may be interpreted to govern both θεοῦ and κυρίου, in effect connecting the two titles and associating them with Jesus. The only other place in Paul where he appears to call Jesus "God" occurs is Rom 9:5 (and perhaps Tit 2:13). See Bruce Metzger, "The Punctuation of Rom. 9:5," in *Christ and Spirit in the New Testament: Studies in Honour of C. F. D. Moule*, ed. Barnabas Lindars and Stephen S. Smalley (Cambridge: Cambridge University Press, 1973), 95-112.

Second Corinthians 3:16

Second Corinthians 3:7-18 contains several allusions to Exod 34:29-35.[312] It expands the meaning of 3:6 which contrasts the written code (γράμμα) and the Spirit (πνεῦμα). On the one hand, it characterizes the γράμμα as the "dispensation of death" (3:7) and "condemnation" (3:9); on the other hand, it describes the πνεῦμα as life giving (3:6), the dispensation of righteousness (3:9).

In 2 Cor 3:1-3 Paul criticised his opponents for carrying letters of commendation. The focus of his argument suggests that they held Moses and the written code in too high regard. It may further reveal that they linked their authority with that of Moses, a claim which Paul countered by asserting that Moses' ministry faded and gave way to the new covenant.[313]

Paul argued that Moses veiled his face so fellow Israelites would be unaware of the covenant's fading glory (3:13). That same veil remains, metaphorically speaking, when the Israelites read the old covenant (3:14). In Paul's mind the veil symbolized the spiritual blindness of the Jews which could only be removed by Christ (ἐν Χριστῷ, 3:14).[314]

At this juncture in his argument, Paul explained how the veil is taken away when he wrote (3:16): ἡνίκα δὲ ἐὰν ἐπιστρέψῃ πρὸς κύριον περιαιρεῖται τὸ κάλυμμα ("but when a man turns to the Lord the veil is removed"). This is an allusion[315] to Exod 34:34 which reads: ἡνίκα δ' ἂν εἰσεπορεύετο Μωυσῆς ἔναντι κυρίου (יהוה) λαλεῖν αὐτῷ, περιῃρεῖτο τὸ κάλυμμα ("but when Moses went in before the Lord to speak to him, he removed the veil").

[312.] 2 Cor 3:7 (Exod 34:30); 3:13 (Exod 34:33, 35); 3:16 (Exod 34:34). Dunn, *Unity*, 88, went too far to call it a commentary or allegory.

[313.] *Contra* Georgi, *Opponents*, 258-82, who held that the key to interpreting this passage is its polemical thrust against the "divine man" theology of Paul's opponents. He believed that they had an understanding of Exodus 34 which presented Moses as a "divine man." Accordingly, he maintained that Paul's exposition both included and refuted their claims. For a critique of Georgi's position, see Furnish, *II Corinthians*, 244.

[314.] This metaphorical meaning is rendered certain by 2 Cor 4:3-4. Evidently opponents claimed Paul's gospel was veiled or difficult to understand. Paul countered, however, saying it was veiled only to those who are perishing, for Satan had blinded their eyes so they could not see the light of the gospel. In Luke's account of Paul's conversion (Acts 9, 22, 26) the apostle receives a special revelation of Jesus and is blinded by a bright light.

[315.] Ellis, *Paul's Use*, 153; Cerfaux, "Kyrios," 183, called it a *"citation virtuelle."*

By "Lord," did Paul mean the Lord Jesus or God? Both possibilities have been argued vigorously by scholars.[316] Yet those who contend that the allusion refers to God do so, it appears, because they assume that κύριος in Paul's quotations and allusions typically refer to θεός, not Χριστός.[317] This project calls that assumption into question and demonstrates that Paul did not hesitate to apply Old Testament Yahweh texts to Christ. Several contextual factors indicate that he understood the κύριος to be Christ here in this allusion.

(1) 3:14 appears to parallel 3:16.[318] The former explains that only "in Christ" is the veil taken away (ὅτι ἐν Χριστῷ καταργεῖτα). In the latter the veil is removed when a man turns to the Lord (πρὸς κύριον), an obvious reference to repentance and conversion.[319]

(2) 3:17 apparently identifies κύριος with the πνεῦμα.[320] Since 3:3 the πνεῦμα and the new covenant have been the crux of his argument. Whereas Paul often associated πνεῦμα with θεός (Rom 8:9, 11, 14; 1 Cor 2:10-14; 3:16; 6:11; 7:40; 2 Cor 3:3), it was not unusual for him to relate πνεῦμα with Χριστός (Rom 8:9-11; 1 Cor 6:17; 12:13; Phil 1:19; Gal 4:6). That he did so here is strengthened by the phrase, "where the Spirit of the Lord is, there is freedom," for Paul characteristically connected freedom (ἐλευθερία) with Christ (Rom 8:1-2; Gal 2:4; 5:1, 13-15).[321]

(3) 3:18 relates that believers (ἡμεῖς δὲ πάντες) behold "the glory of the Lord" (τὴν δόξαν κυρίου) and are being transformed into the same image (τὴν αὐτὴν εἰκόνα μεταμορφούμεθα). The phrase "the glory of the Lord," while frequent in the LXX (e.g., Exod

---

[316] For a review of these positions see J. D. G. Dunn, "2 Corinthians III. 17—'The Lord is the Spirit,'" *JTS* 21 (1970): 309-20.

[317] In particular, Dunn, "2 Cor III. 17," 309-20; and C. F. D. Moule, "2 Cor 3:18, καθάπερ ἀπὸ κυρίου πνεύματος," in *Neues Testament und Geschichte: Historisches Geschehen und Deutung im Neuen Testament Oscar Cullmann zum 70. Geburtstag*, ed. Heinrich Baltensweiler and Bo Reicke (Zurich: Theologischer Verlag; Tübingen: J. C. B. Mohr, 1972), 231-37.

[318] Bruce, *Corinthians*, 192-93; and Kim, *Origin*, 12-13.

[319] Kim, *Origin*, 12; and Furnish, *II Corinthians*, 211.

[320] The statement, ὁ δὲ κύριος τὸ πνεῦμά ἐστιν, establishes the closest relationship between "the Lord" and "the Spirit" that language can express. Robertson, *Grammar*, 768, noted: "When the article occurs with the subject and predicate, both are definite, treated as identical, one and the same, and interchangeable."

[321] Note the relationship between "Spirit" and "freedom" in Rom 7:6; 8:2-21; and Gal 5:16-18.

16:7; 24:17; 40:34-35; Lev 9:23), is nevertheless rare in Paul. It occurs only here and in 2 Cor 8:19 where, according to 8:23, it refers to Christ (δόξα Χριστοῦ). Moreover, Paul's use in 3:18 is clarified by 4:4 when he wrote: "in their case the god of this world has blinded the minds of the unbelievers, to keep them from seeing the light of the gospel of the glory of Christ (τῆς δόξης τοῦ Χριστοῦ), who is the likeness of God." Regarding the believer's transformation into the "same image," it should be noticed that elsewhere Paul describes their conformity to Christ (Rom 8:29; Phil 3:20-21).

(4) Perhaps the most convincing evidence that κύριος in 3:16 refers to Jesus comes from 4:5. Since 3:1 Paul has been combatting the influence of rivals who carry letters of commendation and evidently exalt Moses and the Law. He contrasted his ministry with theirs (3:1-6; 4:1-6) and declared that, over against those who preach themselves, he preached Jesus Christ as Lord (Ἰησοῦν Χριστὸν κύριον).

While some might disagree, these facts suggest that in 2 Cor 3:16 Paul applied the title (κύριος) to Christ.[322]

Philippians 2:10-11

Philippians 2:6-11 is generally considered by scholars to be a traditional hymn[323] arising from the setting of Jewish Christianity.[324]

[322.] Cerfaux, "Kyrios," 183; Bruce, *Paul*, 121; Kreitzer, *Jesus and God*, 113; Bultmann, *2 Corinthians*, 89; and Kim, *Origin*, 12-13.

[323.] Arguments for the traditional form include: (1) antithetical parallelism (μορφῇ θεοῦ/μορφήν δούλου; ἐταπείνωσεν/ὑπερύψωσεν), (2) hapax legomena (e.g., ἁρπαγμόν), (3) the use of participles, (4) chiasmus (ἑαυτὸν ἐκένωσεν/ἐταπείνωσεν ἑαυτόν), (5) διὸ καί dividing the piece in half, part one on humiliation and part two on exaltation, (6) the absence of theological ideas customarily associated with Paul (e.g., resurrection), (7) the presence of theological ideas not found elsewhere in Paul (e.g., "equality with God" and the three-fold division of the universe), and (8) contextual evidence, i.e., language and style which differs from surrounding verses. Jacob Jervell, *Imago Dei: Gen. i. 26f. im Spätjudentum, in der Gnosis und in den paulinischen Briefen* (Göttingen: Vandenhoeck & Ruprecht, 1960), 209, noted that while vv. 6-8 illustrate 2:1-4, vv. 9-11 serve no hortatory function.

[324.] Longenecker, *Christology*, 58-62, 125-27; Otfried Hofius, *Der Christushymnus Philipper 2, 6-11*, WUNT 17 (Tübingen: J. C. B. Mohr, 1976); G. G. Stroumsa, "Form(s) of God: Some Notes on Metatron and Christ," *HTR* 76 (1983): 282; Ralph Martin, *Carmen Christi: Philippians 2:5-11 in Recent Interpretation and in the Setting of Early Christian Worship*, rev. ed. (Grand Rapids: Eerdmans, 1983), xxxiv, concluded: "We are on firm ground in stating that Philippians ii. 6-11 represents a hymnic specimen, taken over by Paul as a *paradosis* from some early Christian source with a Jewish background but slanted to address questions that faced the

While some believe Paul is its author,[325] most conclude that the force of the argument is against Pauline authorship.[326] Nevertheless, its presence in Philippians demonstrates his general agreement with its theology. As W. D. Davies said: "There is nothing in the text to indicate that Paul is quoting the work of any other person; he employs the hymn as if it were part and parcel of his customary exhortation."[327] To put it another way, the hymn expresses Paul's Christology.

Of particular interest here is the second half of the hymn (2:9-11), which depicts the exaltation of the crucified Jesus in language formulated according to coronation ceremonies in the Ancient East (cf. 1 Tim 3:6; Heb 1:3-13; Rev 5:6-14).[328] It declares that God has highly exalted him (ὁ θεὸς αὐτὸν ὑπερύψωσεν) and given him the name above every name (τὸ ὄνομα τὸ ὑπὲρ πᾶν ὄνομα). The rare verb ὑπερύψωσεν, translated "highly exalted" (RSV), describes both the resurrection and the ascension. Although the prefix (ὑπερ-) could render its meaning "exalted to a rank not previously known,"[329] it seems best to understand it as "exalted to the highest office."[330]

The phrase "the name which is above every name" further amplifies God's exaltation of Christ to the highest rank. In the Old Testament the Hebrew word for "name" (שֵׁם) carried with it the idea of office, rank, or dignity.[331] The new name, then, which is revealed only at the climax of the hymn in the acclamation, "Jesus Christ is Lord,"[332] refers to Christ's exalted office.

---

church as it moved out to confront the larger Hellenistic world of Graeco-Roman society." Those who place it within a Hellenistic context include Fuller, *Foundations*, 205; and Kramer, *Christ, Lord, Son*, 65-71.

[325]. Kim, *Origin*, 147-49.

[326]. Martin, *Carmen Christi*, 51.

[327]. Davies, *Paul*, 42.

[328]. Goppelt, *Theology*, 2:84, described the coronation as taking place in three stages: (1) the presentation of the ruler, (2) the proclamation of his name, and (3) worship and acclamation.

[329]. Cullmann, *Christology*, 180-81.

[330]. Martin, *Carmen Christi*, 239.

[331]. Ibid., 235.

[332]. Most scholars consider the name above every name to be κύριος: Kramer, *Christ, Lord, Son*, 75; Black, "Christological Use," 7; Kreitzer, *Jesus and God*, 115-16; Martin, *Carmen Christi*, 255; and Bornkamm, *Early Christian Experience*,

The result of Christ's exaltation is the universal acclamation described in 2:10-11 in the language of Isa 45:23 (LXX), which, as stated earlier, was applied to Christ in Rom 14:11 in the context of eschatological judgment. A comparison of the texts reveals the following similarities:

Phil 2:10-11	Isa 45:23
ἵνα ἐν τῷ ὀνόματι Ἰησοῦ	ὅτι ἐμοὶ
<u>πᾶν γόνυ κάμψῃ</u>	<u>κάμψει πᾶν γόνυ</u>
ἐπουρανίων καὶ ἐπιγείων καὶ καταχθονίων	
<u>καὶ πᾶσα γλῶσσα ἐξομολογήσηται</u>	<u>καὶ ἐξομολογήσεται</u> <u>πᾶσα γλῶσσα</u>
ὅτι	[τῷ θεῷ]
κύριος Ἰησοῦς Χριστός	

The claim that "every knee shall bow" and "every tongue confess" belongs to one of the more important monotheistic passages of the Old Testament and referred originally to Yahweh. Although the Philippian hymn alters and expands the text to accomodate Christian eschatological and christological views, there can be little doubt that Jewish believers would have recognized the core phrases as Old Testament language reserved for Yahweh and now, as a result of the exaltation, applied to the Lord Jesus.[333] Furthermore, they would certainly be aware that these phrases have been applied to the Risen Lord *along with the divine name* (κύριος). They would probably assume that Jesus reigns, not as a second God but as One who shares full equality and divinity with God.[334] Jesus would thereby be viewed as an object of worship and veneration.[335] Such a high view of Jesus,

---

116-18. Otherwise Cerfaux, *Christ*, 477, thought "name" summed up the whole nature of a being and had both ontological and functional import. For him, κύριος was not the name. He wrote: "One has to look further than the title of *Kyrios*, to a deeper reality, an inaccessible, unspeakable name."

[333]. Kreitzer, *Jesus and God*, 116, remarked: "it is difficult to imagine any first-century Jew or Christian even remotely familiar with Isaiah 45 hearing this final stanza of Phil 2.9-11 without recognizing that words of theistic import have now been applied to Jesus Christ."

[334]. Martin, *Carmen Christi*, 274-76.

[335]. Fuller, *Foundations*, 213, approached the proper conclusion when he wrote: "For this is no unreflective transference to the Exalted one of a LXX text about Yhwh, but a conscious and deliberate transference of the 'name'. It is not just a *functional* identity between the Exalted one and Yahweh, but an *ontic*, though not

however, does not threaten God's position since (1) Jesus is exalted by God and (2) the universal adoration awaiting Jesus as Lord will be "to the glory of God the Father."

Implications for Paul's Christology

Paul quoted Old Testament Yahweh texts fourteen times, particularly in Romans and 1 Corinthians. Seven of these he retained as descriptions of God's person and work. The other seven he used to portray the person and work of Christ. Whenever he alluded to Yahweh texts, he applied the texts to the Lord Jesus.

It is now necessary to discuss some implications of Paul's use of Yahweh texts. To do so without addressing the work of Lucien Cerfaux on this matter, however, would be a serious oversight. The following section will evaluate the work of Cerfaux and offer some modifications to his methods and results.

The Contribution of Lucien Cerfaux

In 1943 Lucien Cerfaux published an article entitled "<<Kyrios>> dans les citations pauliniennes de l'Ancien Testament."[336] His insights into how Paul used κύριος quotations have been generally accepted by scholars with little modification.[337]

Having briefly investigated Pauline quotations which contain the κύριος predicate, Cerfaux classified them as "texts applied to God" and "texts applied to Christ."[338] He concluded that when Paul quoted a passage explicitly, he retained κύριος as a designation for God. Paul generally prefaced such citations with an introductory formula and often added a reference to the author (e.g., "David says," Rom 4:7-8; "Isaiah cries out," Rom 9:27-28; "Isaiah said before," Rom 9:29). Quotations with God as referent, he noticed, tended to be verbatim

---

yet ontological, identity: 'Name declares dignity and nature, radiates being and makes it manifest.'" Nevertheless, he stopped short of the claim that Paul and the early churches identified Jesus with Yahweh. *Contra* George Howard, "Phil. 2.6-11 and the Human Christ," *CBQ* 40 (1978): 368-87, who held the transference to Jesus of the "name" had functional, not ontic, overtones.

[336.] First published in *Ephemerides Theologicae Lovanienses* 20 (1943), 5-17. It is available also in *Recueil Lucien Cerfaux*, vol. 1 (Gemblux: J. Duculot, 1954).

[337.] E.g., Kramer, *Christ, Lord, Son*, 156-57.

[338.] Cerfaux did not differentiate, as the present writer has done, from quotations (or allusions) which referred originally to Yahweh and those which did not.

from the LXX, while quotations applied to Christ had less verbal affinity with the original. Cerfaux listed four thematic emphases in Pauline quotations which retain κύριος for God: (1) the call of God, (2) justification, (3) the role of the Gentiles, and (4) the fundamental rights of God.[339]

Regarding passages which apply κύριος to Christ, Cerfaux concluded that when Paul quoted from memory or when he alluded loosely to a text, he *may have* had Christ in mind (as with the expressions: "the table of the Lord" and "the fear of the Lord," "the word of the Lord," "the day of the Lord"). In general he thought Paul's κύριος citations with Christ as referent were rare and, with one or two exceptions, not explicit quotations. He admitted, however, that Paul at times interpreted the texts christologically and read κύριος consciously as Christ. Paul's practice, he believed, indicated that the apostle understood Christ as performing divine functions, functions attributed in the Old Testament to Yahweh. God, however, remained supreme for Paul and themes of justification, creation, etc., were kept in his domain. According to Cerfaux, the application of κύριος quotations to Christ probably occurred before Paul's conversion, since the earliest traditions utilize κύριος as a christological title.[340]

Cerfaux isolated three categories in which Paul applied κύριος quotations to Christ. First, he did so in descriptions of Christ's parousia (Rom 10:13; Phil 2:10-11; 1 Thess 2:19; 4:6; 2 Thess 1:9, 12; 2:8, 14). These quotations were often derived from Old Testament texts which have in view a theophany at the end of time and were not quoted explicitly; they were simply allusions designed evidently to provide descriptive elements to the consummation.[341] Included within this category were passages which deal with judgment, eschatological salvation, and glory. Second, he applied κύριος quotations to Christ in typological exposition of Old Testament events (1 Cor 10:9, 22; 2 Cor 3:16), especially events in the desert which proleptically portrayed the Church. Third, he read κύριος as Christ in citations which speak of the glory and wisdom of God, since for Paul Christ is the wisdom of God (1 Cor 1:31; 2:16; 2 Cor 10:17).[342]

[339.] Cerfaux, "Kyrios," 177, 186-87; idem, *Christ*, 470-72. Cerfaux held that there were only a few exceptions to the rules he enumerated.

[340.] Idem, "Kyrios," 177, 187; idem, *Christ*, 470-72.

[341.] Idem, "Kyrios," 178, questioned whether Paul was the first to collect these texts or whether he was dependent upon some Jewish-Christian tradition. He decided Paul was not the creator of these Christian apocalypses.

This present investigation demonstrates that Cerfaux's method and presuppositions were erroneous and consequently his results need modification. First, Cerfaux classified the "texts applied to God" and "texts applied to Christ" on the basis of little exegetical and contextual analysis. A more rigorous exegetical method and a more comprehensive appraisal of Paul's κύριος Christology in view of each passage's context would have yielded more accurate results.

Second, Cerfaux apparently operated upon the assumption that, unless specified otherwise, κύριος in Pauline citations referred to God.[343] This presupposition caused him to attribute more texts to God than is in fact the case. The present investigation reveals the opposite conclusion, that is, unless otherwise specified, κύριος in Pauline quotations refers to Christ. When Paul wanted the reader to understand that he meant God and not the Lord Jesus, he indicated so clearly in the context (e.g., Rom 4:7-8; 11:34; 15:9, 11; 1 Cor 3:20; 2 Cor 6:18).

Third, Cerfaux seems to have confused the distinction between an explicit and a verbatim quotation. For Paul an explicit quotation had less to do with verbal affinity and more to do with purpose. A good example of this is 1 Cor 1:31. Although it differs significantly from the LXX, the introductory formula demonstrates that Paul intended it to be an explicit citation. Unfortunately these problems render Cerfaux's work less helpful than it might otherwise have been and distort some of the results. Some modifications to Cerfaux's conclusions are therefore in order.

Some Modifications to Cerfaux's Conclusions

When Paul retained an Old Testament Yahweh text to refer to God the Father, (1) he often prefaced it with an introductory formula[344] and quoted the text more or less verbatim. It was also possible, however, for him to alter the text significantly (e.g., Rom 9:27; 2 Cor 6:18). Nevertheless, he apparently never alluded to a Yahweh text with God in mind. (2) He reserved Yahweh texts for God primarily in theocentric passages, such as the bulk of Romans 9-11, which have little christological content. (3) Whenever he added other titles or descriptive language to the κύριος title, as in "Lord of Hosts"

[342.] Ibid., 187.

[343.] Foerster, *TDNT*, 3:1087.

[344.] The only exception to this is Rom 11:34, which, since it is a doxology, would apparently be beyond this criterion.

or "Lord Almighty," he retained these for God (Rom 9:27-29; 2 Cor 6:18). (4) As stated above, when Paul wanted the reader to understand God the Father rather than the Lord Jesus, he stated so in the introductory formula or in the context so there would be no confusion. (5) He reserved God as referent for Old Testament Yahweh texts under the themes (a) justification (Rom 4:7-8), (b) divine wisdom (Rom 11:34; 1 Cor 3:20), (c) the Fatherhood of God (2 Cor 6:18), (d) ethical considerations (2 Cor 6:18), and especially (e) the relationship of Jews and Gentiles (Rom 9:27, 29; 15:9, 11).[345]

When Paul applied Yahweh texts to Christ, he exercised great variety in style, context, and theme. (1) He was able to quote either verbatim (1 Cor 10:26), with slight (Rom 10:13; 14:11; 1 Cor 2:16; 2 Tim 2:19), or substantive differences (1 Cor 1:31 = 2 Cor 10:17). (2) With three of seven quotations, he included an introductory formula (Rom 14:11; 1 Cor 1:31; 2 Tim 2:19).[346] (3) In contrast to his practice regarding Yahweh texts with God as referent, he seldom offered a straightforward sign that he intended to refer to Christ. One derives the referent primarily from the context and appeal to Paul's overall understanding of Christ as κύριος. (4) He applied Yahweh texts to Christ in passages with a christocentric focus under the themes, (a) the universality of the gospel (Rom 10:13; Phil 2:10-11), (b) eschatological salvation, coming, and judgment (Rom 10:13; 14:11; 1 Thess 3:13; 4:6; 2 Thess 1:8-12; 2 Cor 3:16), (c) Christian conduct and belongingness to Christ (Rom 14:11; 1 Thess 4:6), (d) divine wisdom, particularly understood in terms of "Christ crucified" (1 Cor 1:31; 2:16; and perhaps passages related to the Lord's Supper including 1 Cor 10:21, 26),[347] (e) the role of the Spirit in the believer's life (1 Cor 2:16; 2 Cor 3:16), and (f) Paul's apostolic authority (2 Cor 3:16; 10:17; 2 Tim 2:19).

[345.] Krister Stendahl, *Paul among Jews and Gentiles* (Philadelphia: Fortress Press, 1976), 1-7, felt scholars have wrongly interpreted Paul for centuries by their emphasis upon justification by faith. For Stendahl, Paul was concerned primarily with the relation between Jews and Gentiles, not with the "introspective conscience." This present work bears out Stendahl's thesis, particularly as it impacts the Roman letter.

[346.] While it may be admitted that the quotation formula of 2 Tim 2:19 differs significantly from the norm, there can be little doubt that he intended it to function that way.

[347.] Divine wisdom related to God stands in contrast to divine wisdom in relation to Christ. In the former (Rom 11:34; 1 Cor 3:20) it is more ethereal and connected with God's mysterious plan of the ages, while in the latter it is more concrete, related to specific saving events.

Jesus Is Yahweh

The use of κύριος to translate the divine name (יהוה) in the LXX and other contemporary Jewish writings indicates that this term had a firm place within first century Jewish religious life. Paul used it primarily as a christological title in declarations of religious devotion and worship to Jesus. In many cases he employed it to apply to Christ concepts and functions which Yahweh is expected to fulfill according to the Old Testament.

Paul's application of Yahweh texts to Christ, therefore, has significant christological implications. It implies that he considered Jesus to be more than man. It suggests that he believed that Christ was in some sense Yahweh himself, manifest as the Messiah.

This understanding of Paul's Christology corresponds to other evidence in the epistles which demonstrates that Jesus was the object of veneration, not only at some secondary stage but from the beginning. Paul bears witness to this fact by utilizing traditional materials,[348] some of which go back to the Palestinian churches (e.g., 1 Cor 16:22).

Several factors in Paul's letters indicate that Jesus was the focus of worship and devotion in the early churches. (1) The churches formulated credal statements with Christ as their object (e.g., Rom 1:3-4; 10:9-10). (2) They prayed to Christ for his return (1 Cor 16:22) and referred to themselves as those who call upon the name of the Lord Jesus Christ (1 Cor 1:2). (3) They composed hymns which centered upon his person and work in creation, redemption, and eschatological salvation (Col 1:15-20; Phil 2:6-11). (4) They considered their worship services as gatherings in the Lord's name (1 Cor 5:4). (5) They baptized new converts in Jesus' name (Rom 6:3; Gal 3:27). (6) They celebrated a sacred meal which they called the "Lord's Supper" (1 Cor 11:20; cf. 10:21). These practices imply that early Christians worshiped Jesus and thought of him in the way that one thinks of God.[349]

Since this was in fact the case, is it not probable that early Christians believed him to be God? Moreover, since Christianity first grew and developed in a Jewish milieu in which God bore the name

---

[348]. Rom 1:3-4; 10:9-13; Phil 2:6-11; Col 1:15-20. See Ellis, "Traditions in 1 Corinthians," 481-502; idem, "Traditions in the Pastoral Epistles," 239-46.

[349]. France, "Uniqueness," 203-17; idem, "The Worship of Jesus," 17-36; and Moule, *Origin*, 54-69.

Yahweh (= κύριος), is it not conceiveable that they identified him with Yahweh?

Certain scholars argue that the application of Yahweh texts to Jesus was possible only in the setting of Diaspora Hellenistic Jewish Christianity.[350] They contend that Palestinian believers differentiated strictly between Jesus and God due to the constraints of their monotheistic heritage. In the Hellenistic sphere, they explain, the barrier was on the way down and it was possible for Jesus to take on divine status. Even at this point, however, the referential shift from God to Christ represented functional, not ontological dimensions. Fuller said:

> At this stage all that is involved is the transference of *functions* from God to the exalted Jesus. Or rather, it is precisely *through* the exalted Jesus that God carries out these functions.[351]

Why is such a thesis necessary, however, if this "shift" represents merely functional identity? Were not divine functions attributed to divine agents in Palestine? Indeed they were as Larry Hurtado argued.[352] It is necessary because Paul's christological use of Yahweh texts implies more than function; it implies that he considered Jesus to be one with God.

Several factors militate against attributing the application of Yahweh texts to Christ at a later stage of first-century Christianity. First, the Maranatha invocation (1 Cor 16:22) demonstrates convincingly that Aramaic-speaking believers within Palestine invoked Jesus in prayer as "Lord."[353] That this practice is known and understood in Greek-speaking Corinth in the mid-50s suggests an early date. Second, the Philippian hymn (Phil 2:6-11), a pre-formed tradition adopted by Paul, contains a Yahweh text applied to Christ with regard to Isa 45:23, a prominent monotheistic passage in the Old Testament. As indicated above,[354] it is likely that this hymn originated in a Jewish-Christian setting, perhaps in Palestine. Third, the boundaries between theocentrism and christocentrism in early Christianity were not drawn so rigidly as some assume.[355] In Kreitzer's

---

[350] E.g., Fuller, *Foundations*, 186; and Hahn, *Titles*, 107-8.

[351] Fuller, *Foundations*, 186.

[352] Hurtado, *One God*, 17-92.

[353] See above pp. 43-47 and Hurtado, *One God*, 106-7.

[354] See above pp. 157-60.

words, a "conceptual overlap" existed between God and Christ so that the boundary between them was fluid.[356] Kreitzer found evidence that the barrier was already on the way down before the advent of Christianity with regard particularly to eschatological schemes in Jewish Pseudepigrapha.[357] Thus, the "conceptual overlap" was not exclusive to Paul; rather, it appears to have been part and parcel of the Jewish culture around him. It appears then that Paul's practice of attributing Old Testament Yahweh texts to Christ is indicative of exegesis carried out in early Christianity and should not be relegated to some secondary stage.[358]

Further evidence for a Palestinian origin of this practice comes from the Essenes of Qumran who could transfer Old Testament passages originally referring to God to a redeemer figure. In 11QMelchizedek,[359] an angelic figure, identified with the priest-king

---

[355.] See Sanders, *Paul, the Law, and the Jewish People* (Philadelphia: Fortress, 1983), 41-42.

[356.] Kreitzer, *Jesus and God*, 165-69.

[357.] *1 Enoch* provides some good examples with regard to judgment. In *1 Enoch* 47:3 and 60:1-3 God sits upon the throne. In *1 Enoch* 45:3-6; 51:3; 55:4; 61:8; 62:2-5; and 69:29 the Messiah sits upon the throne. In *1 Enoch* 46:1 both God and the Messiah come to the judgment seat. Cf. 4Q161; 4Q174; *T.Abr.* 13:1-2. In *T.Moses* 10:1-2 Michael executes judgment, while in vv. 3-7 God executes judgment. From his analysis of the Jewish pseudepigraphical literature (*1 Enoch*; 4 Ezra; *2 Apoc. Bar.*), Kreitzer, *Jesus and God*, 90, concluded: (1) the Pseudepigrapha demonstrate a great deal of diversity in eschatology without concern for consistency; (2) with regard to final judgment, they portray a "functional overlap between any intermediary agent and God himself as that activity is discharged"; (3) this "overlap" creates confusion in the textual tradition which gives rise to many textual variants; and (4) with those documents which speak of the Messiah, the functional overlap is so complete between the Messiah and God that they seem to slide into one another, despite the strong monotheistic character of the texts (e.g., *2 Apoc. Bar.* 21:7-10). A pre-Christian origin for *1 Enoch* 37-71 and the Testaments is disputed. See H. W. Hollander and M. de Jongue, *The Testaments of the Twelve Patriarchs: A Commentary* (Leiden: E. J. Brill, 1985), 82-85; also Matthew Black, *The Book of Enoch or 1 Enoch* (Leiden: E. J. Brill, 1985), 181-88.

[358.] Cerfaux, "Kyrios," 188. France, "Uniqueness," 206-7, offered an interesting thesis when he suggested that Paul's tendency to identify Jesus with God via Old Testament Yahweh texts may have arisen from Jesus' practice of comparing himself to Old Testament figures used for Yahweh (e.g., shepherd, sower, lord, king, etc.). This thesis will be treated below.

[359.] For *editio princeps* consult A. S. van der Woude, "Melchisedek als himmlische Erlösergestalt in den neugefundenen eschatologischen Midraschim aus Qumran Höhle XI," *Oudtestamentische Studien* 14 (1965): 354-73; see also M. de Jonge and A. S. van der Woude, "11QMelchizedeq and the New Testament," *NTS* 12 (1965/66):

Melchizedek (Gen 14:18-20), appears as the eschatological judge, the conqueror of evil, and issues in the year of jubilee. He is called אלוהים in a quotation taken from Ps 82:1 (l. 10): "concerning him [Melchizedek] in the hymns of David who says: *The heavenly one* [אלוהים] *standeth in the congregation of God; among the heavenly ones he judgeth.*"[360] Likewise, the same word is attributed to him in an allusion to Isa 52:7 (l. 26): *"Thy heavenly one* [אלוהים] *is king."*[361] He appears here as the victorious counterpart to Belial (בליעל), prince of darkness. In both cases אלוהים stood originally as a designation for God.

It was thus possible for Jews within Palestine to apply Old Testament passages originally referring to God to a redeemer figure. But one significant difference remains; Christian exegetes applied to Christ scripture texts which originally referred to יהוה not אלהים. Given the rather broad use of אלהים in Jewish writings, it is not surprising that Jewish exegetes would attribute אלהים texts to redeemer figures who acted as God's agent.[362] On the other hand, given the contemporary view of the divine name in Jewish life, it is amazing that Jewish-Christian exegetes in Palestine would attribute Yahweh texts to Jesus, a man recently crucified. Such a development appears to have been unprecedented in Jewish life.

Paul's Christological Use of Yahweh Texts and Monotheism

The question must now be addressed: How did Paul, who claimed to be a monotheist, accomodate the application of Yahweh texts to Jesus? Further, how can Jesus be both identified with Yahweh and yet distinct from him?

One answer suggests such veneration of Jesus could occur only outside Palestine where the constraints of Jewish monotheism were

---

301-26; Joseph A. Fitzmyer, "Further Light on Melchizedek from Qumran Cave 11," chap. in *Essays on the Semitic Background of the New Testament* (London: Geoffrey Chapman, 1971), 245-67; and J. T. Milik, "Milki-sedeq et Milki-resa dans les anciens écrits juifs et chrétiens," *JJS* 23 (1972): 95-144.

[360] Translation from de Jonge and van der Woude, "11QMelchizedek," 303.

[361] Ibid.

[362] E.g., in Ps 45:3 אלהים refers to the king not יהוה. In Exod 4:16 God refers to Moses as *elohim* (לאלהים). Job 38:7 and Ps 96:7 (LXX) present angels as *elohim* (אלהים). In the present context Ps 82:1 portrays a scene where gods (אלהים) are judged. Cf. 4Q400; 4Q402 4.11-15. Note also Qumran's reluctance even to write יהוה except in the Temple Scroll. See Fitzmyer, *Genesis Apocryphon*, 159.

not pervasive. This solution, however, separates early Christian faith and practice from later developments. As chapter one demonstrated, this view is far from satisfactory.

<u>Judaism's Concept of Divine Agency</u>

Another answer has recently been offered by Larry Hurtado in his book, *One God, One Lord*. Hurtado analyzed traditional evidence embedded in Paul's letters and concluded that Palestinian churches worshiped Jesus as Lord at an early date. Taking his cue from 1 Cor 8:6, which he asserted represents the "binitarian shape" of early Christian devotion, he asked: How did Jewish Christians accomodate the worship of Jesus alongside God? For him the solution lay in the divine agency concept of Judaism which the first Christians borrowed and developed into their own unique "mutation"[363] of Jewish monotheism.

To demonstrate his hypothesis Hurtado examined Jewish documents which depict heavenly figures as divine agents. He concluded that many groups within Judaism believed that God had a chief agent, second only to him in rank, who functioned as God in creating and sustaining the world, redemption, administering divine rule, and the final judgment. He classified these agents into three main categories: (1) divine attributes, e.g., Wisdom and Logos, (2) exalted patriarchs, e.g., Enoch and Moses, and (3) principal angels, e.g., Michael, Melchizedek, and Yahoel. According to Hurtado, these divine agents never posed a threat to the exclusivistic monotheism of the Jews since they were never objects of worship.[364] They simply reflected the acceptance of divine agency within the world of Judaism.

Hurtado surveyed selected New Testament texts and argued that early Christians understood Jesus' relationship to God in terms of Jewish divine agency. Yet he contended that they also demonstrate a sudden and significant restructuring of the concept which included placing Jesus at the center of worship alongside God to form a "binitarian shape" to early Christian devotion.[365] This is demonstrated above all in worship practices including hymns and prayers to Christ, confessing Jesus, and prophecy uttered in his name.[366] The catalyst for this Christian "mutation" of the Jewish divine agency

---

[363] Hurtado, *One God*, 2-12.

[364] Ibid., 40, 67, 82-83.

[365] Ibid., 93-99.

[366] Ibid., 100-114.

concept, according to Hurtado, was (1) Jesus' earthly ministry and its impact upon his followers, (2) the belief in the resurrection and the exalted status of Jesus, and (3) Jewish opposition to Christianity, which apparently worked to refine early Christian belief.

Professor Hurtado has written an interesting and provocative study which has a great deal to commend it. Little doubt exists that post-exilic Judaism viewed God as having divine agents. Furthermore, New Testament writers did use language which appears at times to present Jesus as God's redemptive agent. But to assert that divine agency alone accounts for early Christianity's view of Christ's relationship to God, as Hurtado has done, is to fail to grasp the implications of various early Christian practices. Three objections regarding Hurtado's argument need to be addressed: (1) the conclusion that early Christians worshiped Jesus alongside God, (2) the claim that Christianity reshaped monotheism, and (3) the assumption that pre-Christian monotheism was exclusivistic.

(1) Hurtado analyzed various New Testament passages and concluded that early Christians worshiped Jesus alongside God. The present study, however, suggests that early Christians not only worshiped Jesus *alongside God*, they worshiped him *as God*. Not every credal statement is binitarian. Some focus solely upon Jesus (Rom 1:3-4; 10:9-10). Others indicate prayers were directed to him (1 Cor 16:22). Still others suggest that the early church composed hymns to his honor and conducted baptism, worship, and the Lord's Supper in his name (1 Cor 5:4; 10:21; 11:20; Rom 6:3; Gal 3:27; Col 1:15). By attributing to Jesus the divine name, functions, and Yahweh texts, it is apparent that early believers considered Jesus to be both identified with God and distinct from him.

This was true not only with early Christianity but also with Judaism's understanding of Yahweh's divine agents, in particular, the elusive and mysterious figure of the angel of Yahweh. This perplexing character appears frequently in the Old Testament. In some texts he is only God's representative and therefore distinct from Yahweh (2 Kgs 19:35; 1 Kgs 19:7). In others he is indistinguishable from God as a manifestation of Yahweh in human form (Gen 16:10, 13; 21:17, 19; 22:11). Thus to see the angel of Yahweh is to see Yahweh himself (Gen 16:13; 32:30; 48:15-16; Judg 13:22). The angel of Yahweh also bears the divine name and indicates Yahweh's presence (Exod 23:20-23; 32:34; cf. 33:14; Isa 63:9). He is frequently therefore presented as a theophany, God revealed in time and space for a redemptive purpose.[367]

A. B. Davidson saw messianic elements in the angel of Yahweh as Yahweh's manifestation of himself in redeeming power. Such theopanies, he said, awakened the hope and longing for a more permanent abiding of God with man.[368] Accordingly, Gerhard von Rad wrote: "The figure of the angel of the Lord has conspicuous Christological qualities."[369] Likewise he said: "He is a type, a 'shadow' of Jesus Christ."[370]

During the post-exilic period, Jewish writers became more interested in angels and developed a hierarchy of angels with an emphasis upon certain named angels which serve as God's agents (e.g., Michael and Melchizedek).[371] Whether these chief angels ought to be identified with the angel of Yahweh is uncertain.[372] Nevertheless, Jews continued to have a high regard for the angel of Yahweh as indicated particularly in the *Apocalypse of Abraham*.

In this Jewish document, written in the first centuries of this era,[373] Abraham encounters God, who promises to be his protector and instructs him to sacrifice upon the mountain (9:1-10). Abraham, shocked by the revelatory voice and devoid of strength, falls prostrate to the ground. God responds to his plight and says, "Go, Iaoel of the same name, through the mediation of my ineffable name, consecrate this man for me and strengthen him against his trembling" (10:3). Iaoel[374] comes "in the likeness of a man" (10:4) and reveals to Abraham his role as a ruler over angels and other living creatures

---

[367.] Davidson, *Theology*, 296-300.

[368.] Ibid.

[369.] Gerhard von Rad, *Genesis: A Commentary*, trans. John H. Marks (London: SCM Press, Ltd., 1961), 189.

[370.] Ibid. On the relationship between pre-Christian Judaism and Jewish Christian angelomorphic Christology see Jean Daniélou, *The Theology of Jewish Christianity*, trans. and ed. John A. Baker (London: Darton, Longman & Todd, 1964), 117-46.

[371.] Perhaps Ezek 1:26-28; 8:2-4; Dan 7:9-14; 10:2-9; "Michael" in *1 Enoch* 9:1; 10:1; 40:9-10; *2 Enoch* 22:6; 33:10; 71:28; 72:5; 1QM 13.10; 17.6-8; "Raphael" in Tob 12:15; "Melchizedek" in 11QMelchizedek.

[372.] Hurtado, *One God*, 75-92.

[373.] R. Rubinkiewicz, "Apocalypse of Abraham (First to Second Century A.D.): A New Translation and Introduction," in *The Old Testament Pseudepigrapha: Apocalyptic Literature and Testaments*, vol. 1, ed. James H. Charlesworth (Garden City, NY: Doubleday, 1983), 683.

[374.] Yahoel and Iaoel are variant spellings of the same angelic figure from the *Apocalypse of Abraham*.

(10:5-17). Abraham describes the appearance of his angelic visitor (11:2-3):

> The appearance of his body was like sapphire, and the aspect of his face was like chrysolite, and the hair of his head like snow. And a kidaris (was) on his head, its look that of a rainbow, and the clothing of his garments (was) purple; and a golden staff (was) in his right hand.[375]

Iaoel promises Abraham: "I will go with you visible until the sacrifice, but after the sacrifice invisible forever" (11:5). Later, after they arrive at the mountain, they see fire approaching them and hear a voice from the midst of the fire. Both Iaoel and Abraham bow down in worship, and Iaoel tells Abraham to recite the song that he taught him (17:1-7). Abraham does just as the angel instructed (17:8-14):

> Eternal One, Mighty One, Holy El, God autocrat
> self-originate, incorruptible, immaculate,
> unbegotten, spotless, immortal,
> self-perfected, self-devised,
> without mother, without father, ungenerated,
> exalted, fiery,
> just, lover of men, benevolent, compassionate, bountiful,
> jealous over me, patient one, most merciful.
> Eli, eternal, mighty one, holy, Sabaoth,
> most glorious El, El, El, El, Iaoel,
> you are he my soul has loved, my protector.

The song continues for several more lines, but the important feature of the song for this discussion is the naming of Iaoel along with other names and attributes of God as Abraham worshiped. By naming Iaoel in the "song," Abraham includes him in the worship which is directed to God. Subsequently, Iaoel departs to bring peace to some troubled angels. In chapter nineteen the dialogue continues between Abraham and the voice from the midst of the fire, the voice of the "Eternal, Mighty One." Recalling once again *Apoc. Abr.* 11:5, Iaoel promised to go with Abraham visible to the sacrifice and thereafter invisible. One may reasonably conclude that the voice of the Eternal, Mighty One is to be identified with Iaoel, who is now invisible but with Abraham.

---

[375]. *Apoc. Abr.* 11:2-3. The description of Iaoel's hair like snow resembles the description of the Ancient of Days in Dan 7:9.

Several conclusions may be drawn from this apocalypse. (1) Iaoel apparently belongs to the angel of Yahweh tradition rooted in the Old Testament. His name most likely is a composite of Yah (יה) and El (אל). The address "Go, Iaoel of the same name, through the mediation of my ineffable name" in 10:3 reinforces this understanding. (2) Iaoel is distinct from God. (3) He nevertheless functions as God (cf. 9:4 with 10:3-5). (4) He is worshiped as God (17:13). Iaoel, therefore, as the angel of Yahweh, is identified with God since he bears the divine name, carries out divine functions, and is the object of worship.

Professor Hurtado placed a great deal of significance upon the Yahoel tradition and found evidence therein to support his thesis. He apparently ignored the fact, however, that Abraham worshiped Yahoel, for he quickly asserted that principal angels as divine agents do not threaten monotheism since they are never worshiped.[376] If Abraham does worship Yahoel as *Apoc. Abr.* 17:13 suggests, a significant aspect of Hurtado's thesis is called into question.

(2) Along this line, Hurtado claimed that Jewish Christianity modified pre-Christian Jewish monotheism. He failed, however, to explain why, if principal angels were only servants or agents of God, the later rabbis looked upon them with suspicion. Alan Segal noted that rabbis in the second century A.D. and beyond considered the principal angel figures to be a threat to monotheism;[377] he found little, however, in pre-Christian speculation which would support the classification of these ideas as heretical.[378] This suggests that a modification of monotheism did come, not in the first century with Christianity as Hurtado suggests, but in later centuries with the rabbis. Apparently, they felt it necessary to define monotheism in stricter terms and thus separate themselves from Christians and Gnostics.

(3) Related to this, Hurtado assumed pre-Christian Jewish monotheism to be exclusivistic and unitarian in nature.[379] He apparently looked to the rabbis for his definition of monotheistic faith and constructed his thesis accordingly. However, can one look to the rabbis to understand pre-Christian monotheism? If the argument above is correct, the rabbis modified monotheism through their

---

[376]. Hurtado, *One God*, 82-83.

[377]. Segal, *Two Powers*, 33-155.

[378]. Ibid., 187-201.

[379]. Hurtado, *One God*, 22-29.

conflict with Christians and other "heretical" groups who viewed monotheism in more fluid terms.

The argument has therefore come full-circle to the basic question which began this section on the nature of pre-Christian Jewish monotheism. How can one account for Paul's christological use of Yahweh texts? What kind of monotheism would allow for Christ to be both identified with God and yet distinct from him? Was there a category within Judaism which would accomodate these seemingly antithetical notions? Perhaps the answer may be found in Judaism's understanding of Yahweh as a corporate person.

Yahweh As a Corporate Person

A. R. Johnson in his book, *The One and the Many in the Israelite Conception of God*,[380] stated concisely and clearly a view of Hebrew theology which has been adopted by a considerable number of scholars.[381] Believing Hebrew anthropology informed Hebrew theology, he began with the Israelite concept of man as possessing "an indefinable 'extension' of the personality" or corporate dimension.[382] Since the Hebrews conceived of God in largely anthropomorphic terms and believed man was created in God's image (Gen 1:26), he argued that they viewed their one God, Yahweh, as having extensions of his own person. He found evidence for this in the concept of the Spirit (רוּחַ),[383] the divine Word (דבר),[384] the Name (שֵׁם),[385] and the Ark of the Covenant.[386] He discovered further evidence for Yahweh's "manyness" in (1) the ambiguity involved in the plural אלהים,[387] (2) the

---

[380] A. R. Johnson, *The One and the Many in the Israelite Conception of God* (Cardiff: University of Wales Press, 1961).

[381] Ellis, "Biblical Interpretation," 716-20; R. P. Shedd, *Man in Community: A Study of St. Paul's Application of Old Testament and Early Jewish Conceptions of Human Solidarity* (London: Epworth Press, 1958); and H. Wheeler Robinson, *Corporate Personality in Ancient Israel*, rev. ed. (Philadelphia: Fortress, 1980). Otherwise see J. W. Rogerson, *Anthropology and the Old Testament* (Atlanta: John Knox, 1979).

[382] Johnson, *One and Many*, 2; pp. 1-13 *passim*.

[383] 1 Kgs 22:19ff.; Judg 6:34; 15:14; 1 Sam 10:6, 10; Ezek 2:1-2; Isa 11:1-3; 61:1-2; cf. Luke 4:16-19.

[384] Isa 55:10-11; 1 Sam 3:11; and Ezek 12:21-28.

[385] Num 6:22-27; Psalm 20; and Deut 12:5, 11, 21.

[386] Num 10:35-36; 1 Sam 4:5-8; and 6:20.

[387] 1 Sam 4:5-8; and Ps 58:11-12.

Angel of Yahweh figure,[388] and (3) the Old Testament concept of the prophet as God's spokesman or Yahweh in person.[389] Johnson concluded that the Israelites, within a monotheistic framework, conceived of their one God as having plural manifestations.

Given this background, it was possible for Jews like Paul and other early Christians to consider Messiah Jesus to be a manifestation of Yahweh.[390] The Hebrew concept of Yahweh as a corporate person provided the category which made possible the application of Old Testament Yahweh texts to Jesus. Apparently Paul believed Jesus was not just a divine agent but God himself, manifest as the Messiah. Although there were other ways to express his unity with God,[391] the application of Yahweh texts to Jesus more than any other title or phrase asserted his identification with Yahweh.

The Catalysts for Paul's Christological Use of Yahweh Texts

The discussion thus far has suggested that Paul's christological use of Yahweh texts implies that he identified Jesus with Yahweh. It has also posited that Judaism's concept of Yahweh as a corporate person provided the category which made this identification possible. Yet the mere presence of this antecedent category in Judaism does not account sufficiently for the application of Yahweh texts to Jesus. Judaism may have provided the seed bed, but it did not provide the cause.

There were at least two catalysts for this unprecedented use of scripture and the divine name. First, the immediate background for Paul's christological use of Yahweh texts may be found in his own religious experiences. Paul began his contact with Christianity as its primary opponent. He persecuted the Church (Phil 3:6), a fact which apparently plagued him all his life (1 Cor 15:9). Nevertheless, Paul was transformed from the Church's primary opponent to its greatest missionary. The transforming event was likely Paul's Damascus road experience,[392] which is recounted in Acts (9:1-9; 22:6-11; and

---

[388]. Gen 16:7-14; Genesis 18-19; Judg 6:11-24; and Hos 12:4-5.

[389]. Jer 9:1; 23:21-23; and Deut 29:2-6.

[390]. Ellis, "Biblical Interpretation," 719.

[391]. E.g., the ambivalence in Paul's expressions, "Spirit of God" and "Spirit of Christ," in Rom 8:9; see also 2 Cor 3:16-18; the title "Son of God" in Matt 11:27; Rom 1:3-4; 8:3; Heb 1:2; "image of God" in 2 Cor 4:4 and Col 1:15; see Kim, *Origin*, 137-41; "wisdom of God" in 1 Cor 1:24, cf. 1:30.

26:12-18) and alluded to by Paul on more than one occasion (e.g., 1 Cor 9:1; 15:8).[393] That life changing revelation, however, was not to be his last. According to his own testimony, he had further visions and revelations of the Lord (2 Cor 12:1-10), although he was unable to determine the exact nature of the event ("whether in the body or out of the body I do not know, God knows").

One of the most provocative and insightful books on Paul's religious experience to appear recently is Alan Segal's *Paul the Convert*.[394] Segal investigates Paul's writings as well as Jewish mystical and apocalyptic texts in order to comprehend his conversion to Christianity. Since the apostle was the only Pharisaic Jew to leave behind a written record, he views Paul as a major source for reconstructing first century Jewish religious life.[395] According to Segal, Paul is a "convert" in the modern sense of the word, even though he never used the term. The most accurate term to describe Paul's experience is "transformation," a term often used in Jewish mystic circles.[396]

To understand Paul's visionary and ecstatic experience, Segal insists, one must inquire into the character of first century Jewish mysticism. He finds considerable affinity between Paul's mystical, apocalyptic experiences and what came to be known later as *merkabah* mysticism. The term *merkabah* derives from certain Jewish mystical traditions from the third century A.D. and describes the throne-chariot vision in Ezekiel 1 and the man-like figure who appears therein. *Merkabah* mysticism emphasized God's manifestations of himself as this man-like figure, the *Kavod*.[397] Although it appeared in its developed form only later, Paul probably represents incipient *merkabah* mysticism or perhaps a tradition which ultimately gave rise to it.

[392.] Kim, *Origin*, 51-100, 223-33, 330-35.

[393.] Ibid., 3-31. Kim related numerous Pauline passages which may refer to his Damascus road experience including 1 Cor 9:1; 15:5-10; Gal 1:13-17; Phil 3:4-11; 2 Cor 3:4-4:6; and 5:16-21.

[394.] Alan Segal, *Paul the Convert: The Apostolate and Apostasy of Saul the Pharisee* (New Haven and London: Yale University Press, 1990).

[395.] Ibid., xi-xiii.

[396.] Ibid., 20-21.

[397.] Ibid., 39-52. Segal notes considerable evidence from Jewish texts which describe this man-like appearance of God.

Segal argues that Luke described Paul's conversion in language reminiscent of Ezekiel's call. During the time Ezekiel lived among the exiles by the Chebar river, he received a spectacular vision which included, among other things, a man-like figure seated on a throne. He called this figure "the appearance of the likeness of the glory of the Lord (יהוה)" (Ezek 1:28). Brilliant lights accompanied the vision, surrounding it and emanating from it. When he saw it, he fell to the ground and heard the Lord calling him to go and preach to the rebellious nation of Israel (2:1ff.). In similar fashion, according to Segal, Luke narrated Paul's conversion and call. As Saul approached Damascus to engage in further campaigns against "the Way," he was blinded by a brilliant light, fell to the ground, and heard the risen Jesus charge him to go to the Gentiles (another rebellious people) with a new message of salvation. If Segal is correct, Luke intentionally constructs his account to imply that Paul's encounter with Jesus was, in reality, his encounter with the Glory of the Lord (*Kavod Yahweh*).[398]

Further support for this understanding of Paul's conversion is present in the apostle's own writings as he links aspects of glory with Christ (e.g., Phil 3:21; 4:19; 1 Cor 2:8; Rom 6:4; 9:23). In particular he alluded to his conversion and on-going transformation utilizing "glory" terminology (2 Cor 3:18): "and we all, with unveiled face, beholding the glory of the Lord, are being changed into his likeness from one degree of glory to another; for this comes from the Lord who is the Spirit." Later in the same passage he united light imagery with his description of the Lord's glory (2 Cor 4:4-6):

> In their case the god of this world has blinded the minds of the unbelievers, to keep them from seeing the light of the gospel of the glory of Christ, who is the likeness of God. . . . For it is the God who said, "Let light shine out of darkness," who has shone in our hearts to give the light of the knowledge of the glory of God in the face of Christ.

Believers, Paul affirmed, reflect the Lord's glory—understood to be Christ[399]—and are being transformed into his likeness (cf. Rom 8:29). Unbelievers, however, cannot see this light, which he further explained as the gospel of the glory of Christ, the image of God. The contrast is obvious. Whereas the god of this age blinds unbelieving minds, the God of Paul's gospel causes the light to shine in believing

---

[398.] Ibid., 9-11.

[399.] See above pp. 155-57.

hearts and thereby effects transformation. While this text has great import for a number of Pauline teachings, our concern is twofold: (1) he described this transformation as effected by the believer's encounter with "glory" and (2) he connected this experience of "glory" with Christ ("the glory of God in the face of Christ"). This suggests that Paul understood his revelation of Christ as an experience with the glory of the Lord, the *Kavod Yahweh*. This being the case, it is likely that he would identify Christ as Yahweh manifest and therefore readily quote Yahweh texts and apply them to Christ.

Therefore, Segal concludes that Paul's transformation and his mystical ascension form the basis of his theology. He writes:

> His language shows the marks of a man who has learned the contemporary vocabulary for expressing a theophany and then has received one. This language of vision has informed his thought in a number of crucial respects. First, it has allowed him to develop a concept of the divinity of Christ or the messiah both as a unique development within the Jewish mystical tradition and as characteristically Christian. Second, he used this Jewish mystical vocabulary to express the transformation experienced by believers.[400]

Apparently, the apostle Paul became convinced through his personal experiences with the risen Lord on the Damascus road and beyond that in Jesus he had encountered the glory of Yahweh. Therefore, he identified Jesus with the God of scripture. He emphasized this identity by attributing to Jesus (1) his name (= Yahweh), (2) his work, and (3) scripture texts reserved originally for Yahweh.

Second, since Paul believed that the risen Christ was identical with Jesus of Nazareth, the ultimate source for the conviction that the Messiah was Yahweh manifest lay in Jesus' own words and ministry. What Jesus did and said, accompanied by their experience of his resurrection, caused the first disciples to believe that he was not only the Messiah, but God himself manifest for their salvation. Several aspects of Jesus' earthly ministry provide sufficient warrant for this conclusion.

(1) According to the Gospels, Jesus performed miracles which caused amazement among his disciples. Miracles, especially healing miracles, were apparently common enough in the ancient world,[401]

---

[400] Ibid., 69.

[401] France, "Uniqueness," 207.

but it seems that in particular his nature miracles and his ability to raise the dead caused his disciples to wonder who he really was (e.g., Mark 4:35-41; 5:42; John 2:19-21.).[402]

(2) Related to this is Jesus' claim that he would raise himself from the dead. Most Gospel passages say simply that Jesus (the Son of Man) will arise (ἀναστῆναι, Mark 8:31; ἀναστήσεται, Mark 9:31, 10:34, Luke 18:33) or be raised (ἐγερθῆναι, Matt 16:21, Luke 9:22; ἐγερθήσεται, Matt 17:23, 20:19) apparently by God (Acts 2:32). In the passion narrative, however, at Jesus' trial before the high priest, his accusers said: "We heard him say, 'I will destroy this temple that is made with hands, and in three days I will build another, not made with hands'" (Mark 14:58; cf. Mark 15:29; and par.). Mark referred to these accusers as false, not because their testimony was untrue but because they misrepresented Jesus' saying and portrayed him as a seditious criminal. In all likelihood the saying is authentic, and the reference is to Jesus' resurrection as it establishes the new eschatological community.[403]

(3) Jesus also claimed to forgive sins (Mark 2:1-12; Matt 9:1-8; and Luke 5:17-26). Even though the disciples' reaction to this claim is not recorded, the scribes who heard Jesus forgive the sins of the paralytic (Mark 2:5) charged him with blasphemy for usurping the prerogative of God ("who can forgive sins but God alone?"). No doubt the followers of Jesus on this occasion were well aware of the opposition to their master and the cause for it.

(4) Jesus also seemed to possess a special, intimate relationship with God. This is expressed above all in his unique use of *Abba* for God (Mark 14:36) and his instruction for followers to pray "Our Father" (Matt 6:9; cf. Luke 11:2; Rom 8:15; Gal 4:6).[404] It is further

---

[402]. Not all, of course, regard the miracles as historical. Albert Schweitzer, *The Quest for the Historical Jesus*, trans. W. Montgomery (New York: MacMillan, 1968), 1-222, surveyed various explanations of Jesus' miracles among nineteenth century rationalists and liberal scholars. R. Bultmann, *The History of the Synoptic Tradition*, trans. John Marsh (Oxford: Basil Blackwell, 1968, 215-45, noting parallels in pagan literature, denied their historicity. Other scholars affirm them as real events in history including Alan Richardson, *The Miracle-Stories of the Gospels* (London: SCM Press, 1941), 20-37, 123-38; Colin Brown, *Miracles and the Critical Mind* (Grand Rapids: Eerdmans, 1984); H. van der Loos, *The Miracles of Jesus* (Leiden: E. J. Brill, 1965), 699-706.

[403]. James D. G. Dunn, *Jesus and the Spirit: A Study of the Religious and Charismatic Experience of Jesus and the First Christians As Reflected in the New Testament* (Philadelphia: Westminster, 1975), 186; and E. E. Ellis, "Background and Christology of John's Gospel: Selected Motifs," *SWJT* 31 (1988): 28-29.

demonstrated by Jesus' teaching in Matt 11:27: "All things have been delivered to me by my Father; and no one knows the Son except the Father, and no one knows the Father except the Son and any one to whom the Son chooses to reveal him." Certainly Jesus' filial consciousness influenced those first disciples.

(5) Jesus applied to himself concepts and texts which the Old Testament applied to Yahweh.[405] (a) In Mark 13:31 (par. Matt 24:35; Luke 21:33) Jesus, speaking of his own teaching ministry, said: "Heaven and earth will pass away, but my words will not pass away." This saying recalls Isa 40:8 which refers to the enduring affect of Yahweh' words. (b) Following the cleansing of the temple, Jesus' opponents became indignant because of the praise he received. Jesus responded to them with the question: "Have you never read, 'Out of the mouth of babes and sucklings thou hast brought perfect praise'?" (Matt 21:16). His response seems to be a rather explicit quotation of Ps 8:2. In this Old Testament passage Yahweh uses the praise of children to silence his enemies. Jesus adopted it as his defense against the chief priests and scribes. (c) In Luke 10:19, following the return of the seventy, Jesus said that he had given them "authority to tread upon serpents and scorpions, and over all the power of the enemy." His words are reminiscent of Ps 91:13, a passage in which Yahweh promises that his followers will tread on the lion and the serpent. As Yahweh protects his people, Jesus protects his disciples. (d) Jesus concluded the parable of the wicked tenants by alluding to Dan 2:34-35, 44-45 and Isa 8:14-15 (Luke 20:18). In the latter, Isaiah warned that Yahweh would become "a stone of offense, and a rock of stumbling to both houses of Israel." Furthermore, he said: "and many shall stumble thereon; they shall fall and be broken." It is clear that Isaiah considered Yahweh to be the stone. Jesus, however, alluded to these texts and applied them to himself as the son of the vineyard owner (God). He believed he would be rejected by the tenants (the Jews), but would be vindicated by his Father. Jesus then quoted Ps 118:22: "The very stone which the builders rejected has become the head of the corner" (Luke 20:17). He therefore considered himself not only the rejected Son but also the rejected stone, a stone which will

---

[404.] See Joachim Jeremias, *The Prayers of Jesus* (London: SCM Press, 1967), 54-62; idem, *New Testament Theology: The Proclamation of Jesus*, vol 1 (London: SCM Press, 1971), 1:62-67; and Dunn, *Jesus*, 21-26.

[405.] R. T. France, *Jesus and the Old Testament: His Application of Old Testament Passages to Himself and His Mission* (Downers Grove, IL: Inter-Varsity Press, 1971), 150-59.

be established by God and upon which many will stumble and be broken.

In a similar fashion Jesus referred to John the Baptist and his ministry in terms of Mal 3:1 and 3:23-24 (4:5-6).[406] In Mal 3:1 Yahweh speaks and promises to send "my messenger" (מלאכי) to prepare the way for him. In Mal 3:23-24 Yahweh says that he will send Elijah the prophet prior to the coming of the Day of Yahweh. Given their similar function, it is likely that that these two figures represent the same "forerunner."[407] Nevertheless, Jesus adopted these prophecies and related them to the ministry of John the Baptist. If Jesus considered John to be this promised forerunner, in all probability he saw his own ministry as the coming of Yahweh.

Still other dominical sayings portray the Son of Man in images typical of Yahweh in the Old Testament. In particular Matt 25:31-46 contains allusions to Dan 7:9, Zech 14:5, and Joel 3:1-2. Each of these Old Testament passages portrays aspects of the Day of Yahweh. On that day Yahweh (or the Ancient of Days) will sit upon the throne surrounded by an angelic retinue and judge the nations. Jesus applied these same images to himself as the coming Son of Man in Matt 25:31-46.[408]

These examples imply that Jesus saw his own ministry in terms of images and concepts which the Old Testament reserves for Yahweh. They further imply that his disciples first experienced the impressions of his oneness with God through his teaching ministry.

Even if some scholars dismiss many of Jesus' sayings and deeds as inventions of the early Church, they cannot dismiss all of them. Likewise they cannot discount the rapid rise of devotion to him in a largely Palestinian context. A Jesus who said and did nothing worth remembering or recording could hardly have influenced his followers

---

[406.] Matt 11:10, 14; 17:11-12; Mark 9:12-13; Luke 7:27.

[407.] France, *Jesus*, 91-92.

[408.] The relationship of Jesus to the Son of Man has long been debated. Some deny the authenticity of the Son of Man sayings in the Gospels, e.g., Conzelmann, *Outline*, 131-37. Others believe Jesus expected another figure who would be the Son of Man, including Bultmann, *Theology*, 1:28-32; Fuller, *Foundations*, 119-25; Hahn, *Titles*, 15-53; and particularly H. E. Tödt, *The Son of Man in the Synoptic Tradition*, trans. D. M. Barton (Philadelphia: Westminster Press; London: SCM Press, 1965). Still others consider the Son of Man sayings to be not only authentic but expressive of Jesus' own self-understanding, e.g., Kim, *Son of Man*, 7-14; and Lindars, *Jesus Son of Man*, 1-17.

in such a way that they worshiped him so soon after his crucifixion. Indeed the impact he made upon them should not be underestimated.

These deeds and sayings by Jesus, therefore, in conjunction with the belief that he had conquered death, may well have been the ultimate catalyst for the conviction that Jesus the Messiah occupied divine status as Yahweh.[409] The first believers apparently saw in his coming the coming of God into the world.

The apostle Paul probably persecuted the early Church for such beliefs[410] and was not convinced of their validity until the risen Christ apprehended him upon the Damascus road. Following that transforming encounter, however, he became a bold proponent of a gospel which centered upon a crucified Messiah whom he identified with the risen Lord.

Paul's "High" Christology

Paul's christological use of Yahweh texts calls into question the construct that Christianity moved from a "low" Christology, represented by Paul's letters, to a "high" Christology, represented by the Fourth Gospel. This construct is based upon the supposition that, during the decades which separated these writings, significant changes occurred with regard to Christians' thinking about Christ. It is also based upon the conclusion that Paul never explicitly called Jesus "God"—apart from debated texts including Rom 9:5 and Tit 2:13—and John asserted clearly the unity of the Father and the Son (John 1:1-18; 5:17-19; 10:37-38; 14:9-11; perhaps also the "I am" sayings in John 4:26; 6:35; 8:12, 58; 10:11; 11:25; and 14:6). For example, in the prologue John wrote (1:1): "the Word was God" (θεὸς ἦν ὁ λόγος). Likewise, following the resurrection, Thomas saw Jesus and addressed him (20:28): "My Lord and my God!" (ὁ κύριος μου καὶ ὁ θεός μου). These texts, along with others, indicate that the author thought Jesus was God.[411] It is supposed, however, that Paul never took that step and never identified Christ with God in any substantial way.[412]

Upon close examination, however, one sees that Paul shared some important similarities with John in his view of Christ. For example,

---

[409.] Ellis, "Biblical Interpretation," 718-19.

[410.] Marxsen, *IDBS*, 149.

[411.] Scroggs, *Christology*, 65-67.

[412.] Ibid., 52.

as argued above, Paul's christological use of Yahweh texts indicates that he considered his Lord Jesus to be equal with God or, to put it in Johannine language, to be one with him (John 1:1-18; 5:17-19; 10:37-38; and 14:9-11). At the same time, Paul asserted that Jesus was distinct from God, a notion also reflected in the Fourth Gospel. John wrote (1:1): "the Word was with God" (ὁ λόγος ἦν πρὸς τὸν θεόν). This statement clearly implies individual existence distinct from God. Furthermore, Paul claimed that in some sense Jesus was subordinate to God the Father (e.g., 1 Cor 3:23; 15:25-28). Likewise, John wrote (5:19): "Jesus said to them, 'Truly, truly, I say to you, the Son can do nothing of his own accord, but only what he sees the Father doing; for whatever he does, that the Son does likewise.'" Later, quoting Jesus again, he wrote (5:30): "'I can do nothing on my own authority; as I hear, I judge; and my judgment is just, because I seek not my own will but the will of him who sent me.'" These words upon Jesus' lips indicate the subordination of the Son to the Father. He has no independent will. He has no authority of his own. He does only what he sees the Father doing. Yet Christ's subordination to God does not undermine thoughts of his equality with God. While these may at first appear to be antithetical notions, the biblical writers apparently did not think so. Upon the basis of these Johannine texts Scroggs concluded: *"Complete subordination means complete equality!"*[413]

Certainly differences exist between Paul's and John's Christologies, yet they are mainly terminological. John, who wrote late in the first century, utilized terms and expressions with which Paul may not have been familiar. Moreover, he was writing a Gospel not an epistle. Likewise, Paul ministered at a different time and among different people than did John, and the terms he brought to bear upon his understanding of Christ were naturally different. The substance of their Christologies, however, were the same, namely, Jesus is God and yet he is distinct from and subordinate to God.

Most interpreters agree that several decades separate the composition of Paul's letters from the writing of the Fourth Gospel. As one reads the Gospel and letters attributed to John, it is apparent that what is in danger of being lost is not the divinity of Jesus but his humanity. Therefore, the author insists that only deceivers and anti-Christs deny that Jesus came in the flesh (John 1:14; 1 John 4:2-3; 2 John 7); true believers continue to hold to that important doctrine. The problem facing John then is a Christology which is too

---

[413.] Ibid., 79; with regard to Pauline theology see Ellis, *Pauline Theology*, 57-61.

high, a Christology which, among certain circles, denies Jesus' humanity. Since this is true, it is difficult to understand how some interpret early Christianity and its most prominent spokesman, the apostle Paul, as representing a "low Christology." Or, to put it another way, could Paul's "low Christology"—as some would have it—have evolved so quickly to a Christology which denied Jesus' humanity? The evidence from Paul's letters and particularly his use of Yahweh texts suggests that he identifies Jesus as Yahweh manifest and thus his Christology is already "high."

These factors demonstrate that Paul's and John's Christologies have more in common than has sometimes been allowed. It indicates further that certain theories of christological development—for example, the "evolutionary" view of the History of Religions School[414]—actually misinterpret much of the evidence. The differences between Paul's and John's Christologies are not due to the gradual accumulation of foreign ideas which were not inherent from the beginning; rather they arose as successive generations of Christians sought to unfold the mystery of Jesus' person and to defend it against misunderstanding. As Moule wrote, the words they used were: "only attempts to describe what was already there from the beginning."[415]

[414.] Moule, *Origin*, 1-10.

[415.] Ibid., 3.

Conclusion

This volume has analyzed Paul's use of Old Testament Yahweh texts and proposed some implications for Paul's Christology. The conclusion will serve to summarize and highlight aspects of this study.

Chapter one dealt with contributions scholars in this century have made toward understanding the origin and content of κύριος as a christological designation. First, it discussed the theory held by Bousset, Hahn, and others that the christological use of κύριος arose outside Palestine. Proponents of this theory considered Jewish monotheism in Palestine too exclusivistic to allow the application of a term connoting deity to be applied to Jesus. Second, it treated the theory advanced by Machen, Rawlinson, Cullmann, and others that Palestinian Jewish believers called Jesus κύριος in the full sense of divinity. Proponents of this theory argued against the importance of Greco-Roman influences on early Christianity and upheld its Jewish background as the dominant factor in the formation of its Christology. Chapter one then went on to analyze the presuppositions upon which the Hellenistic theory was based and concluded that the theory of a Palestinian origin for the christological use of κύριος appears to be in harmony with evidence in Paul's letters and the rest of the New Testament.

The Septuagint used κύριος as both a human designation and a translation for Yahweh, the special name for God in the Old Testament. While the LXX exercised great latitude in employing κύριος and drew little distinction between sacred and secular uses of the term, the majority of occurrences are translations of the divine name. This fact suggests, among other things, that κύριος had a firm place within first century Jewish religious worship practices.

Paul used κύριος as a designation for men in authority, the God of Israel, pagan gods, and Jesus Christ. He employed the title as a christological designation more than any other title, with the exception of Χριστός. Chapter two classified and analyzed Paul's use of κύριος with the goal of formulating Paul's κύριος Christology. It found that (1) Paul inherited this designation from early Christianity, (2) he considered Jesus' Lordship to be cosmic in scope, (3) he based Jesus' Lordship upon his resurrection and exaltation to the right hand of God, (4) he used κύριος to underscore the unique relationship between God the Father and Jesus, (5) he employed the title frequently in ethical admonitions, (6) he utilized κύριος in his discussions of the Lord's Supper, and (7) he applied κύριος to Jesus when discussing eschatological events such as (a) the Day of the Lord, (b) the Second Coming, and (c) the final judgment. One implication of Paul's κύριος Christology is that he used κύριος as a christological title to apply to Jesus concepts and functions originally reserved for Yahweh in the Old Testament.

The final chapter engaged in a contextual and exegetical study of Pauline quotations and allusions to Yahweh texts. It observed that Paul quoted Old Testament Yahweh texts fourteen times. It explored each quotation in light of its context and Paul's κύριος Christology in order to determine the referent for each Yahweh text. It classified them as "Yahweh Texts with God As Referent" and "Yahweh Texts with Christ As Referent."

Chapter three also presented some implications for Paul's use of Yahweh texts. It suggested that the application of Yahweh texts to Christ occurred within the churches in Palestine at an early date and was not an innovation of the later Greek churches. In this regard it proposed that Paul's use of Yahweh texts reflected a fluid boundary between God and Christ in Palestinian Judaism, a fact recently noted and designated a "conceptual overlap" by L. Joseph Kreitzer. The application of divine functions and Old Testament texts to redeemer figures in the Pseudepigrapha and the Dead Sea Scrolls demonstrates that this "conceptual overlap" was already an aspect of Jewish exegesis prior to Paul's time.

Some may disagree whether a certain text refers to God or to Christ; but it is clear that Paul, as well as the traditions from which he drew, occasionally applied to Jesus texts originally referring to Yahweh. Given his high regard for scripture, this exegetical practice means that Paul considered Jesus to be a manifestion of Yahweh. It means that he identified Jesus with Yahweh in a substantive way despite the opinion of some to the contrary.[1]

For Paul, Christ was not simply a man, nor was he merely an intermediary figure popular in Jewish apocalyptic writings.[2] He was more than God's agent to effect redemption in the world. He remained distinct, yet fully identified with the Yahweh.[3]

---

[1] E.g., Scroggs, *Christology*, 52.

[2] Hurtado, *One God*, 17-92.

[3] France, "Worship," 25; Kreitzer, *Jesus and God*, 16. First Corinthians 8:6 gives

Conclusion

The understanding of Christ as Yahweh manifest explains many aspects of early Christian practice and doctrine. It explains why early Christians offered prayers and hymns to Christ and placed him at the center of their worship. It gives a basis for the application of the title θεός to Jesus (e.g., Rom 9:5; and Tit 2:13). It clarifies why early Christians gave the words of Jesus authoritative status equal to Old Testament scripture. Furthermore, the conviction that Jesus occupies divine status as Yahweh accounts for other christological notions such as his pre-existence, his role in creation, and his role as the coming eschatological Savior and Judge.

The amazing fact of Paul's religion is that he considered Jesus, a man who died a scandalous death and who, for a short period of time, was contemporary with him, to be divine. Had Paul been a polytheist, this would have been far less significant. But he was a Jew, a monotheist, who looked with contempt upon polytheists and idolators (1 Cor 8:4-6; 10:14-22). For a monotheist to call Jesus "Lord" and to apply to him Old Testament texts originally reserved for Yahweh is astounding. Machen stated: "Yet it was this monotheist sprung of a race of monotheists, who stood in a full religious relation to a man who had died but a few years before; it was this monotheist who designated that man, as a matter of course, by the supreme religious term 'Lord,' and did not hesitate to apply to Him the passages in the Greek Old Testament where that term was used to translate the most awful name of the God of Israel!"[4] Could there indeed be a "higher" Christology?

---

evidence of this binitarian devotion to God the Father and the Lord Jesus Christ. If Paul understood Jesus to be the κύριος of 2 Cor 3:16, then subsequent verses identifying "Lord" with "Spirit" may suggest the beginnings of trinitarian devotion. This possibility is strengthened by the concluding verse of 2 Corinthians (13:14): "the grace of the Lord Jesus Christ and the love of God and the fellowship of the Holy Spirit be with you all."

[4.] Machen, *Origin*, 22-24.

Bibliography

Abbott, T. K. *A Critical and Exegetical Commentary on the Epistles to the Ephesians and to the Colossians.* The International Critical Commentary. Edinburgh: T. & T. Clark, 1909.

Aletti, Jean-Noel. *Colossiens 1:15-20.* Rome: Biblical Institute, 1981.

Allegro, J. M. "Fragments of a Qumran Scroll of Eschatological Midrashim." *Journal of Biblical Literature* 77 (1958): 350-54.

Anderson, B. W. "Lord of Hosts." *The Interpreter's Dictionary of the Bible*, 3:151.

Bailey, K. E. "Recovering the Poetic Structure of I Cor. i 17 - ii 2: A Study in Text and Commentary." *Novum Testamentum* 17 (1975): 265-96.

Balch, David. "Backgrounds of I Cor VII: Sayings of the Lord in Q; Moses as an Ascetic *theios aner* in II Cor III." *New Testament Studies* 18 (1972): 351-64.

Barrett, C. K. *A Commentary on the Epistle to the Romans.* Harper's New Testament Commentaries. New York: Harper & Row, 1957.

──────. *A Commentary on the Second Epistle to the Corinthians.* Harper's New Testament Commentaries. New York: Harper & Row, 1973.

──────. *Essays on Paul.* Philadelphia: Westminster Press, 1982.

──────. *The First Epistle to the Corinthians.* Harper's New Testament Commentaries. New York: Harper & Row, 1968.

──────. *From First Adam to Last.* New York: Charles Scribner's Sons, 1962.

──────. *The Pastoral Epistles.* The New Clarendon Bible. Oxford: Clarendon Press, 1963.

Barth, Karl. *The Epistle to the Romans.* Translated by Edwyn C. Hoskyns. 6th ed. London: Oxford University Press, 1933.

Baudissin, Wolf Wilhelm Graf. *Kyrios als Gottesname im Judentum und seine Stelle in der Religionsgeschichte.* Giessen: Töpelmann, 1929.

Bauernfeind, Otto. "μάταιος." *Theological Dictionary of the New Testament*, 4:519-22.

Beare, F. W. *A Commentary on the Epistle to the Philippians.* Black's New Testament Commentaries. London: Adam and Charles Black, 1959.

_____. *The Earliest Records of Jesus.* New York: Abingdon Press, 1962.

Beasley-Murray, G. R. *Baptism in the New Testament.* Grand Rapids: Eerdmans, 1962.

_____. *Jesus and the Kingdom of God.* Grand Rapids: Eerdmans, 1986.

Beasley-Murray, Paul. "Colossians 1:15-20; An Early Christian Hymn Celebrating the Lordship of Christ." In *Pauline Studies: Essays Presented to Professor F. F. Bruce on His 70th Birthday,* ed. Donald A. Hagner and Murray J. Harris, 169-83. Grand Rapids: Eerdmans, 1980.

Bedale, Stephen. "The Meaning of *kephale* in the Pauline Epistles." *Journal of Theological Studies* 5 (1954): 211-15.

Behm, Johannes. "νοῦς." *Theological Dictionary of the New Testament,* 4:951-60.

Beker, J. Christiaan. *Paul the Apostle: The Triumph of God in Life and Thought.* Philadelphia: Fortress, 1980.

Benz, Ernst. *Paulus als Visionär.* Wiesbaden: Akademie der Wissenschaften und der Literatur, 1952.

Bernard, J. H. *The Pastoral Epistles.* Cambridge: Cambridge University Press, 1899; reprint, Grand Rapids: Baker, 1980.

Bertram, Georg. "στερεός." *Theological Dictionary of the New Testament,* 7:609-614.

Best, Ernest. *A Commentary on the First and Second Epistles to the Thessalonians.* Black's New Testament Commentaries. London: Adam and Charles Black, 1972.

Betz, Hans Dieter. "2 Cor 6:14-7:1: An Anti-Pauline Fragment?" *Journal of Biblical Literature* 92 (1973): 88-108.

Beyer, Hermann W. "εὐλογέω." *Theological Dictionary of the New Testament.* 2:754-65.

Bietenhard, Hans. "ὄνομα [κτλ]." *Theological Dictionary of the New Testament,* 5:242-83.

Black, Matthew. "The Christological Use of the Old Testament in the New Testament." *New Testament Studies* 18 (1971): 1-14.

_____. "The Maranatha Invocation and Jude 14, 15 (1 Enoch 1:9)." In *Christ and Spirit in the New Testament: Studies in Honor of C. F. D. Moule,* ed. Barnabas Lindars and Stephen S. Smalley, 189-96. Cambridge: Cambridge University Press, 1973.

_____. *Romans.* In the New Century Bible. Greenwood, SC: The Attic Press, 1973.

_____. *The Scrolls and Christian Origins: Studies in the Jewish Background of the New Testament.* New York: Charles Scribner's Sons, 1961.

Boers, Hendrikus. "Jesus and the Christian Faith: New Testament Christology Since Bousset's *Kyrios Christos.*" *Journal of Biblical Literature* 89 (1970): 450-56.

Borchert, Gerald L. *Paul and His Interpreters: An Annotated Bibliography.* Madison, WI: Theological Studies Fellowship, 1985.

Bornkamm, Günther. *Early Christian Experience.* New York: Harper & Row, 1969.

_____. "μυστήριον." *Theological Dictionary of the New Testament,* 4:802-823.

_____. *Paul.* Translated by D. M. G. Stalker. New York: Harper & Row, 1969.

Bousset, Wilhelm. *Kyrios Christos: A History of the Belief in Christ from the Beginnings of Christianity to Irenaeus.* Translated by John E. Steely. Nashville: Abingdon, 1970.

Boyd, Glenn E. "A Brief Background to Recent Christology." *Restoration Quarterly* 26 (1983): 129-43.

Branick, V. P. "Source and Redaction Analysis of 1 Corinthians 1-3." *Journal of Biblical Literature* 101 (1982): 251-69.

Brooks, James A., and Carlton L. Winbery. *Syntax of New Testament Greek.* Washington, DC: University Press of America, 1979.

Brown, R. E. "Does the New Testament Call Jesus God?" *Theological Studies* 26 (1965): 545-73.

Brownlee, William H. *The Midrash Pesher of Habukkuk.* Society of Biblical Literature Monograph Series, no. 24. Missoula, MT: Scholars Press, 1979.

Bruce, F. F. *1 and 2 Corinthians.* The New Century Bible Commentary. Grand Rapids: Eerdmans, 1971.

_____. "Colossian Problems Part 2: The Christ Hymn of Colossians 1:15-20." *Bibliotheca Sacra* 141 (1984): 99-111.

_____. *The Epistles to the Colossians, to Philemon, and to the Ephesians.* The New International Commentary on the New Testament. Grand Rapids: Eerdmans, 1984.

_____. *The Epistle of Paul to the Romans.* Tyndale New Testament Commentaries. Grand Rapids: Eerdmans, 1963.

_____. "Jesus is Lord." In *Soli Deo Gloria: New Testament Studies in Honor of William Childs Robinson,* ed. J. McDowell Richards, 23-36. Richmond, VA: John Knox Press, 1968.

_____. *New Testament Development of Old Testament Themes.* Grand Rapids: Eerdmans, 1968.

_____. *Paul: Apostle of the Heart Set Free.* Grand Rapids: Eerdmans, 1971.

Büchsel, Friedrich. "παραδίδωμι." *Theological Dictionary of the New Testament,* 2:169-72.

Bultmann, Rudolf. "ἀφίημι [κτλ]." *Theological Dictionary of the New Testament,* 1:509-12.

_____. "γινώσκω." *Theological Dictionary of the New Testament,* 1:689-719.

_____. "καύχομαι [κτλ]." *Theological Dictionary of the New Testament,* 3:645-54.

_____. "Karl Barth, The Resurrection of the Dead." Chap. in *Faith and Understanding.* Translated by Louise Pettibone Smith. New York: Harper & Row, 1969.

_____. "Das Problem der Ethik bei Paulus." *Zeitschrift für die neutestamentliche Wissenschaft* 23 (1924): 123-40.

_____. *The Second Letter to the Corinthians.* Translated by Roy A. Harrisville. Minneapolis: Augsburg, 1985.

_____. *Theology of the New Testament.* 2 Vols. Translated by Kendrick Grobel. New York: Charles Scribner's Sons, 1951-55.

Bultmann, Rudolf and Dieter Lührmann. "ἐπιφαίνω [κτλ]." *Theological Dictionary of the New Testament,* 9:7-10.

Burney, C. F. "Christ as the *ARCHE* of Creation." *Journal of Theological Studies* 27 (1926): 160-77.

Burton, Ernest DeWitt. *A Critical and Exegetical Commentary on the Epistle to the Galatians.* The International Critical Commentary. Edinburgh: T & T Clark, 1921.

Caird, G. B. "The Development of the Doctrine of Christ in the New Testament." In *Christ for Us Today,* ed. Norman Pittenger, 66-80. London: SCM Press, 1968.

Casey, Maurice. "Chronology and the Development of Pauline Christology." In *Paul and Paulinism: Essays in Honor of C. K. Barrett,* ed. M. D. Hooker and S. G. Wilson, 124-34. London: S.P.C.K., 1982.

Cate, Robert L. *Old Testament Roots for New Testament Faith.* Nashville: Broadman, 1982.

Cerfaux, Lucien. *Christ in the Theology of Paul.* Translated by Geoffrey Webb and Adrian Walker. New York: Herder and Herder, 1959.

_____. "<<Kyrios>> dans les citations pauliniennes de l'Ancien Testament." Chap. in *Recueil Lucien Cerfaux: Etudes d'exégèse et d'histoire religieuse de Monseigneur Cerfaux.* Vol. 1. Gemblux: J. Duculot, 1954.

_____. "Vestiges d'un florilège dans I Cor. 1.18-3.24?" *Revue d'historie ecclesiastique* 27 (1931): 521-34.

Chamberlain, J. V. "The Functions of God as Messianic Title in the Complete Qumran Isaiah Scroll." *Vetus Testamentum* 5 (1955): 366-72.

Clements, Ronald E. "'A Remnant Chosen by Grace' (Romans 11:5): The Old Testament Background and Origin of the Remnant Concept." In *Pauline Studies: Essays Presented to Professor F. F. Bruce on His 70th Birthday,* ed. Donald A. Hagner and Murray J. Harris, 106-21. Exeter: Paternoster Press, 1980.

Collins, Raymond F. *Studies on the First Letter to the Thessalonians.* Leuven: University Press, 1984.

Conzelmann, Hans. *First Corinthians.* Hermeneia. Translated by James W. Leitch. Philadelphia: Fortress, 1975.

_____. *An Outline of the Theology of the New Testament.* New York: Harper & Row, 1969.

Cowley, Arthur Ernest. *Aramaic Papyri of the Fifth Century B.C.* Oxford: Clarendon Press, 1923.

Craddock, Fred B. "All Things in Him: A Critical Note on Col. 1:15-20." *New Testament Studies* 12 (1965): 78-80.

_____. *The Pre-existence of Christ in the New Testament.* Nashville: Abingdon, 1968.

Cranfield, C. E. B. *A Critical and Exegetical Commentary on the Epistle to the Romans.* The International Critical Commentary. 2 Vols. Edinburgh: T. & T. Clark, 1975.

Cullmann, Oscar. *Christ and Time: The Primitive Christian Conception of Time and History.* Translated by Floyd V. Filson. Philadelphia: Westminster, 1950.

_____. *The Christology of the New Testament.* Translated by Shirley Guthrie and Charles A. M. Hall. Philadelphia: Westminster, 1959.

_____. *The Earliest Christian Confessions.* Translated by J. K. S. Reid. London: Lutterworth Press, 1949.

Daniélou, Jean. *The Theology of Jewish Christianity.* Translated and edited by John A. Baker. London: Darton, Longman & Todd, 1964.

Davidson, A. B. *The Theology of the Old Testament*. Edinburgh: T. & T. Clark, 1904.

Davies, W. D. *Paul and Rabbinic Judaism: Some Rabbinic Elements in Pauline Theology*. 4th ed. Philadelphia: Fortress, 1980.

———. *Torah in the Messianic Age and/or the Age to Come*. Philadelphia: Society of Biblical Literature, 1952.

Davis, Philip G. "The Mythic Enoch: New Light on Early Christology." *Studies in Religion/Sciences religieuses* 13 (1984): 335-43.

Deichgräber, Reinhard. *Gotteshymnus und Christushymnus in der frühen Christenheit: Untersuchungen zu Form, Sprache und Stil der frühchristlichen Hymnen*. Göttingen: Vandenhoeck & Ruprecht, 1967.

Deissmann, Adolf. *Light from the Ancient East: The New Testament Illustrated by Recently Discovered Texts of the Graeco-Roman World*. Translated by Lionel R. M. Strachan. 4th ed. New York: Harper & Brothers, 1922.

de Jongue, Marinus. *Christology in Context: The Earliest Christian Response to Jesus*. Philadelphia: Westminster Press, 1988.

de Jongue, Marinus and A. S. van der Woude. "11QMelchizedek and the New Testament." *New Testament Studies* 12 (1966): 301-26.

de Lacey, D. R. "Image and Incarnation in Pauline Christology." *Tyndale Bulletin* 30 (1979): 3-28.

———. "'One Lord' in Pauline Christology." In *Christ the Lord: Studies in Christology Presented to Donald Guthrie*, ed. Harold H. Rowdon, 191-203. Leicester, UK: Inter-Varsity Press, 1982.

Delling, Gerhard. "ἡμέρα." *Theological Dictionary of the New Testament*, 2:947-53.

———. "παραλαμβάνω." *Theological Dictionary of the New Testament*, 4:11-14.

———. "πλήρωμα." *Theological Dictionary of the New Testament*, 6:298-305.

———. "συμβιβάζω." *Theological Dictionary of the New Testament*, 7:763-66.

———. "συντελέω." *Theological Dictionary of the New Testament*, 8:62-64.

———. *Worship in the New Testament*. Translated by Percy Scott. Philadelphia: Westminster, 1962.

Dibelius, Martin and Hans Conzelmann. *The Pastoral Epistles*. Hermeneia. Translated by Philip Buttolph and Adela Yarbro. Philadelphia: Fortress, 1972.

Dodd, C. H. *According to the Scriptures: The Substructure of New Testament Theology.* London: Nisbet & Co., 1952.

──────. *The Epistle of Paul to the Romans.* The Moffatt New Testament Commentary. New York: Harper & Brothers, 1932.

Doty, William G. *Letters in Primitive Christianity.* Guides to Biblical Scholarship Series. Philadelphia: Fortress, 1973.

Duling, Dennis C. "The Promises to David and Their Entrance into Christianity—Nailing Down a Likely Hypothesis." *New Testament Studies* 20 (1974): 55-77.

Dungan, David. *The Sayings of Jesus in the Churches of Paul.* Philadelphia: Fortress, 1971.

Dunn, James D. G. "2 Corinthians III.17—'The Lord is the Spirit'." *Journal of Theological Studies* 21 (1970): 309-20.

──────. *Christology in the Making: A New Testament Inquiry into the Origins of the Doctrine of the Incarnation.* Philadelphia: Westminster, 1980.

──────. *Jesus and the Spirit: A Study of the Religious and Charismatic Experience of Jesus and the First Christians As Reflected in the New Testament.* Philadelphia: Westminster, 1975.

──────. "Paul's Understanding of the Death of Jesus." In *Reconciliation and Hope: New Testament Essays on Atonement and Eschatology Presented to L. L. Morris on His 60th Birthday*, ed. R. J. Banks, 125-41. Exeter: Paternoster Press, 1974.

──────. "'Righteousness from the Law' and 'Righteousness from Faith': Paul's Interpretation of Scripture in Romans 10:1-10." In *Tradition and Interpretation in the New Testament: Essays in Honor of E. Earle Ellis*, ed. Gerald F. Hawthorne and Otto Betz, 216-28. Grand Rapids: Eerdmans, 1987.

──────. "Some Clarifications on Issues of Method: A Reply to Holladay and Segal." In *Christology and Exegesis: New Approaches*, ed. Robert Jewett, 97-104. Semeia 30. Decatur, GA: Society of Biblical Literature, 1985.

──────. *Unity and Diversity in the New Testament: An Inquiry into the Character of Earliest Christianity.* Philadelphia: Westminster, 1977.

──────. "Was Christianity a Monotheistic Faith from the Beginning?" *Scottish Journal of Theology* 35 (1982): 303-36.

Dupont, Jacques. "'Le Seigneur de tous' (Ac 10:36; Rm 10:12): Arrière-fond scripturaire d'une formule christologique." In *Tradition and Interpretation in the New Testament: Essays in Honor of E. Earle*

Ellis, ed. Gerald F. Hawthorne and Otto Betz, 229-36. Grand Rapids: Eerdmans, 1987.

Easton, B. S. *The Pastoral Epistles*. New York: Charles Scribner's Sons, 1947.

Ellis, E. Earle. "Biblical Interpretation in the New Testament Church." In *Mikra: Text, Translation, Reading and Interpretation of the Hebrew Bible in Ancient Judaism and Early Christianity*. Compendia rerum iudaicarum ad novum testamentum, ed. Martin Jan Mulder, 691-725. Vol. 2, no. 1. Philadelphia: Fortress, 1988.

_____. Review of *Christology in Paul and John*, by Robin Scroggs. In *Southwestern Journal of Theology* 31 (1989): 55.

_____. *Paul and His Recent Interpreters*. Grand Rapids: Eerdmans, 1961.

_____. *Paul's Use of the Old Testament*. Grand Rapids: Baker, 1957.

_____. *Prophecy and Hermeneutic in Early Christianity: New Testament Essays*. Grand Rapids: Eerdmans, 1978.

_____. *Pauline Theology: Ministry and Society*. Grand Rapids: Eerdmans, 1989.

_____. "Traditions in 1 Corinthians." *New Testament Studies* 32 (1986): 481-502.

_____. "Traditions in the Pastoral Epistles." In *Early Jewish and Christian Exegesis*, ed. C. A. Evans and William F. Stinespring, 239-46. Atlanta: Scholars Press, 1987.

Evans, C. F. *Resurrection and the New Testament*. London: SCM Press, 1970.

Fee, Gordon D. "II Corinthians vi.14-vii.1 and Food Offered to Idols." *New Testament Studies* 23 (1977): 140-61.

_____. *The First Epistle to the Corinthians*. The New International Commentary on the New Testament. Grand Rapids: Eerdmans, 1987.

Feuillet, André. *Le Christ Sagesse de Dieu d'apres les epitres pauliniennes*. Paris: Librairie Lecoffre, 1966.

_____. *Christologie paulinienne et tradition biblique*. Paris: Desclée De Brouwer, 1973.

Fitzer, Gottfried. "σφραγίς." *Theological Dictionary of the New Testament*, 7:939-53.

Fitzmyer, Joseph A. "The Contribution of Qumran Aramaic to the Study of the New Testament." *New Testament Studies* 20 (1974): 382-407.

---. *The Dead Sea Scrolls: Major Publications and Tools for Study.* Missoula, MT: Scholars Press, 1977.

---. *Essays on the Semitic Background of the New Testament.* London: Geoffrey Chapman, 1971.

---. *The Genesis Apocryphon of Qumran Cave 1: A Commentary.* Rome: Pontifical Biblical Institute, 1966.

---. *Pauline Theology: A Brief Sketch.* Englewood Cliffs, NJ: Prentice-Hall, 1967.

---. *A Wandering Aramean: Collected Aramaic Essays.* Society of Biblical Literature Monograph Series, no. 25. Missoula, MT: Scholars Press, 1979.

---. "The Use of Explicit Old Testament Quotations in Qumran Literature and in the New Testament." *New Testament Studies* 7 (1961): 297-333.

Flusser, David. "At the Right Hand of the Power." *Immanuel* 14 (1982): 42-46.

Flusser, David, and Shmuel Safrai. "The Essene Doctrine of Hypostasis and Rabbi Meir." *Immanuel* 14 (1982): 47-57.

Foerster, Werner. "κυριακός." *Theological Dictionary of the New Testament*, 3:1095-96.

---. "κύριος." *Theological Dictionary of the New Testament*, 3:1039-58, 1081-95.

Fortna, Robert T. "Rom 8:10 and Paul's Doctrine of the Spirit." *Anglican Theological Review* 41 (1959): 77-84.

Fossum, Jarl E. *The Name of God and the Angel of the Lord: Samaritan and Jewish Concepts of Intermediation and the Origin of Gnosticism.* Wissenschaftliche Untersuchungen zum Neuen Testament, no. 36. Tübingen: J. C. B. Mohr, 1985.

Foulkes, Francis. *The Epistle of Paul to the Ephesians: An Introduction and Commentary.* Tyndale New Testament Commentaries. Grand Rapid: Eerdmans, 1963.

Frame, James E. *A Critical and Exegetical Commentary on the Epistles of St. Paul to the Thessalonians.* The International Critical Commentary. Edinburgh: T. & T. Clark, 1912.

France, R. T. "The Uniqueness of Christ." *Churchman* 95 (1981): 200-217.

---. "The Worship of Jesus: A Neglected Factor in Christological Debate?" In *Christ the Lord: Studies in Christology Presented to Donald Guthrie*, ed. Harold H. Rowdon, 17-36. Leicester, UK: Inter-Varsity Press, 1982.

Fuller, Reginald. "Aspects of Pauline Christology." *Review and Expositor* 71 (1974): 5-17.

———. *Foundations of New Testament Christology*. New York: Charles Scribner's Sons, 1965.

———. "Pre-Existence Christology: Can We Dispense With It?" *Word and World* 2 (1982): 29-33.

Funk, Robert W. *Language, Hermeneutic and Word of God: The Problem of Language in the New Testament and Contemporary Theology*. New York: Harper & Row, 1966.

Furnish, Victor Paul. *II Corinthians*. The Anchor Bible. Garden City, NY: Doubleday, 1984.

———. "The Jesus-Paul Debate: From Baur to Bultmann." *Bulletin of the John Rylands University Library at Manchester* 47 (1965): 342-81.

———. *Theology and Ethics in Paul*. Nashville: Abingdon Press, 1968.

Gadd, C. J. *Ideas of Divine Rule in the Ancient East*. London: Oxford University Press, 1948.

Gamble, Harry. *The Textual History of the Letter to the Romans: A Study in Textual and Literary Criticism*. Studies and Documents Series, no. 42. Grand Rapids: Eerdmans, 1977.

Gaster, Theodor H. *The Dead Sea Scriptures*. 3d ed. Garden City, NY: Anchor Press, 1976.

Georgi, Dieter. *The Opponents of Paul in Second Corinthians*. Philadelphia: Fortress, 1986.

Gibbs, John G. *Creation and Redemption: A Study in Pauline Theology*. London: E. J. Brill, 1971.

Glasson, T. Francis. *The Second Advent: The Origin of the New Testament Doctrine*. London: Epworth Press, 1945.

———. "Two Notes on the Philippian Hymn." *New Testament Studies* 21 (1974): 133-39.

Gnilka, Joachim. "2 Cor 6:14-7:1 in Light of the Qumran Texts and the Testaments of the Twelve Patriarchs." In *Paul and Qumran: Studies in New Testament Exegesis*, ed. Jerome Murphy-O'Connor, 48-68. Chicago: Priory Press, 1968.

Godet, Frederick L. *Commentary on St. Paul's Epistle to the Romans*. Vol. 1. Translated by A. Cusin. Edinburgh: T. & T. Clark, 1880.

Goppelt, Leonhard. *Theology of the New Testament*. Vol. 2, *The Variety and Unity of the Apostolic Witness to Christ*. Translated by John Alsup. Grand Rapids: Eerdmans, 1982.

Goudge, H. L. *The First Epistle to the Corinthians*. Westminster Commentaries. London: Methuen & Co., 1903.

Gourgues, M. *A la droite de Dieu: Resurrection de Jesus et actualisation du Psaume 110:1 dans le Nouveau*. Paris: Librairie Lecoffre, 1978.

Grant, F. C. *Roman Hellenism and the New Testament*. New York: Charles Scribner's Sons, 1962.

Grant, Robert M. *Gods and the One God*. Library of Early Christianity. Edited by Wayne A. Meeks. Philadelphia: Westminster, 1986.

Green, William Scott, ed. *Approaches to Ancient Judaism: Theory and Practice*. Brown Judaic Studies, no. 1. Missoula, MT: Scholars Press, 1978.

Greenwood, David. "'The Lord is Spirit': Some Considerations of 2 Cor 3:17." *Catholic Biblical Quarterly* 34 (1972): 467-72.

Griffiths, D. R. "The Lord is the Spirit." *Expository Times* 55 (1943): 81-83.

Grosheide, F. W. *Commentary on the First Epistle to the Corinthians*. The New International Commentary on the New Testament. Grand Rapids: Eerdmans, 1953.

Grundmann, Walter. "δεξιός." *Theological Dictionary of the New Testament*, 2:37-40.

_____. "στήκω, ἵστημι." *Theological Dictionary of the New Testament*, 7:636-53.

Gundry, R. H. *'Soma' in Biblical Theology with Emphasis on Pauline Anthropology*. Cambridge: University Press, 1976.

Hahn, Ferdinand. *The Titles of Jesus in Christology: Their History in Early Christianity*. Translated by Harold Knight and George Ogg. New York: World Publishing Company, 1969.

Hammerton-Kelly, R. G. *Pre-existence, Wisdom, and the Son of Man: A Study of the Idea of Pre-existence in the New Testament*. Cambridge: University Press, 1973.

Hanse, Hermann. "ἔχω [κτλ]." *Theological Dictionary of the New Testament*, 2:816-32.

Hanson, A. T. "The Midrash on II Corinthians 3: A Reconsideration." *Journal for the Study of the New Testament* 9 (1980): 2-28.

_____. *Studies in Paul's Technique and Theology*. Grand Rapids: Eerdmans, 1974.

_____. *The Pastoral Epistles*. The New Century Bible Commentary. Grand Rapids: Eerdmans, 1982.

Hanson, R. P. C. "St. Paul's Quotations of the Book of Job." *Theology* 53 (1950): 250-53.

Harmon, Allan M. "Aspects of Paul's Use of the Psalms." *Westminster Theological Journal* 32 (1969): 1-23.

Harris, Murray J. "Titus 2:13 and the Deity of Christ." In *Pauline Studies: Essays Presented to Professor F. F. Bruce on His 70th Birthday,* ed. Donald A. Hagner and Murray J. Harris, 262-77. Grand Rapids: Eerdmans, 1980.

Harrison, P. N. *Paulines and Pastorals.* London: Villiers, 1964.

_____. *The Problem of the Pastoral Epistles.* London: Oxford, 1921.

Hatch, Edwin and Henry A. Redpath. *A Concordance to the Septuagint and Other Greek Versions of the Old Testament.* 2 Vols. Graz, AUS: Akademische Druck- u. Verlagsanstalt, 1954.

Hawthorne, Gerald F. "The Role of Christian Prophets in the Gospel Tradition." In *Tradition and Interpretation in the New Testament: Essays in Honor of E. Earle Ellis,* ed. Gerald F. Hawthorne and Otto Betz, 119-33. Grand Rapids: Eerdmans, 1987.

Hay, David M. *Glory at the Right Hand: Psalm 110 in Early Christianity.* Nashville: Abingdon Press, 1973.

Hays, Richard B. *Echoes of Scripture in the Letters of Paul.* New Haven and London: Yale University Press, 1989.

Hegermann, Harald. *Die Vorstellung vom Schopfungsmittler im hellenistischen Judentum und Urchristentum.* Berlin: Akademie, 1961.

Heitmüller, Wilhelm. "Zum Problem Paulus und Jesus." *Zeitschrift für die neutestamentliche Wissenschaft* 13 (1912): 320-37.

Hengel, Martin. *Between Jesus and Paul: Studies in the Earliest History of Christianity.* Translated by John Bowden. Philadelphia: Fortress, 1983.

_____. *Judaism and Hellenism: Studies in their Encounter in Palestine during the Early Hellenistic Period.* 2 Vols. Translated by John Bowden. Philadelphia: Fortress, 1974.

_____. *The Son of God: The Origin of Christology and the History of Jewish Hellenistic Religion.* Translated by John Bowden. Philadelphia: Fortress, 1976.

Hering, Jean. *The Second Epistle of St. Paul to the Corinthians.* Translated by A. W. Heathcote and P. J. Allcock. London: Epworth Press, 1967.

Hermann, Ingo. *Kyrios und Pneuma: Studien zur Christologie der paulinischen Hauptbriefe.* Studien zum Alten und Neuen Testament. Edited by Vinzenz Hamp and Josef Schmid. München: Dösel-Verlag, 1961.

Herntrich, Volkmar. "κρίνω." *Theological Dictionary of the New Testament*, 3:923-33.

Higgins, A. J. B. Review of *The Foundations of New Testament Christology*, by Reginald H. Fuller. In *Journal of Biblical Literature* 85 (1966): 360-62.

Hill, David. *Greek Words and Hebrew Meanings: Studies in the Semantics of Soteriological Terms*. Cambridge: University Press, 1967.

_____. *New Testament Prophecy*. Atlanta: John Knox Press, 1979.

Hofius, Otfried. *Der Christushymnus Philipper 2,6-11*. Wissenschaftliche Untersuchungen zum Neuen Testament, no. 17. Tübingen: J. C. B. Mohr, 1976.

Holladay, Carl R. *The First Letter of Paul to the Corinthians*. Austin, TX: Sweet Publishing Company, 1979.

_____. "New Testament Christology: Some Considerations of Method." *Novum Testamentum* 25 (1983): 257-78.

_____. *Theios Aner in Hellenistic-Judaism: A Critique of the Use of This Category in New Testament Christology*. Society of Biblical Literature Dissertation Series, no. 40. Missoula, MT: Scholars Press, 1977.

Horsley, R. A. "The Background of the Confessional Formula in 1 Cor. 8:6." *Zeitschrift für die neutestamentliche Wissenschaft* 69 (1978): 130-37.

_____. "Wisdom of Word or Words of Wisdom in Corinth." *Catholic Biblical Quarterly* 39 (1977): 224-39.

Howard, George. "Phil. 2.6-11 and the Human Christ." *Catholic Biblical Quarterly* 40 (1978): 368-87.

_____. "The Tetragram and the New Testament." *Journal of Biblical Literature* 96 (1977): 63-83.

Hughes, Philip Edgcumbe. *Paul's Second Epistle to the Corinthians*. The International Critical Commentary on the New Testament. Grand Rapids: Eerdmans, 1962.

Hunter, A. M. *Paul and His Predecessors*. 2d ed. London: SCM Press, 1961.

Hurtado, L. W. "Jesus as Lordly Example in Philippians 2:5-11." In *From Jesus to Paul: Studies in Honour of Francis Wright Beare*, ed. Peter Richardson and John C. Hurd, 113-26. Waterloo, Ont.: Wilfrid Laurier University Press, 1984.

_____. "New Testament Christology: Retrospect and Prospect." In *Christology and Exegesis: New Approaches*, ed. Robert Jewett, 15-27. *Semeia* 30. Decatur, GA: Society of Biblical Literature, 1985.

———. *One God, One Lord: Early Christian Devotion and Ancient Jewish Monotheism*. Philadelphia: Fortress, 1988.

Irwin, William A. *The Old Testament: Keystone of Human Culture*. New York: Abelard-Schuman, n.d.

Jacob, Edmond. *Theology of the Old Testament*. Translated by Arthur W. Heathcote and Philip J. Allcock. London: Hodder & Stoughton, 1955.

Jenni, Ernst. "Day of the Lord." *The Interpreter's Dictionary of the Bible*, 1:784-85.

Jeremias, Joachim. *Die Briefe an Timotheus und Titus*. Göttingen: Vandenhoeck & Ruprecht, 1949.

———. "Chiasmus in den Paulusbriefen." In *Abba: Studien zur neutestamentlichen Theologie und Zeitgeschichte*, 276-90. Göttingen: Vandenhoeck & Ruprecht, 1966.

———. *The Eucharistic Words of Jesus*. Translated by Norman Perrin. Philadelphia: Fortress, 1966.

———. *Jerusalem in the Time of Jesus*. Philadelphia: Fortress, 1969.

———. *New Testament Theology: The Proclamation of Jesus*. Vol. 1. London: SCM Press, 1971.

———. *The Prayers of Jesus*. London: SCM Press, 1967.

———. "Zur Gedankenführung in den paulinischen Briefen." In *Studia Paulina: In Honorem Johannis de Zwaan*, 146-54. Haarlem: De Erven F. Bohn, 1953.

Jervell, Jacob. *Imago Dei: Gen. i. 26f. im Spätjudentum, in der Gnosis und in den paulinischen Briefen*. Göttingen: Vandenhoeck & Ruprecht, 1960.

Jewett, Robert. "The Redaction and Use of an Early Christian Confession in Romans 1:3-4." In *The Living Text*, ed. D. E. Groh, 99-122. Lanham, MD: University Press of America, 1985.

———. *The Thessalonian Correspondence: Pauline Rhetoric and Millenarian Piety*. Philadelphia: Fortress, 1986.

Johnson, Aubrey R. *The One and the Many in the Israelite Conception of God*. Cardiff: University of Wales Press, 1961.

———. *Sacral Kingship in Ancient Israel*. 2d ed. Cardiff: University of Wales Press, 1967.

———. *The Vitality of the Individual in the Thought of Ancient Israel*. Cardiff: University of Wales Press, 1949.

Johnson, S. Lewis, Jr. "Christ Pre-eminent." *Bibliotheca Sacra* 119 (1962): 12-19.

Käsemann, Ernst. *Commentary on Romans*. Translated by Geoffrey W. Bromiley. Grand Rapids: Eerdmans, 1980.

_____. "A Critical Analysis of Philippians 2:5-11." In *God and Christ: Existence and Province*. New York: Harper & Row, 1968.

_____. *Essays on New Testament Themes*. Philadelphia: Fortress, 1982.

_____. *Perspectives on Paul*. Translated by Margaret Kohl. Philadelphia: Fortress, 1971.

Kee, Howard C. Review of *Christologische Hoheitstitel*, by Ferdinand Hahn. In *Journal of Biblical Literature* 83 (1964): 191-93.

Kehl, Nikolaus. *Der Christushymnus im Kolosserbrief*. Stuttgart: Katholisches Bibelwerk, 1967.

Kelly, J. N. D. *A Commentary on the Pastoral Epistles*. Thornapple Commentaries. New York: Harper & Row, 1963; reprint, Grand Rapids: Baker, 1981.

_____. *Early Christian Creeds*. 3d ed. New York: D. McKay Co., 1972.

Kim, Seyoon. *The Origin of Paul's Gospel*. Grand Rapids: Eerdmans, 1981.

_____. *The Son of Man As the Son of God*. Grand Rapids: Eerdmans, 1983.

Knox, John. *The Humanity and Divinity of Christ: A Study of Pattern in Christology*. Cambridge: University Press, 1967.

Köhler, Ludwig. *Old Testament Theology*. Translated by A. J. Todd. Philadelphia: Westminster, 1957.

Köster, Helmut. "ὀρθοτομέω." *Theological Dictionary of the New Testament*, 8:111-12.

Kramer, Werner R. *Christ, Lord, Son of God*. Translated by Brian Hardy. Naperville, IL: A. R. Allenson, 1966.

Kreitzer, L. Joseph. *Jesus and God in Paul's Eschatology*. Sheffield, UK: Academic Press, 1987.

Kuhn, K. G. "μαραναθά." *Theological Dictionary of the New Testament*, 4:466-72.

Kümmel, Werner Georg. *Introduction to the New Testament*. Translated by Howard C. Kee. Nashville: Abingdon, 1975.

Ladd, George Eldon. *A Theology of the New Testament*. Grand Rapids: Eerdmans, 1974.

Lagrange, Marie Joseph. *Saint Paul: Epitre aux Romains*. Paris: J. Gabalda, 1922.

Lambrecht, J. "Paul's Christological Use of Scripture in 1 Cor. 15:20-28." *New Testament Studies* 28 (1982): 505-27.

Lane, William R. "A New Commentary Structure on 4QFlorilegium." *Journal of Biblical Literature* 78 (1959): 343-46.

Lightfoot, J. B. *Biblical Essays*. London: MacMillan, 1904.

———. *St. Paul's Epistles to the Colossians and to Philemon*. London: MacMillan, 1916.

———. *Saint Paul's Epistle to the Philippians*. London: MacMillan, 1912.

Lindars, Barnabas. *Jesus Son of Man: A Fresh Examination of the Son of Man Sayings in the Gospels in the Light of Recent Research*. Grand Rapids: Eerdmans, 1983.

———. *New Testament Apologetic: The Doctrinal Significance of the Old Testament Quotations*. London: SCM Press, 1961.

Lock, Walter. *A Critical and Exegetical Commentary on the Pastoral Epistles*. The International Critical Commentary. Edinburgh: T. & T. Clark, 1924.

Lohmeyer, Ernst. *Die Briefe an die Philipper, an die Kolosser und an Philemon*. Göttingen: Vandenhoeck & Ruprecht, 1956.

———. *Kyrios Jesus: Eine Untersuchung zu Phil. 2.5-11*. 2d ed. Heidelberg: Carl Winter Universitäts-verlag, 1961.

Lohse, Eduard. *Colossians and Philemon*. Hermeneia. Translated by William R. Poehlmann and Robert J. Karris. Philadelphia: Fortress, 1971.

———. "Zu I Cor 10.26, 31." *Zeitschrift für die neutestamentliche Wissenschaft* 47 (1956): 277-80.

Longenecker, Richard N. *Biblical Exegesis in the Apostolic Period*. Grand Rapids: Eerdmans, 1975.

———. *The Christology of Early Jewish Christianity*. London: SCM Press, 1970; reprint, Grand Rapids: Baker, 1981.

———. *Paul: Apostle of Liberty*. New York: Harper & Row, 1964; reprint, Grand Rapids: Baker, 1976.

Losie, Lynn Allan. "A Note on the Interpretation of Phil. 2.5." *The Expository Times* 90 (1978): 52-53.

Machen, J. Gresham. *The Origin of Paul's Religion*. New York: MacMillan, 1923.

Marshall, I. Howard. *1 and 2 Thessalonians*. The New Century Bible. Grand Rapids: Eerdmans, 1983.

———. "The Divine Sonship of Jesus." *Interpretation* 21 (1967): 87-103.

———. *The Origins of New Testament Christology*. Leicester, UK: Inter-Varsity Press, 1976.

_____, "Palestinian and Hellenistic Christianity: Some Critical Comments." *New Testament Studies* 9 (1973): 173-87.

Martin, Ralph. *Carmen Christi: Philippians 2:5-11 in Recent Interpretation and in the Setting of Early Christian Worship.* Rev. ed. Grand Rapids: Eerdmans, 1983.

_____. *Colossians and Philemon.* The New Century Bible Commentary. Grand Rapids: Eerdmans, 1973.

_____. "An Early Christian Hymn." *Evangelical Quarterly* 36 (1964): 195-205.

_____. *The Epistle of Paul to the Philippians: An Introduction and Commentary.* Tyndale New Testament Commentaries. Grand Rapids: Eerdmans, 1959.

_____. "The Opponents of Paul in 2 Corinthians: An Old Issue Revisited." In *Tradition and Interpretation in the New Testament: Essays in Honor of E. Earle Ellis,* ed. Gerald W. Hawthorne and Otto Betz, 279-89. Grand Rapids: Eerdmans, 1987.

_____. *Worship in the Early Church.* Rev. ed. Grand Rapids: Eerdmans, 1974.

Marxsen, Willi. "Christology in the NT." *The Interpreter's Dictionary of the Bible: Supplementary Volume,* 146-56.

Mayer, Reinhold. "Jesus—Messias Israels—Christus der Kirche." *Judaica* 40 (1984): 248-58.

McCown Wayne. "The Hymnic Structure of Colossians 1:15-20." *Evangelical Quarterly* 51 (1979): 156-62.

McKelvey, R. J. "Christ the Cornerstone." *New Testament Studies* 8 (1962): 352-59.

_____. *The New Temple: The Church in the New Testament.* London: Oxford University Press, 1969.

Meeks, Wayne A. *The First Urban Christians: The Social World of the Apostle Paul.* New Haven: Yale University Press, 1983.

_____. "Judgment and the Brother: Romans 14:1-15:13." In *Tradition and Interpretation in the New Testament: Essays in Honor of E. Earle Ellis,* ed. Gerald W. Hawthorne and Otto Betz, 290-300. Grand Rapids: Eerdmans, 1987.

Metzger, Bruce M., ed. *Index to Periodical Literature on the Apostle Paul.* Leiden: E. J. Brill, 1960.

_____. *The New Testament: Its Background, Growth, and Content.* 2d ed. Nashville: Abingdon, 1983.

_____. "The Punctuation of Rom. 9:5." In *Christ and Spirit in the New Testament: Studies in Honour of C. F. D. Moule,* ed. Barnabas

Lindars and Stephen S. Smalley, 95-112. Cambridge: University Press, 1973.

———. "A Reconsideration of Certain Arguments Against the Pauline Authorship of the Pastoral Epistles." *Expository Times* 70 (1959/60): 91-94.

———. *The Text of the New Testament: Its Transmission, Corruption, and Restoration*. 2d ed. New York: Oxford University Press, 1968.

———. *A Textual Commentary on the Greek New Testament*. New York: United Bible Societies, 1975.

Michel, Otto. "ὁμολογέω [κτλ]." *Theological Dictionary of the New Testament*, 5:199-220.

Milik, J. T. "*Milki-sedeq* et *Milki-resa* dans les anciens écrits juifs et chrétiens." *Journal of Jewish Studies* 23 (1972): 95-144.

Miller, Merrill P. "Targum, Midrash and the Use of the Old Testament in the New Testament." *Journal for the Study of Judaism* 2 (1971): 29-82.

Mitton, C. Leslie. *Ephesians*. The New Century Bible. London: Marshall, Morgan, & Scott, 1976.

Morris, Leon. "The Emergence of the Doctrine of the Incarnation." *Themelios* 8 (1982): 15-19.

———. *The First and Second Epistles to the Thessalonians*. The New International Commentary on the New Testament. Grand Rapids: Eerdmans, 1959.

Moule, C. F. D. "2 Cor. 3:18b, καθάπερ ἀπὸ κυρίου πνεύματος." In *Neues Testament und Geschichte: Historisches Geschehen und Deutung im Neuen Testament. Oscar Cullmann zum 70. Geburtstag*, ed. Heinrich Baltensweiler and Bo Reicke, 231-37. Zürich: Theologischer Verlag, 1972.

———. *The Birth of the New Testament*. 3d ed. San Francisco: Harper & Row, 1982.

———. *The Epistles of Paul the Apostle to the Colossians and to Philemon*. Cambridge: University Press, 1962.

———. "The Influence of Circumstances on the Use of Christological Terms." *Journal of Theological Studies* 10 (1959): 49-61.

———. "Jesus, Judaism, and Paul." In *Tradition and Interpretation in the New Testament: Essays in Honor of E. Earle Ellis*, ed. Gerald F. Hawthorne and Otto Betz, 43-52. Grand Rapids: Eerdmans, 1987.

———. *The Origin of Christology*. Cambridge: University Press, 1977.

_____. *The Phenomenon of the New Testament: An Inquiry into the Implications of Certain Features of the New Testament.* Naperville, IL: A. R. Allenson, 1967.

_____. "The Problem of the Pastoral Epistles: A Reappraisal." *Bulletin of the John Rylands University Library of Manchester* 47 (1964/65): 430-52.

Moulton, W. F., A. S. Geden, and H. K. Moulton. *A Concordance to the Greek New Testament.* 5th ed. Edinburgh: T. & T. Clark, 1978.

Müller, J. J. *The Epistle of Paul to the Philippians and to Philemon.* The New International Commentary on the New Testament. Grand Rapids: Eerdmans, 1955.

Munck, Johannes. *Paul and the Salvation of Mankind.* Atlanta: John Knox Press, 1959.

Murphy-O'Connor, Jerome. *1 Corinthians.* New Testament Message, no. 10. Wilmington, DE: Michael Glazier, 1979.

_____. "1 Cor. 8:6: Cosmology or Soteriology?" *Revue Biblique* 85 (1978): 253-67.

_____. "Christological Anthropology in Phil. II,6-11." *Revue Biblique* 83 (1976): 25-50.

Murray, John. *The Epistle to the Romans.* The New International Commentary on the New Testament. Grand Rapids: Eerdmans, 1959.

Neufeld, Vernon H. *The Earliest Christian Confessions.* Grand Rapids: Eerdmans, 1963.

Neugebauer, Fritz. "Das paulinische 'in Christo'." *New Testament Studies* 4 (1958): 124-38.

Neusner, Jacob. *What Is Midrash?* Philadelphia: Fortress, 1987.

Newman, Carey. "'The Glory of God in the Face of Jesus': A Traditional-Historical Investigation in Paul's Doxa-Christology." Ph.D. diss., Baylor University, Waco, TX, 1989.

Nock, A. D. *Early Gentile Christianity and Its Hellenistic Background.* New York: Harper & Row, 1964.

_____. "Gnosticism." *Harvard Theological Review* 57 (1964): 255-79.

Norden, Eduard. *Agnostos Theos: Untersuchungen zur Formengeschichte religiöser Rede.* Darmstadt: Wissenschaftliche Buchgesellschaft, 1956.

Oates, John F., Roger S. Bagnall, and William H. Willis. *Checklist of Editions of Greek Papyri and Ostraca.* 2d ed. Missoula, MT: Scholars Press, 1978.

Odeburg, Hugo. *3 Enoch or the Hebrew Book of Enoch*. New York: KTAV Publishing House, 1973.

O'Neill, J. C. *Paul's Letter to the Romans*. Baltimore: Penguin Books, 1975.

Oepke, Albrecht. "ἀποκαλύπτω." *Theological Dictionary of the New Testament*, 3:563-92.

_____. "ἐν." *Theological Dictionary of the New Testament*, 2:537-43.

_____. "παρουσία, πάρειμι." *Theological Dictionary of the New Testament*, 5:858-71.

Orr, William F. and James Arthur Walthar. *1 Corinthians*. The Anchor Bible. Garden City, NY: Doubleday, 1976.

Osborne, Grant. "Christology and New Testament Hermeneutics: A Survey of the Discussion." In *Christology and Exegesis: New Approaches*, ed. Robert Jewett, 49-62. *Semeia* 30. Decatur, GA: Society of Biblical Literature, 1985.

Parry, R. St. John. *The First Epistle of Paul the Apostle to the Corinthians*. 2d ed. Cambridge: University Press, 1926.

Pedersen, Johannes. *Israel: Its Life and Culture*. London: Oxford University Press, 1926.

Pentecost, J. Dwight. *Things to Come*. Grand Rapids: Dunham, 1958.

Perrin, Norman. "New Beginnings in Christology: A Review Article." *The Journal of Religion* 46 (1966): 491-96.

Piper, Otto A. "The Savior's Eternal Work: An Exegesis of Col 1:9-29." *Interpretation* 3 (1949): 286-98.

Plummer, Alfred. *A Critical and Exegetical Commentary on the Second Epistle of St Paul to the Corinthians*. The International Critical Commentary. Edinburgh: T. & T. Clark, 1915.

Pollard, T. E. "Colossians 1:12-20: A Reconsideration." *New Testament Studies* 27 (1981): 572-75.

Porten, Bezadel. "The Address Formulae in Aramaic Letters: A New Collation of Cowley 17." *Revue Biblique* 90 (1980): 396-415.

Porter, J. R. "Legal Aspects of Corporate Personality." *Vetus Testamentum* 15 (1965): 361-80.

Preisker, Herbert. "ἔπαινος." *Theological Dictionary of the New Testament*, 2:586-88.

Quell, Gottfried. "κύριος." *Theological Dictionary of the New Testament*, 3:1058-81

_____. "σπέρμα." *Theological Dictionary of the New Testament*, 7:538-42.

Rawlinson, A. E. J. *The New Testament Doctrine of the Christ.* New York: Longmans, Green, 1926.

Redpath, Henry A. *Concordance to the Septuagint and Other Greek Versions of the Old Testament: Supplement.* Oxford: Clarendon Press, 1906.

Reicke, Bo. "πᾶς." *Theological Dictionary of the New Testament,* 5:886-90, 892-96.

Reule, George. "The Christology of Phil. 2,5-11." *The Springfielder* 35 (1971): 82-85.

Richards, E. R. "The Role of the Secretary in Greco-Roman Antiquity and Its Implications for the Letters of Paul." Ph.D. diss., Southwestern Baptist Theological Seminary, Fort Worth, TX, 1988.

Ridderbos, Herman. "The Earliest Confession of the Atonement in Paul." In *Reconciliation and Hope: New Testament Essays on Atonement and Eschatology Presented to L. L. Morris on His 60th Birthday,* ed. Robert Barks, 76-89. Exeter: Paternoster Press, 1974.

_____. *The Epistle of Paul to the Churches of Galatia.* The New International Commentary on the New Testament. Translated by Henry Zylstra. Grand Rapids: Eerdmans, 1953.

_____. *Paul: An Outline of His Theology.* Translated by John R. de Witt. Grand Rapids: Eerdmans, 1975.

Rigaux, Beda. *The Letters of St. Paul: Modern Studies.* Translated by S. Yonick. Chicago: Franciscan Herald Press, 1968.

_____. *Saint Paul—Les Epitres aux Thessaloniciens.* Paris: Gabalda, 1956.

Robertson, A. T. *A Grammar of the Greek New Testament in Light of Historical Research.* 2d ed. New York: Hodder & Stoughton, 1915.

Robertson, Archibald and Alfred Plummer. *A Critical and Exegetical Commentary on the First Epistle of St Paul to the Corinthians.* The International Critical Commentary. Edinburgh: T. & T. Clark, 1911.

Robinson, H. Wheeler. *Corporate Personality in Ancient Israel.* Rev. ed. Philadelphia: Fortress, 1980.

Robinson, James M. "A Formal Analysis of Colossians 1:15-20." *Journal of Biblical Literature* 76 (1957): 270-87.

Roller, Otto. *Das Formular der paulinischen Briefe.* Stuttgart: W. Kohlhammer, 1933.

Russell, D. S. *The Method and Message of Jewish Apocalyptic*. Philadelphia: Westminster, 1964.

Sabourin, Leopold. "Christ's Pre-existence." *Religious Studies Bulletin* 4 (1984): 22-29.

Sanday, William, and Arthur C. Headlam. *A Critical and Exegetical Commentary on the Epistle to the Romans*. The International Critical Commentary. New York: Charles Scribner's Sons, 1920.

Sanders, E. P. *Paul and Palestinian Judaism*. Philadelphia: Fortress, 1977.

──────. *Paul, the Law, and the Jewish People*. Philadelphia: Fortress, 1983.

Sanders, J. A. "Dissenting Deities and Philippians 2.1-11." *Journal of Biblical Literature* 88 (1969): 279-90.

Sanders, Jack T. *The New Testament Christological Hymns: Their Historical Religious Background*. Cambridge: University Press, 1971.

Sawyer, John F. A. "Biblical Alternatives to Monotheism." *Theology* 87 (1984): 172-80.

Scharlemann, Martin H. "The Scope of the Redemptive Task." *Concordia Theological Monthly* 36 (1965): 291-300.

Schelkle, Karl Hermann. *Paulus: Leben—Briefe—Theologie*. Erträge der Forschung, vol. 152. Darmstadt: Wissenschaftliche Buchgesellschaft, 1981.

Schlier, Heinrich. "αἰνέω." *Theological Dictionary of the New Testament*, 1:177.

──────. "Zu Röm 1,3f." In *Neues Testament und Geschichte: Historisches Geschehen und Deutung im Neuen Testament. Oscar Cullmann zum 70. Geburtstag*, ed. Heinrich Baltensweiler and Bo Reicke, 207-18. Zürich: Theologischer Verlag, 1972.

Schmidt, Karl Ludwig. "ἔθνος." *Theological Dictionary of the New Testament*, 2:369-72.

──────. "ἐπικαλέω." *Theological Dictionary of the New Testament*, 3:496-500.

──────. "θεμέλιος." *Theological Dictionary of the New Testament*, 3:63-64.

──────. "ὁρίζω." *Theological Dictionary of the New Testament*, 5:452-53.

Schmithals, Walter. *Gnosticism at Corinth: An Investigation of the Letters to the Corinthians*. Translated by J. E. Steely. Nashville: Abingdon, 1971.

_____. "Die Korintherbriefe als Briefsammlung." *Zeitschrift für die neutestamentliche Wissenschaft* 64 (1973): 263-88.

Schrenk, Gottlob. "ἀδικία." *Theological Dictionary of the New Testament*, 1:153-57.

_____. "διαλογισμός." *Theological Dictionary of the New Testament*, 2:96-98.

_____. "λεῖμμα [κτλ]." *Theological Dictionary of the New Testament*, 4:209-14.

_____. "πατήρ." *Theological Dictionary of the New Testament*, 5:945-59, 974-1014.

Schulz, Siegfried. "Maranatha und Kyrios Jesus." *Zeitschrift für die neutestamentliche Wissenschaft* 53 (1962): 125-44.

Schweitzer, Albert. *The Mysticism of Paul the Apostle*. Translated by William Montgomery. London: A. & C. Black, 1931.

_____. *Paul and His Interpreters: A Critical History*. Translated by William Montgomery. London: A. & C. Black, 1912.

Schweizer, Eduard. "Der Glaube an Jesus den 'Herrn' in seiner Entwicklung von den ersten Nachfolgern bis zur hellenistischen Gemeinde." *Evangelische Theologie* 17 (1957): 7-21.

_____. *Jesus*. Translated by David E. Green. Atlanta: John Knox Press, 1971.

_____. *The Letter to the Colossians*. Translated by Andrew Chester. Minneapolis: Augsburg, 1976.

_____. "Römer 1,3f. und der Gegensatz von Fleisch und Geist vor und bei Paulus." *Evangelische Theologie* 15 (1955): 564ff.

Scroggs, Robin. *Christology in Paul and John*. Philadelphia: Fortress, 1988.

_____. *The Last Adam: A Study in Pauline Anthropology*. Philadelphia: Fortress, 1966.

_____. "Paul: ΣΟΦΟΣ and ΠΝΕΥΜΑΤΙΚΟΣ." *New Testament Studies* 14 (1967): 33-55.

Segal, Alan F. "'He who did not spare his own son . . .': Jesus, Paul, and the Akedah." In *From Jesus to Paul: Studies in Honour of Francis Wright Beare*, ed. Peter Richardson and John C. Hurd, 169-84. Waterloo, Ont.: Wilfrid Laurier University Press, 1984.

_____. *Paul the Convert: The Apostolate and Apostasy of Saul the Pharisee*. New Haven: Yale University Press, 1990.

_____. *Two Powers in Heaven: Early Rabbinic Reports About Christianity and Gnosticism*. Studies in Judaism in Late Antiquity, vol. 25. Leiden: E. J. Brill, 1977.

Selby, D. J. *Toward an Understanding of St. Paul*. Englewood Cliffs, NJ: Prentice-Hall, 1962.

Sevenster, J. N. *Do You Know Greek? How Much Greek Could the First Jewish Christians Have Known?* Supplements to Novum Testamentum, vol. 19. Leiden: E. J. Brill, 1968.

Shedd, R. P. *Man in Community: A Study of St. Paul's Application of Old Testament and Early Jewish Conceptions of Human Solidarity*. London: Epworth Press, 1958.

Simpson, E. K. and F. F. Bruce. *Commentary on the Epistle to the Ephesians and the Colossians*. The New International Commentary on the New Testament. Grand Rapids: Eerdmans, 1957.

Smith, John M. P., William Hayes Ward, and J. Brewer. *A Critical and Exegetical Commentary on Micah, Zephaniah, Nahum, Habakkuk, Obadiah and Joel*. The International Critical Commentary. New York: Charles Scribner's Sons, 1911.

Stanton, Graham N. *Jesus of Nazareth in New Testament Preaching*. Cambridge: University Press, 1974.

Steele, E. S. "The Use of Jewish Scripture in 1 Thessalonians." *Biblical Theology Bulletin* 14 (1984): 12-17.

Stowers, S. K. *The Diatribe and Paul's Letter to the Romans*. Society of Biblical Literature Dissertation Series, no. 57. Missoula, MT: Scholars Press, 1981.

Strack, Hermann L., and Paul Billerbeck. *Kommentar zum Neuen Testament aus Talmud und Midrasch*. München: C. H. Beck'sche Verlagsbuchhandlung, 1954.

Strathmann, Hermann. "λαός." *Theological Dictionary of the New Testament*, 4:29-57.

Strimple, Robert B. "Philippians 2.5-11 in Recent Studies: Some Exegetical Conclusions." *Westminster Theological Journal* 41 (1978): 247-68.

Stuhlmacher, Peter. "The Hermeneutical Significance of 1 Cor 2:6-16." In *Tradition and Interpretation in the New Testament: Essays in Honor of E. Earle Ellis*, ed. Gerald F. Hawthorne and Otto Betz, 328-47. Grand Rapids: Eerdmans, 1987.

Swete, H. B. *An Introduction to the Old Testament in Greek*. 2d ed. Cambridge: University Press, 1914.

Tabor, James D. *Things Unutterable: Paul's Ascent to Paradise in its Greco-Roman, Judaic, and Early Christian Contexts.* Lanham, MD: University Press of America, 1986.

Takahashi, Masashi. "An Oriental's Approach to the Problems of Angelology." *Zeitschrift für die alttestamentliche Wissenschaft* 78 (1966): 343-50.

Talbert, Charles H. "The Problem of Pre-existence in Philippians 2.6-11." *Journal of Biblical Literature* 86 (1967): 141-53.

Taylor, C. *Hebrew-Greek Cairo Genizah Palimpsests from the Taylor Schechter Collection Including a Fragment of the Twenty-Second Psalm according to Origen's Hexapla.* Cambridge: University Press, 1900.

Taylor, Vincent. "Does the New Testament Call Jesus God?" *Expository Times* 63 (1962): 116-18.

_____. *The Names of Jesus.* New York: St. Martin's Press, 1953.

_____. *The Person of Christ in New Testament Teaching.* New York: MacMillan, 1958.

Thackeray, H. St. John. *Josephus: The Man and the Historian.* New York: Jewish Institute of Religion Press, 1929.

Thrall, Margaret E. "The Problem of II Cor. vi.14-vii.1 in Some Recent Discussion." *New Testament Studies* 24 (1977): 144-48.

Theissen, Gerd. *The Social Setting of Pauline Christianity: Essays on Corinth.* Translated by John H. Schutz. Philadelphia: Fortress, 1982.

Tödt, H. E. *The Son of Man in the Synoptic Tradition.* Translated by D. M. Barton. Philadelphia: Westminster Press; London: SCM Press, 1965.

van Unnik, W. C. "Jesus: Anathema or Kyrios (1 Cor. 12:3)." In *Christ and Spirit in the New Testament: Studies in Honour of C. F. D. Moule*, ed. Barnabas Lindars and Stephen S. Smalley, 113-126. Cambridge: University Press, 1973.

_____. "Jesus the Christ." *New Testament Studies* 8 (1962): 101-16.

Vermes, Geza. *Jesus the Jew: A Historian's Reading of the Gospel.* New York: MacMillan, 1973.

_____. *Scripture and Tradition in Judaism.* 2d ed. Leiden: E. J. Brill, 1974.

Vielhauer, Philipp. "Ein Weg zur neutestamentliche Christologie?" Chap. in *Aufsätze zum Neuen Testament.* München: Chr. Kaiser Verlag, 1965.

Vincent, Marvin. R. *A Critical and Exegetical Commentary on the Epistles to the Philippians and to Philemon.* The International Critical Commentary. Edinburgh: T. & T. Clark, 1897.

von Rad, Gerhard. "ἡμέρα." *Theological Dictionary of the New Testament,* 2:943-47.

_____. *Genesis: A Commentary.* Translated by John H. Marks. London: SCM Press, 1961.

_____. *Old Testament Theology: The Theology of Israel's Historical Traditions.* Translated by D. M. G. Stalker. Vol. 1. New York: Harper & Brothers, 1962.

Waddell, W. G. "The Tetragrammaton in the LXX." *Journal of Theological Studies* 45 (1944): 158-61.

Wainwright, Arthur W. *The Trinity in the New Testament.* London: S.P.C.K., 1962.

Wallis, W. B. "The Use of Psalms 8 and 110 in 1 Corinthians 15:25-27 and in Hebrews 1 and 2." *Journal of the Evangelical Theological Society* 15 (1972): 25-29.

Wedderburn, A. J. M. "The Body of Christ and Related Concepts in 1 Corinthians." *Scottish Journal of Theology* 24 (1971): 74-96.

Wengst, Klaus. *Christologische Formeln und Lieder des Urchristentums.* Gütersloh: Gütersloh Verlagshaus, 1972.

Whiteley, D. E. H. *The Theology of St. Paul.* Philadelphia: Fortress, 1972.

Wilckens, Ulrich. "σοφία [κτλ]." *Theological Dictionary of the New Testament,* 7:465-76, 496-528.

Wilder, Amos. *Early Christian Rhetoric: The Language of the Gospel.* 2d ed. Cambridge: Harvard University Press, 1971.

Willis, Wendell L. *Idol Meat in Corinth: The Pauline Argument of 1 Corinthians 8 and 10.* Society of Biblical Literature Dissertation Series, no. 68. Chico, CA: Scholars Press, 1985.

Wuellner, Wilhelm. "Haggidic Homily Genre in I Corinthians 1-3." *Journal of Biblical Literature* 89 (1970): 199-204.

Yamauchi, Edwin M. *Pre-Christian Gnosticism: A Survey of Proposed Evidences.* 2d ed. Grand Rapids: Baker, 1973.

Zahn, Theodor. *Introduction to the New Testament.* Translated by John Moore Trout et al. 3 vols. 1909: reprint, Grand Rapids: Kregel, 1953.

Index of Passages Cited

Old Testament

Genesis

1:26	173
4:26	4
14:18-20	167
15:6	91-92
16:10,13	169
16:13	169
21:12	94
21:17,19	169
22:11	169
27:29	34
27:37	34
32:30	169
48:15-16	169

Exodus

3:13-15	3-4
4:16	167
6:2-3	4
15:6,12	58
20:2	4
20:7	5
21:4	35
21:28	35
22:8	35
23:20-21	30
23:20-23	169
32:34	169
34:29-35	155
34:34	155

Leviticus

26:11	114
26:11-12	112

Numbers

16:5	115, 146
21:13	136

Deuteronomy

6:4	60
6:4-6	26
21:23	50
22:6-11	174
25:4	79-80
30:12,14	122
30:12-14	122
30:14	116-117
32:15-26	150
32:17	150
32:19	150
32:21	150
32:43	105

Judges

13:22	169

1 Samuel

1:3,11	99
1:15	35
1:26-28	36
2:10	135

2 Samuel

7:8	113
7:12-16	55
7:14	112
7:14-16	111

1 Kings

19:7	169

2 Kings

19:35	169
23:34	40

1 Chronicles

17:11-13	55

Job

5:13	108
28:23-27	132
38:7	167
41:3	100

Psalms

2:7	55
8:2	179
17:7	58
18:49	104
24:1	142-143, 145
32:1	91
32:1-2	92
45:3	167
60:5	58
61:13	149
82:1	167
89:26	55
91:13	179
93:8	109
94:1	152
94:11	108-109
96:7	167
110:1	14, 17, 36, 53, 57-59
110:3	55
117:1	105
118:22	179

Proverbs

3:4	149
8:22-31	30, 132
8:27-31	60

Isaiah

1:3	35
1:9	94, 98
2:10	153

2:11-17	153	Ezekiel		7:21-23	146
8:13-15	121	1:26-28	170	7:23	146
8:14	121	1:28	176	8:11	81
8:14-15	179	8:2-4	170	9:1-8	178
9:8	30	37:27	112	11:10,14	180
10:21	96			11:27	174, 179
10:22	95	Daniel		16:21	178
10:22-23	98	2:34-35	179	17:11-12	180
11:4	86	2:44-45	179	17:23	178
12:5	38	5:23	45	19:5	30
17:10	37	7:9	171, 180	21:16	179
19:11-12	131	7:9-14	170	22:23-33	81
19:19	42	10:2-9	170	24:30-31	81
24:3	38			25:31-46	59, 180
28:16	118-119, 121	Hosea		27:63	47
29:14	131	2:1	95	Mark	
40:3-11	30	Joel		4:35-41	178
40:8	179	2:32	120, 123	5:42	178
40:13	100-101, 137, 139-140	3:1-2	180	8:31	178
		Amos		9:12-13	180
43:6	113	5:18-20	83	9:31	178
45:23	115, 126-128, 130, 159, 165	Habakkuk		10:11-12	78
		2:4	133	10:34	178
48:13	58	Zechariah		12:9	47
49:18	127	14:5	151, 180	12:35-37	14, 47
52:7	167	Malachi		13:31	179
55:10-11	30	1:7,12	149	14:36	178
59:20	102	3:1	30, 180	14:58	178
63:9	169	3:23-24	180	Luke	
64:4	137			5:17-26	178
65:16	137			7:27	180
66:5	154			9:22	178
66:15	153-154			10:1-12	79
Jeremiah		**New Testament**		10:19	179
9:24	130, 132-133, 135	Matthew		13:27	146
		6:9	178	16:3	47
15:11	38	7:1	125	18:33	178
		7:21	47	20:17	179
				20:18	179

Index

John		4:7-8	90-93, 114, 160, 162-163	11:26	102
1:1	181			11:33-36	99
1:1-18	181	4:8	48	11:34	48, 99-102, 114, 138, 140, 162-163
1:14	182	5:11	134		
2:19-21	178	5:12-19	30		
4:26	181	6:3	70, 164	12:9	126
5:17-19	181	6:3-4	76	12:11	72
5:19	182	6:4	70, 176	12:19	3, 48
5:30	182	6:8	70	13:11-14	129
6:35	181	8:3	174	14:1-15:13	123, 129
8:12	181	8:9	174	14:5-9	72
10:11	181	8:15	178	14:7-9	53-54, 59, 125
10:37-38	181	8:29	157, 176		
13:13-14	13	8:34	57-58	14:8	124
14:6	181	9-11	94	14:10,14	73
14:9-11	181	9:5	154, 181, 186	14:11	123-130, 159, 163
20:28	181				
		9:23	176	15:8	103
Acts		9:27	162	15:9,11	103-6, 115, 162
2:32	178	9:27,29	115		
2:32-36	53	9:27-29	93-99, 106, 160, 163	15:10-12	97
6	22			15:11	48
6:9	21			15:12	103
9:1-9	174	9:28-29	48	15:20	148
10:9-23	142	9:29	97	16:20	66
11:2-3	142	9:30-32	116	16:22	7
19:13	148	9:32-33	148		
25:26	47	9:33	97, 118, 121	1 Corinthians	
26:12-18	175			1:1	7
		10:4	122	1:2	164
Romans		10:6-7	122	1:7	85
1:2	5	10:8	116	1:8	84
1:3-4	54-57, 68, 164, 169, 174	10:9	50	1:9	136
		10:9-10	169	1:10-4:21	130
		10:9-12	116	1:18	131
1:6	70	10:13	116-123, 161, 163	1:18-25	108
1:16	17, 132			1:18-31	131
2:6	149	10:16	3	1:23	121, 131
3:1-2	5	11:1-5	97	1:24	132, 134, 174
4:1-12	90	11:3	3, 48		
		11:4-5	98	1:30	132, 134
		11:17-19	102		

1:31	48, 130-136, 150, 161-163	*10:16-17*	30, 149	*2 Corinthians*	
		10:17	141	*1:1*	7
		10:19-22	145	*1:3*	64
2:1,2	137	*10:20*	17, 25, 49, 141, 150	*2:17*	28
2:6-16	137			*3:4-4:6*	175
2:8	76, 176	*10:21*	74, 143, 149	*3:7-18*	155
2:10-15	139			*3:13-14*	155
2:16	100, 136-140, 161, 163	*10:21,26*	163	*3:14-17*	156
		10:22	150-151	*3:16*	48, 155-157, 161, 163, 185
		10:22,26	48		
3:5	110	*10:23-24*	141		
3:16-17	107, 112	*10:26*	140-145, 163	*3:16-18*	51, 140, 174
3:18	110				
3:18-23	106	*10:30*	142	*3:18*	156, 176
3:19	100, 108	*11:17-26*	74	*4:2*	28
3:20	48, 106-111, 114, 162-163	*11:20*	74, 164	*4:3-4*	155
		11:23-25	82	*4:4*	157, 174
		11:26	76, 150	*4:4-6*	176
3:23	70, 182	*11:27-32*	75	*4:5*	51, 117, 157
4:4-5	86, 110	*12*	117		
5:1-5	72	*12:3*	50, 117	*5:10*	126
5:4	164	*12:12-13*	30	*5:16-21*	175
5:9-11	111	*14:21*	3, 126	*6:14-7:1*	111
6:11	70	*15:3*	124	*6:16-18*	126
7:1	79	*15:8*	27, 175	*6:17*	48
7:10-11	78	*15:9*	174	*6:18*	111-114, 162-163
7:25	79	*15:22*	30, 69		
8:1-11:1	140-141	*15:23*	70	*8:19*	157
8:4-6	15, 49, 144, 186	*15:24-27*	68	*8:21*	48, 149
		15:25	57	*8:23*	27
8:4-13	141	*15:25-28*	182	*10:2-12*	27
8:5-6	16	*15:33*	17	*10:7*	70
8:6	59, 62, 144, 168, 185	*15:52*	81	*10:8*	51, 136
		15:58	72	*10:17*	48, 130, 133, 135-136, 150, 161, 163
9:1	27, 51, 175	*16:19*	71		
9:5	81	*16:21*	7		
9:8-14	79	*16:22*	10, 15, 17-18, 31, 33, 43-47, 50, 164-165, 169	*10:18*	136
10:2	30			*11:4*	26-28, 135
10:4	148			*11:13*	27
10:9	161			*11:22*	26, 28
10:14-22	15, 75, 186	*16:23*	66	*11:30-31*	65
10:16	144			*12:1-10*	175

13:10	51, 136	*2:11*	50, 117, 126	*4:6*	152, 161, 163
13:14	66, 185	*3:1*	71	*4:14*	124, 151
Galatians		*3:3*	134	*4:15-17*	80-81
1:6	27	*3:4-6*	17	*5:2-3*	84
1:6-9	25, 28	*3:4-11*	175	*5:9*	84
1:13-14	17, 26, 52	*3:5*	52, 115	*5:27*	63, 71
1:13-17	175	*3:5-6*	25	*5:28*	66
1:18	82	*3:6*	174	*2 Thessalonians*	
1:19	15, 81	*3:8*	51		
2:20	70	*3:20-21*	157	*1:1*	7
3:13	50	*3:21*	176	*1:5-6*	87
3:27	70, 76, 164	*4:1*	71	*1:5-7*	152
3:29	48, 70	*4:4*	71	*1:5-10*	87
4:1	48	*4:19*	176	*1:7-10*	151
4:6	178	*4:23*	66	*1:8*	153-154
5:24	70	*Colossians*		*1:8-12*	163
6:11	7			*1:9*	48, 84, 153
6:14	76, 134	*1:1*	7	*1:9,12*	161
6:18	66	*1:3*	64	*1:10*	84
Ephesians		*1:15*	174	*1:12*	154
		1:15-20	60, 164	*2:8*	85
1:3	64	*1:18-20*	61	*2:8,14*	161
1:20	57-58	*3:1*	57-58	*3:14*	7
1:21	148	*3:17*	72	*3:18*	66
2:6	70	*3:18-4:1*	73	*1 Timothy*	
2:14-15	120	*3:22-24*	47		
5:31	30	*3:23*	47	*5:18*	80
6:1	71	*3:24*	52	*6:21*	67
6:23-24	66	*4:1*	47	*2 Timothy*	
Philippians		*4:16*	63		
		4:18	7, 67	*1:9-10*	86
1:1	7	*1 Thessalonians*		*2:7*	145
1:6	84			*2:18*	147
2:5-8	76	*1:1*	7	*2:19*	48, 115, 145-149, 163
2:6-11	128, 157, 164-165	*2:19*	161		
		3:11-13	65	*3:16*	5, 88
2:9	115	*3:13*	151, 163	*4:22*	66
2:9-11	122, 148, 158	*4:1*	71	*Titus*	
2:10-11	61, 157-160, 161, 163	*4:1-7*	152	*1:12*	17
		4:3	152		

2:13	154, 181, 186	12:9	22	*Pss. Sol.*	
		14:9	22	17:36	30
3:15	67	*4 Maccabees*		*T. Abr.*	
Philemon		5:2	142	13:1-2	166
1	7			*T. Moses*	
19	7			10:1-7	166
1 Peter		## Pseudepigrapha		*T. Sim.*	
3:6	47	*Apoc. Abr.*		6:5	30
1 John		9:1-10:17	170	*T. Levi*	
4:2-3	182	10:3-4	30	5:2	30
2 John		11:2-3	171	*T. Jud.*	
7	182	11:5	171	22:2	30
		17:8-14	171		
Revelation		17:13	30, 172	*T. Naph.*	
1:10	74	*2 Apoc. Bar.*		8:3	30
22:20	43	21:7-10	166	*T. Asher*	
		1 Enoch		7:3	30
## Apocrypha		9:1	170		
		10:1	170		
2 Esdras		40:9-10	170	## Josephus	
7:28-30	55	45:3-6	166	*Antiquities*	
Tobit		46:1	166	1.5	42
12:15	170	47:3	166	1.20	42
Wisdom		51:3	166	1.72	42
7:21	60	55:4	166	2.270	42
7:21-27	30	60:1-3	166	4.40	42
7:22-8:1	132	61:8	166	5.41	42
9:1-7	132	62:2-5	166	5.95	42
Sirach		69:29	166	8.111	42
13:1-3, 17-18	112	105:1-2	55	11.64-65	42
24:3-12	132	106:11	45	12.189	22
2 Maccabees		*2 Enoch*		13.68	42
4	22	22:6	170	20.11	21
4:11	22	33:10	170	20.90	42
		71:28	170		

Index

Philo

De mutatione nominum

15	42
24	42

Legum allegoriarum

1.95-96	42

De plantatione

86-89	42

De somniis

1.163	42
1.244	110

Dead Sea Scrolls

CD (Zadokite Document)

1.13-14	99
4:7-8	96
4.12-18	99
6.3	136
6.11-14	99
6.13	113
6.14-18	111
7.15-16	94
7.15-21	99
8.9	113
8.9-16	99
8:14	96
11.20	108, 126
19:1	99
19:26-27	96

1QpHab

1.11	113
5.6-8	116
6.8	116
7.3-5	116
10.2-4	116
12.2-10	116
12.6-7	94

1QM

1.1-9	111
1.1-13	111
10.1	96
13.2-4	111
13.5-6	111
13.10	170
17.6-8	170

1QS

1.9-11	111
2.16-17	111
3.3-25	111
5.13-17	111
9.8-9	111

1QapGn

2.4	45
7.7	45
12.7	45
20.12-13	45
20.12-15	45
20.15	45
22.21	45

4QFlor

1.2-3	99
1.9	111
1.10-13	55
1.11	111
1.11-14	94
1.14-17	99

11QMelch

l. 10	167
l. 26	111, 167

11QtgJob

24.6-7	45

1Q20

2.5	45

Rabbinic Writings

m. Abod. Zar.

2.3	142

m. Sanh.

38	30

b. Ber.

35	142

b. Hul.

13	142

b. Sanh.

90	103

t. Abod. Zar.

4.6	142

t. Ber.

4.1	142

Pesiqta Rabbati

33:7	91
44:7	91

Early Christian Writings

Irenaeus
Against Heresies

2.17.7	8
3.3.3	8

Polycarp
Philippians
4.1   8

Tertullian
Against Marcion
2.21   8

Didache
10:6   43

Other Writings

Cowley
AP
30:15   45

Epictetus
Dissertationes
1.10.2   91
4.1.12   12
4.10.5   91

Marcus Aurelius
Meditations
4.23   102

Plutarchus
De Iside et Osiride
2.367   12

Wissenschaftliche Untersuchungen zum Neuen Testament

*Alphabetical index
of the first and the second series*

Appold, Mark L.: The Oneness Motif in the Fourth Gospel. 1976. *Volume II/1.*
Bachmann, Michael: Sünder oder Übertreter.1991.*Volume 59.*
Bammel, Ernst: Judaica. 1986. *Volume 37.*
Bauernfeind, Otto: Kommentar und Studien zur Apostelgeschichte. 1980. *Volume 22.*
Bayer, Hans Friedrich: Jesus' Predictions of Vindication and Resurrection. 1986. *Volume II/20.*
Betz, Otto: Jesus, der Messias Israels. 1987. *Volume 42.*
– Jesus, der Herr der Kirche. 1990. *Volume 52.*
Beyschlag, Karlmann: Simon Magnus und die christliche Gnosis. 1974. *Volume 16.*
Bittner, Wolfgang J.: Jesu Zeichen im Johannesevangelium. 1987. *Volume II/26.*
Bjerkelund, Carl J.: Tauta Egeneto. 1987. *Volume 40.*
Blackburn, Barry Lee: 'Theios Anēr' and the Markan Miracle Traditions. 1991. *Volume II/40.*
Bockmuehl, Markus N. A.: Revelation and Mystery in Ancient Judaism and Pauline Christianity. 1990. *Volume II/36.*
Böhlig, Alexander: Gnosis und Synkretismus. Part 1. 1989. *Volume 47* – Part 2. 1989. *Volume 48.*
Büchli, Jörg: Der Poimandres – ein paganisiertes Evangelium. 1987. *Volume II/27.*
Bühner, Jan A.: Der Gesandte und sein Weg im 4. Evangelium. 1977. *Volume II/2.*
Burchard, Christoph: Untersuchungen zu Joseph und Aseneth. 1965. *Volume 8.*
Cancik, Hubert (Ed.): Markus-Philologie. 1984. *Volume 33.*
Capes, David B.: Old Testament Yaweh Texts in Paul's Christology. 1992. *Volume II/47.*
Caragounis, Chrys C.: The Son of Man. 1986. *Volume 38.*
Dobbeler, Axel von: Glaube als Teilhabe. 1987. *Volume II/22.*
Ebertz, Michael N.: Das Charisma des Gekreuzigten. 1987. *Volume 45.*
Eckstein, Hans-Joachim: Der Begriff der Syneidesis bei Paulus. 1983. *Volume II/10.*
Ego, Beate: Im Himmel wie auf Erden. 1989. *Volume II/34.*
Ellis, E. Earle: Prophecy and Hermeneutic in Early Christianity. 1978. *Volume 18.*
– The Old Testament in Early Christianity. 1991. *Volume 54.*
Feldmeier, Reinhard: Die Krisis des Gottessohnes. 1987. *Volume II/21.*
Fossum, Jarl E.: The Name of God and the Angel of the Lord. 1985. *Volume 36.*
Garlington, Don B.: The Obedience of Faith. 1991. *Volume II/38.*
Garnet, Paul: Salvation and Atonement in the Qumran Scrolls. 1977. *Volume II/3.*
Gräßer, Erich: Der Alte Bund im Neuen. 1985. *Volume 35.*
Green, Joel B.: The Death of Jesus. 1988. *Volume II/33.*
Gundry Volf, Judith M.: Paul and Perseverance. 1990. *Volume II/37.*
Hafemann, Scott J.: Suffering and the Spirit. 1986. *Volume II/19.*
Heckel, Ulrich: see *Hengel.*
Heiligenthal, Roman: Werke als Zeichen. 1983. *Volume II/9.*
Hemer, Colin J.: The Book of Acts in the Setting of Hellenistic History. 1989. *Volume 49.*
Hengel, Martin: Judentum und Hellenismus. 1969, ³1988. *Volume 10.*
Hengel, Martin and *Ulrich Heckel* (Ed.:) Paulus und das antike Judentum. 1991.*Volume 58.*
Hengel, Martin and *Anna Maria Schwemer* (Ed.): Königsherrschaft Gottes und himmlischer Kult. 1991. *Volume 55.*
Herrenbrück, Fritz: Jesus und die Zöllner. 1990. *Volume II/41.*
Hofius, Otfried: Katapausis. 1970. *Volume 11.*
– Der Vorhang vor dem Thron Gottes. 1972. *Volume 14.*
– Der Christushymnus Philipper 2,6–11. 1976, ²1991. *Volume 17.*
– Paulusstudien. 1989. *Volume 51.*
Holtz, Traugott: Geschichte und Theologie des Urchristentums. Ed. by Eckart Reinmuth and Christian Wolff. 1991. *Volume 57.*
Hommel, Hildebrecht: Sebasmata. Volume 1. 1983. *Volume 31.* – Volume 2. 1984. *Volume 32.*
Kamlah, Ehrhard: Die Form der katalogischen Paränese im Neuen Testament. 1964. *Volume 7.*
Kim, Seyoon: The Origin of Paul's Gospel. 1981, ²1984. *Volume II/4.*
– »The ›Son of Man‹« as the Son of God. 1983. *Volume 30.*
Kleinknecht, Karl Th.: Der leidende Gerechtfertigte. 1984, ²1988. *Volume II/13.*

Klinghardt, Matthias: Gesetz und Volk Gottes. 1988. *Volume II/32.*
Köhler, Wolf-Dietrich: Rezeption des Matthäusevangeliums in der Zeit vor Irenäus. 1987. *Volume II/24.*
Kuhn, Karl G.: Achtzehngebet und Vaterunser und der Reim. 1950. *Volume 1.*
Lampe, Peter: Die stadtrömischen Christen in den ersten beiden Jahrhunderten. 1987, ²1989. *Volume II/18.*
Maier, Gerhard: Mensch und freier Wille. 1971. *Volume 12.*
- Die Johannesoffenbarung und die Kirche. 1981. *Volume 25.*
Marshall, Peter: Enmity in Corinth: Social Conventions in Paul's Relations with the Corinthians. 1987. *Volume II/23.*
Meade, David G.: Pseudonymity and Canon. 1986. *Volume 39.*
Mengel, Berthold: Studien zum Philipperbrief. 1982. *Volume II/8.*
Merkel, Helmut: Die Widersprüche zwischen den Evangelien. 1971. *Volume 13.*
Merklein, Helmut: Studien zu Jesus und Paulus. 1987. *Volume 43.*
Metzler, Karin: Der griechische Begriff des Verzeihens. 1991. *Volume II/44.*
Niebuhr, Karl-Wilhelm: Gesetz und Paränese. 1987. *Volume II/28.*
Nissen, Andreas: Gott und der Nächste im antiken Judentum. 1974. *Volume 15.*
Okure, Teresa: The Johannine Approach to Mission. 1988. *Volume II/31.*
Pilhofer, Peter: Presbyteron Kreitton. 1990. *Volume II/39.*
Probst, Hermann: Paulus und der Brief. 1991. *Volume II/45.*
Räisänen, Heikki: Paul and the Law. 1983, ²1987. *Volume 29.*
Rehkopf, Friedrich: Die lukanische Sonderquelle. 1959. *Volume 5.*
Reinmuth, Eckhardt: see *Holtz.*
Reiser, Marius: Syntax und Stil des Markusevangeliums. 1984. *Volume II/11.*
Richards, E. Randolph: The Secretary in the Letters of Paul. 1991. *Volume II/42.*
Riesner, Rainer: Jesus als Lehrer. 1981, ³1988. *Volume II/7.*
Rissi, Mathias: Die Theologie des Hebräerbriefs. 1987. *Volume 41.*
Röhser, Günter: Metaphorik und Personifikation der Sünde. 1987. *Volume II/25.*
Rüger, Hans Peter: Die Weisheitsschrift aus der Kairoer Geniza. 1991. *Volume 53.*
Sänger, Dieter: Antikes Judentum und die Mysterien. 1980. *Volume II/5.*
Sandnes, Karl Olav: Paul – One of the Prophets? 1991. *Volume II/43.*
Sato, Migaku: Q und Prophetie. 1988. *Volume II/29.*
Schimanowski, Gottfried: Weisheit und Messias. 1985. *Volume II/17.*
Schlichting, Günter: Ein jüdisches Leben Jesu. 1982. *Volume 24.*
Schnabel, Eckhard J.: Law and Wisdom from Ben Sira to Paul. 1985. *Volume II/16.*
Schutter, William L.: Hermeneutic and Composition in I Peter. 1989. *Volume II/30.*
Schwartz, Daniel R.: Studies in the Jewish Background of Christianity. 1992. *Volume 60.*
Schwemer, A. M. – see *Hengel.*
Siegert, Folker: Drei hellenistisch-jüdische Predigten. Part 1. 1980. *Volume 20.* – Part 2. 1992.
- Nag-Hammadi-Register. 1982. *Volume 26.*
- Argumentation bei Paulus. 1985. *Volume 34.*
- Philon von Alexandrien. 1988. *Volume 46.*
Simon, Marcel: Le christianisme antique et son contexte religieux I/II. 1981. *Volume 23.*
Snodgrass, Klyne: The Parable of the Wicked Tenants. 1983. *Volume 27.*
Speyer, Wolfgang: Frühes Christentum im antiken Strahlungsfeld. 1989. *Volume 50.*
Stadelmann, Helge: Ben Sira als Schriftgelehrter. 1980. *Volume II/6.*
Strobel, August: Die Studie der Wahrheit. 1980. *Volume 21.*
Stuhlmacher, Peter (Ed.): Das Evangelium und die Evangelien. 1983. *Volume 28.*
Tajra, Harry W.: The Trial of St. Paul. 1989. *Volume II/35.*
Theißen, Gerd: Studien zur Soziologie des Urchristentums. 1979, ³1989. *Volume 19.*
Thornton, Claus-Jürgen: Der Zeuge des Zeugen. 1991. *Volume 56.*
Wedderburn, A. J. M.: Baptism and Resurrection. 1987. *Volume 44.*
Wegner, Uwe: Der Hauptmann von Kafarnaum. 1985. *Volume II/14.*
Wilson, Walter T.: Love without Pretense. 1991. *Volume II/46.*
Wolff, Christian: see *Holtz.*
Zimmermann, Alfred E.: Die urchristlichen Lehrer. 1984, ²1988. *Volume II/12.*

For a complete catalogue please write to
J. C. B. Mohr (Paul Siebeck), P. O. Box 2040, D-7400 Tübingen

www.ingramcontent.com/pod-product-compliance
Lightning Source LLC
Chambersburg PA
CBHW030342240426
43661CB00052B/1714